Analyzing Narrative

The socially minded linguistic study of storytelling in everyday life has been rapidly expanding. This book provides a critical engagement with this dynamic field of narrative studies, addressing long-standing questions such as definitions of narrative and views of narrative structure but also more recent preoccupations such as narrative discourse and identities, narrative language, power and ideologies. It also offers an overview of a wide range of methodologies, analytical modes and perspectives on narrative from conversation analysis to critical discourse analysis, to linguistic anthropology and ethnography of communication. The discussion engages with studies of narrative in multiple situational and cultural settings, from informal–intimate to institutional. It also demonstrates how recent trends in narrative analysis, such as small stories research, positioning analysis and sociocultural orientations, have contributed to a new paradigm that approaches narratives not simply as texts, but rather as complex communicative practices intimately linked with the production of social life.

ANNA DE FINA is Associate Professor of Italian Language and Linguistics at Georgetown University.

ALEXANDRA GEORGAKOPOULOU is Professor of Discourse Analysis and Sociolinguistics at King's College London.

T0370772

Analyzing Narrative

Discourse and Sociolinguistic Perspectives

Anna De Fina and Alexandra Georgakopoulou

CAMBRIDGE
UNIVERSITY PRESS

CAMBRIDGE
UNIVERSITY PRESS

32 Avenue of the Americas, New York NY 10013-2473, USA

Cambridge University Press is part of the University of Cambridge.

It furthers the University's mission by disseminating knowledge in the pursuit of education, learning and research at the highest international levels of excellence.

www.cambridge.org
Information on this title: www.cambridge.org/9780521715133

© Anna De Fina and Alexandra Georgakopoulou 2012

First published 2011, 2012
Second Edition 2012
Reprinted 2013

A catalogue record for this publication is available from the British Library

Library of Congress Cataloguing in Publication data
De Fina, Anna.
  Analyzing narrative : discourse and sociolinguistic perspectives /
Anna De Fina, Alexandra Georgakopoulou.
    p. cm.
  Includes bibliographical references and index.
  ISBN 978-0-521-88716-8 – ISBN 978-0-521-71513-3 (pbk.)
  1. Narration (Rhetoric) 2. Discourse analysis–Social aspects.
  3. Sociolingusitics. I. Georgakopoulou, Alexandra. II. Title.
  PN212.D4 2012
  808.036–dc23
  2011040409

ISBN 978-0-521-88716-8 Hardback
ISBN 978-0-521-71513-3 Paperback

Contents

Acknowledgments

This book is the result of many years of collaboration between us, but our work has also benefited immensely from the open dialogue that we have established throughout the years with colleagues and students. We would like to extend our thanks for their participation and critical insights to colleagues and audiences in the various conference panels that we have organized in both continents over the years. We are particularly grateful to Molly Andrews, Michael Bamberg, Mike Baynham, Jan Blommaert, Arnulf Deppermann, Mark Freeman, Matti Hyvärinen, Cathy Riessman, Deborah Schifrrin, Stef Slembrouck, Corinne Squire and Stanton Wortham for many a constructive exchange. We also want to thank all our students at Georgetown and at King's College London, particularly those on the MA course in Linguistic Approaches to Narrative Analysis (King's College London) for their critical engagement and enthusiasm. For help with the editing of this volume, special thanks to Leslie Cohran (Georgetown University) and to Anna Charalambidou (King's College London). Helen Barton from Cambridge University Press showed much encouraging enthusiasm at the initial stages of this book, and we are indebted to her for that. To Inder, Emiliano and Silvio Ruprah, and to Alex, Eliana and Christopher Nunes, we continue to be grateful for unfailingly enriching our lives and making it all worthwhile.

Preface

Writing this book has been a wonderful, even though somewhat humbling experience. The idea for the volume was born out of a need for a language and discourse-oriented introduction to the field that we had identified as scholars and, more importantly, as teachers of narrative. We both felt that, although scholars from sociolinguistics, discourse analysis, linguistic anthropology, social and discursive psychology, just to name some of the fields covered in this book, had produced a vast body of research and theoretical reflection on narrative, a comprehensive and critical evaluation of their work was lacking. This was in stark contrast to the proliferation of textbooks and resource books that present sociological, cultural studies and literary approaches to narrative. Our aim was to redress the balance by highlighting the specificities of a language and discourse-focused perspective on narrative but also its important place within the narrative turn in the social sciences.

The journey of writing this book involved a great deal of discussion, reflection and rethinking as we navigated our way within a body of research that tends to be fragmented and dispersed and as, in the process, we had to make difficult decisions of selection, representation and even "construction" of coherence. Most of our transatlantic exchanges were made possible by the affordances of new technologies (with skyping playing a major role!), but this distance factor made the occasional face-to-face interactions even more rewarding and hugely anticipated. In the process of this intense intellectual engagement, not only did we need to rethink issues and questions posed by the book's organization, but we also needed to explore meeting points in terms of our dissimilar "narrative" experiences and backgrounds, which had shaped our views about how to conceive of and analyze narratives. At the end of this process, we feel we have fundamentally grown together.

This book does not attempt to be exhaustive. Instead, it reflects our interest in two overarching themes that we believe have inadvertently shaped the development of language and discourse approaches to narrative: on the one hand, we focus on the investigation of narrative as textually and discursively constituted and organized. On the other hand, we highlight the analysis of storytelling as a social practice shaped by and shaping multiple social contexts. The latter leads us to questions of power, ideology and identity both in institutional and everyday environments and in the research context. The separation between these two areas is in many ways artificial, and indeed one of the most important questions that we discuss in this book is the tension between text and context in narrative and the difficulties of reconciling a focus on narratives as structurally defined texts and a focus on narratives as discourse embedded in micro- and macro-contexts. The presence of these two themes can be traced in the different chapters that compose the book. While Chapters 1 and 2 are more concerned with issues related to definitions, units of analysis and structural components, Chapters 3 to 6 are centered on different aspects of the relationship between narrative and social life. Another central concern of the volume is interaction. We emphasize the study of oral narratives told in interactional contexts at the expense of literary narratives, as we feel that the latter have been amply represented in the expansive narratological literature.

Overview of chapters

In Chapter 1 we introduce some of the most debated questions related to the definition of narrative and some of the methodological differences between approaches. We review attempts at formalizing the study of narrative based on structural dimensions. In particular, we critically discuss the criteria that have been proposed within narratology and story grammars and the debates over the nature of "narrativity." We also discuss attempts to look at narrative as a particular text-type and to distinguish it from other text-types. We then extend the overview to conceptions of storytelling that go beyond the search for punctual criteria but regard narrative as a mode, a frame for apprehending reality. We reflect on the narrative turn in the social sciences and on conflicting views of narrative as a mode of expression and knowledge, as an epistemology and as a method of inquiry. In the last section of the chapter, we review typologies that attempt to capture the different methodologies used in narrative research and we propose parameters that can be useful to distinguish between different orientations while also providing a guide for our readers in the classification and critical evaluation of the authors and trends presented in the book.

In Chapter 2 we review linguistic approaches to narrative structure that focus on ordinary storytelling, and that analyze the linguistic and discursive means through which structural organization is achieved. In particular, we discuss three approaches to narrative that have been particularly influential in discourse-oriented narrative perspectives: Labov's model of analysis of narratives of personal experience, ethnopoetics and conversation analysis. We describe the assumptions and criteria for identifying structural units employed in each of these traditions and assess their strengths and weaknesses. The discussion shows the difficulties involved in the definition and identification of narrative units and in keeping a balance between a focus on local phenomena and an interest in possible generalizations about the nature of narrative organization. In particular, we underscore the foundational nature of Labov's model and its continuing influence on the linguistic study of narrative, but we also point to its limitations: the lack of attention to the interactional dynamics of storytelling, the ambiguity of the coding categories and therefore the difficulties of applying it.

In reviewing ethnopoetics, we highlight the importance of this movement in uncovering the poetic quality of storytelling, its significance in shaping and reflecting cultural forms of expression and culturally shared values. However, we also point to some shortcomings in the ethnopoetic movement: the difficulty of applying it to narratives produced in modern literate societies and the highly interpretive nature of the analysis.

In reviewing the contribution of conversation analysis to the study of storytelling, we underscore the centrality of this movement in proposing a view of narrative as talk-in-interaction that is now prevalent in discourse studies. But we also point to its neglect of the in-between part of a story versus its beginnings and endings, its narrow focus on the here-and-now of conversation and its rejection of any interest in textual structure. We conclude with our own arguments for the development of approaches that recognize the importance of structure in linguistic analysis, together with a greater attention to interactional roles and dynamics.

In Chapter 3 we shift attention to research that centers on the relationships between narrative and context and on the embedding of narrative in social life. In particular, we focus on research that has investigated sociocultural variability distinguishing between:

a. approaches that conceptualize the relationship between narrative and culture in terms of contexts of narrative activity;
b. approaches that see narrative as connected to culture through values and ideas;
c. approaches that focus on communicative styles.

In discussing work that we situate within the first category, we emphasize the importance of the research on oral storytelling in preliterate cultures conducted by anthropologists between the 1960s and the 1980s as their work constituted a break with the structuralist orientation of studies of fables and myths produced before then, for example by Lévi-Strauss and Propp. We review the concept of performance as proposed within the anthropological tradition, paying particular attention to the work of Hymes and to Bauman's framework for analyzing narratives as emergent within communicative events. In the second and third categories, we include sociolinguistic studies of cultural variability that have focused on the differences in story content and storytelling styles among national and ethnic groups. We conclude with a reflection in which we problematize a view of culture as a set of values and styles characterizing a national community, and argue that such conception may result in oversimplification and in a neglect of the multiple ways in which local contexts shape and are shaped by narratives.

In Chapter 4 we look at stories as interactional achievements and we therefore stress the significance of participation structures and of the conversational work done in the moment by moment unfolding of a story's telling. We discuss how studies of storytelling have gradually shifted from an exclusive focus on tellers toward the analysis of tellership and from story as a product to storytelling as a process. In the first part of the chapter, we analyze ways in which storytellers open, sustain and close narratives in interaction, and we illustrate the role of both storytellers and audiences in the unfolding of stories. Thus, we review work on story openings and closings, audience participation and telling roles. We illustrate how even though narratives are often cooperative achievements, they may as often be used by interactants as strategic tools in situations of conflict and/or as argumentative devices to back up controversial positions. We also engage with the notion of telling rights as central to an understanding of different participant configurations in specific storytelling contexts. In the second part of the chapter, we illustrate the variability of storytelling formats presenting different kinds of story types such as counterfactual narratives, habitual narratives, second stories, argumentative narratives. We conclude with a review of *small stories research* as an attempt to unify efforts at broadening the scope of narrative analysis.

In Chapter 5 we turn to the relationship between narratives and power, illustrating how narratives can be sites for the imposition of forms of domination by powerful individuals and institutions, but also how they may be used to negotiate new roles and norms by members of society. We start from a general review of the concept of power, to then illustrate its relation to storytelling in concrete social encounters: we focus on institutional contexts, and in particular on legal settings. We discuss strategies for the exercise and negotiation of power in storytelling and highlight the role of processes of contextualization and entextualization. We then turn to a discussion of how narrative power involves questions of authority and legitimation and to an analysis of ways in which the latter are negotiated in storytelling. As we argue, the study of narrative and power also implies a consideration of the relations between narrative and truth. In connection with the themes of truth, authority and credibility, we examine work that has linked narratives with ideologies and research that has underscored the central role that storytelling has in shaping public opinion through the news. In the last part of the chapter, we extend these questions about truth, ideology and power in storytelling to story ownership. We conclude with a consideration of the implications of our reflection on power for the relationships between researchers and researched and the analysis of their role in data collection and analysis.

In Chapter 6 we discuss how connections between narrative and identities have been conceptualized within different research paradigms and the kinds of problems that research in this field raises. We analyze biographical, socio-linguistic and conversation-analytic work and explore similarities and differences amongst them, using key concepts such as positioning, categorization, self-presentation and indexicality. In the first part of the chapter, we discuss theoretical developments in different disciplines within the social sciences that have constituted the basis for an important shift in the study of identity toward an interactionist and social contructionist paradigm. We then review biographical approaches, discussing the division within this camp between orientations that connect identity to the expression of the self in a coherent and unitary life story and orientations that focus on the positionality of identity as a process of production of identities vis-à-vis specific interlocutors and circumstances.

In the second part of the chapter, we turn to sociolinguistically oriented studies. In particular, early studies on self-presentation and more recent research that has developed around the concept of indexicality. We assess the impact of recent frameworks for the study of identity, such as conversation-analytic/ethnomethodology-oriented (Antaki and Widdicombe 1998a) and socioculturally oriented models (Bucholtz and Hall 2005). We conclude by arguing for the advantages of a middle ground between more macro- and more micro-oriented approaches.

Note on transcription conventions

The following two systems of transcription conventions were used in the examples

System 1

((smiling))	Non-linguistic actions
(...)	Inaudible
(.)	Noticeable pause
.	Falling intonation followed by noticeable pause (as at end of declarative sentence)
?	Rising intonation followed by noticeable pause (as at end of interrogative sentence)
,	Continuing intonation : may be a slight rise or fall in contour (less than "".""" or – "?"); may be not followed by a pause (shorter than """." or "?")
word→	Listing intonation
-	Self-interruption
=	Latched utterances by the same speaker or by different speakers
_____	Emphatic stress
CAPS	Very emphatic stress
::	Vowel or consonant lengthening
[	Overlap between utterances
→ (line)	Highlights key phenomena
@	Laughter

System 2

//	the point in a turn where the utterance of the next speaker begins to overlap
=	two utterances closely connected without a noticeable overlap
( )	speech that can't be deciphered
(text)	analyst's guess at speech that's hard to decipher

(( ))	stage directions
(.)	micro-pause, not timed
(1.)	approximate length of a pause in seconds
> <	faster than normal speech
::	extended speech
?	Question
↑↓	Rising Falling Intonation

1   Narrative definitions, issues and approaches

1.0   Introduction

More than numerous objects of inquiry, *narrative* resists straightforward and agreed-upon definitions and conceptualizations. Instead, its study tends to be a minefield of multiple and at times competing perspectives in a wide array of humanities and social science fields. This is a sign of richness and refreshing pluralism for some, while a sign of deplorable fragmentation for others; but the fact remains that any attempt to present and pull together different strands in the area involves delicate issues of selection and representation. It is with this acute awareness that an exhaustive and evenly balanced overview is close to impossible that we will approach in this chapter the complicated yet fundamental issues of "What is narrative?" and "How is it studied?" That said, two principles have guided our selection of materials in the discussion to follow:

a. The inclusion of approaches that in more or less explicit ways have influenced the assumptions and tools of what will form the main focus of this book, namely socially minded linguistic approaches to narrative.
b. The need to extract and bring to the fore aspects of convergence and even overlapping interests from traditions that on the face of it may have developed separately.

In this attempt to pull threads together, we have seen it fit to pose a working distinction, by no means dichotomous, between views of narrative as a *type of text* and views of narrative as a *mode, epistemology and method*. We will thus map each of the poles of this distinction with specific approaches and what we see as distinct assumptions and ways of analyzing narrative in them.

1.1   Narrative as text-type

Seeing narrative as a text-type inevitably involves a commitment to clear-cut definitional criteria coupled with a belief in the verbal/linguistic aspects of narrative as holding the key to those criteria. This main assumption leads almost by implication to other views too: for instance, a view of narrative as a structured activity with a beginning, middle and an end, and with clearly identifiable units that are amenable to analysis. It is thus no accident that structuralism has been closely associated with approaches to narrative as a text-type. The assumption that strict textual criteria are the main guide to defining narrative and setting it apart from other types of text also goes hand in hand with a belief in the universal properties of narrative. Very simply put, narrative is seen as having textual properties that apply across contexts, and the task for the analyst is both to uncover those and to shed light on what may be culture-specific. Another affiliated focus is on the ways in which the knowledge of how to tell a (good) story is acquired and in turn how stories are understood and processed: this makes some of the approaches here cognitive in epistemological orientation. But let us examine the main approaches to narrative as text-type in more detail.

1.1.1   Narratology and the issue of defining a story

Narratology is one of the most important approaches to narrative as text-type. Below we present a typical definition:

> Narratology is the study of narrative as a genre. Its objective is to describe the constant variables and combinations typical of narrative and to clarify how the characteristics of narrative texts connect with the framework of theoretical models (typologies). (Fludernik 2009: 8)

As is evident from the above, the focus is on the story as a type of text that can be set apart from other genres. It is therefore hardly surprising that the issue of defining what a story is should lie at the center of narratology. Narratologists also generally assume that the definitional criteria of narrative are universally applicable and that narrative can be theorized as such. Narratology is, for the most part, devoted to the study of literary texts, but its influence on linguistic studies of narrative is undeniable. In the light of this, our discussion here will mainly concern itself with issues within narratology which are relevant to the linguistic study of narrative as well.

Most of the classical narratologists[1] (Bal 1985; Genette 1980; Prince 1973) conceived of the story as their object of study and basically defined it as a series of temporally and causally ordered events. Specific definitions varied, but the basic idea that events are the stuff of which a story is made was shared by most researchers in the field. Such a predominance of the action aspects over other story elements in the theorizations about narrative can be traced as far back as Aristotle. The Greek philosopher stated in his *Poetics* (52, VI.14): "The plot, then, is the first principle and, as it were, the soul of a tragedy: character holds the second place." But the succession of events that a reader encounters in a story constitutes just one level of analysis of a story. Classical narratologists inherited from Russian formalists such as Shklovsky and Propp a distinction between what is told in a story (its basic events) and the way it is told. The Russian formalists named the events represented in the story, the *fabula*, and the story as it is put together and narrated by the author, the *syuzhet*. This distinction was later revisited by narratologists who, based on Genette (1980), adopted a distinction between *narration* as the act of narrating, *discourse* (*discours* or *récit*) as the narrative text and *story* (*histoire*) as the basic sequence of events (see Toolan 2001: 15 on this point).

The distinction between *story* and *discourse* is designed to capture the fact that there are some basic stories that do not change even if the circumstances of the telling and the medium through which they are told change. It could be said, for example, that *Snow White* has a basic set of elements that make it look like the same story no matter whether it is written or told in the form of a movie or a series of newspaper strips.[2] These elements constitute its plot, but the ways in which the plot is told will vary according to authors, media and contexts of performance. Of course, the basic tenet that the plot of a story is represented by a set of temporally ordered and causally connected events is in itself highly debatable, but let us take it at face value for the moment. The point is that the distinction between *story* and *discourse* also reflects a basic conception, present in many structuralist treatments, that posits the existence of a surface level (the level of the text as it is accessed by a reader) and a deep structure (the most basic level of actions and roles from which the story is derived).

As we discuss in detail in section 3.1, structuralist studies of literary works (see Barthes 1977; Bremond 1973; Greimas [1966] 1983; Todorov 1969)[3] constituted the immediate precursors not only of narratology, but also of story grammars, and for this reason an analysis of stories based on a rigid division between levels is common to those later developments as well.

Following Vladimir Propp (1968), who had attempted to capture the fundamental structure of Russian folk tales in terms of basic roles and action functions, literary structuralists tried to describe the deep structure of fictional works as a very abstract model from which the narrative was derived. Indeed, structuralists were not so much interested in the surface level of texts as in their deep structure. The latter was described in different ways by different authors. For example, some characterized it in terms of the basic relations between a few concepts such as "love" and "prohibition" (see Greimas 1983), while others saw it as a system of relations between actions, roles and functions (as in Propp 1968 or Barthes 1977). But the common ideal was to find certain basic elements that would allow researchers to reduce the deep structure of stories to a minimal set of universal elements in order to derive from them any surface realization of narratives in any language. In this sense, structural studies of narratives resembled structural linguistics in its quest for minimal units of analysis, in its rigid separation of levels and in its attempt to distinguish between competence and performance. But of course, every time analysts tried to define the basic elements of deep structure, they ended up proposing symbols that were not devoid of meaning but were semantically and culturally loaded (e.g. "life," "death," "love," "prohibition," etc.).

As noted by Herman and Vervaeck (2005), there are significant problems with structuralist narratology. These have to do with the ambiguity of the categories used in the analysis of stories, the rigid separation between levels (such as deep and surface structure) and the lack of specificity on how transitions between them work. The authors conclude (p. 100) that

the creation of unambiguous and generally accepted categories remains a utopian enterprise. Any classification proposed by structuralist narratology gives rise to borderline cases and problems that have yet to be – and probably never will be – solved. In many cases the structuralist is forced to acknowledge that concrete stories always upset the theoretical demarcations.

Of particular interest here is the problem of the definition of a story as a text, which has occupied narratologists for decades and which has been inherited by all text-based approaches to narrative. As already mentioned, for narratologists, a story has to comprise a series of related events. Chatman (1990: 9) pointed to chronological ordering as the main criterion to distinguish stories from other texts or, to put this more specifically, proposed the criterion of double chronology. For a text to qualify as narrative, it has to entail movement through time, not only externally (i.e. through its telling, cf. discourse time) but also internally (through the duration of the sequence of events that constitute its plot, cf. story time). In his *Dictionary of Narratology*, Prince proposed instead that such a link was not only chronological, but also causal. He thus characterized a minimal story as a set of "two states and one event" that are chronologically ordered and causally connected in that the second state is a "reversal"or "modification"of the first state. Thus, the following was classified as a minimal story:

John was happy, then he saw Peter, then, as a result, he was unhappy. (Prince [1987] 2003: 53)

As is evident from these definitions, structuralists and narratologists alike have had little interest in storytelling contexts, given their focus on the text-internal properties of narrative. This lack of interest in the context is not shared by more recent narratological approaches as we will discuss below.

1.1.2   Narrative and cognition

The basic idea that the story is a series of temporally and causally connected events is echoed in story grammars, another set of approaches to narrative as a text-type. Such approaches, however, are not so much focused on the production as on the comprehension and processing of narratives. Researchers in the field look at narrating as a cognitive activity and their main interest is discovering how people understand and remember stories and what criteria determine their judgments about story well-formedness. According to de Beaugrande (1982), although at the beginning of the story-grammar movement it was difficult to distinguish amongst different trends, later on two approaches became identifiable: the story-schema approach (Rumelhart 1975) and the story-grammar approach (Mandler and Johnson 1977, 1980; Mandler 1984). In the story-schema approach a story is defined in cognitive terms as an abstract representation about story structure and content or, in Mandler's terms, as: "a mental structure consisting of sets of expectations about the way in which stories proceed" (1984: 18).

Story-schema theories derive from cognitive models of text processing (see, for example, Schank and Abelson 1977) that regard text comprehension as a process of decoding new information based on previous knowledge. The latter is stored in memory through schemas, frames and scripts representing either constellations of meaning relations (schemas and frames) or stereotypical situations (scripts). Such schemas allow people to make inferences about what they are reading or hearing. In the case of stories, according to story grammars, they are formed by sets of basic components (such as SETTING, THEME, PLOT, etc.) and sets of relationships amongst them.

For some (see Stein and Policastro 1984), story schemas are prototypes (Rosch and Mervis 1975), i.e. kinds of general models with stereotypical characteristics that people keep in mind when judging whether a text is a story. In this view, stories may be closer or further away from the prototype, and in that sense narrativity may be a matter of degree.

Story-grammar models focus more than story schemas on the description of the internal structure of a story and present a type of syntax of story organization based on the combination of the basic story components and their internal ordering. Thus, for example, a story would consist of a combination of elements such as SETTING + INITIATING EVENT + REACTION + ENDING and would specify the position and content of each of those elements. According to de Beaugrande, however, these two approaches are compatible as:

A comparison of the literature indicates that a story grammar can be viewed as a rule-set for relating the ordering of surface-text categories to the underlying schema (cf. 1.13). Thus, the grammar is a theoretical formalization that operates upon the knowledge organized within the schema, with major focus on the arrangement of categories in sequences. (1982: 410)

Thus, there is no contradiction between the conception of a story as a mental schema and its conception as a grammatically well-formed string, since the grammar is a concrete realization of the mental prototype that we have about stories. It is worth noting the recurrence of certain definitional criteria of narrative in the approaches we have seen so far. We have already pointed to the chronological criterion as the *sine qua non* of definitions. Here, we will single out the idea of an initiating (see above) or a complicating event as another pivotal ingredient. The view that to have a narrative, a disruption of sorts is needed, that is, an event or series of events that will introduce some kind of a complication to an initial state of affairs or an equilibrium, is not new. It goes back to Aristotle's notion of *peripeteia* and has been variously described since then (cf. "trouble" in Burke [1950] 1969).

These definitional criteria in story grammars are essential in their aim to construct abstract models of narrative so as to account for the kinds of information that people would expect to find in a story and for the type of organization that characterizes it (see Johnson and Mandler 1980: 51) in order to explain people's comprehension of stories. Thus, story grammars try to represent or even simulate cognitive processes that accompany story comprehension and test them through experimental work.

However, as noted by de Beaugrande and others, such abstract models are fraught with problems. First, the status of the rules created by story grammarians is not clear. Are they true representations of mental processes or are they models devised and used by the analyst? Are they all causally ordered with respect to one another?

Second, story grammars and schema theories (like narratology) have attempted to come up with basic features that need to be present in order for a story to be considered such, but they have not really been able to empirically demonstrate the validity of their hypotheses.

Some of these features have been summarized by Stein and Policastro (1984) who claim that they have found twenty different descriptions of stories. However most of them share the idea that a story

1. represents a series of temporally and causally related events;
2. introduces some form of a complication or disruption;
3. presents (more or less) goal-directed actions and reactions to deal with this disruption;
4. has an animate protagonist.

The last two criteria are related in that definitions that do not consider goal-directed behavior to be a necessary feature for stories (such as Prince 1973) do not include the presence of a protagonist as a defining feature either.

The abstraction and context-independence of many of these definitions has led to different reactions within both story grammars and narratology. Many have also noted that experiments conducted as part of the testing of hypotheses regarding the characteristics of stories have not provided definitive answers. Unsurprisingly, there is still a great deal of controversy about which texts can be regarded as stories. For example, Stein and Policastro (1984) were not able to show in their experiments with children and adults that goal-directed behavior was essential for recognizing a text as a story. In general, they found that "not all constituents of a goal-based episode need be included in a text for it to be classified as a story" (p. 149) and that no definition of story accurately predicted their subjects' behavior.

One point that many within the story-grammar approach have raised is that stories cannot be defined or understood in abstraction from users, and without a consideration of the relative status of narrator and audience in storytelling. Indeed, according to some researchers (in particular Brewer and Lichtenstein 1981, and de Beaugrande and Colby 1979), story-like qualities do not depend exclusively on structural properties of the stories but are attributed to them by audiences. Therefore, for a text to be seen as a story, the audience needs to be emotionally involved and the action must deal with difficulties and obstacles to be overcome, i.e. it must be able to arouse interest and affective participation.

1.1.3   Stories and mental models

This more central role accorded to the reader and the process of interpretation can be seen in recent so-called *post-classical* narratology (see Dolezel 1998; Herman 2002; Ryan 1991; Werth 1999). Recent narratological approaches have started paying more attention to context in the sense that they recognize the role of the reader, in particular of people's knowledge and beliefs in the interpretation of the text. In this respect, they have started to converge with cognitive theories about text processing. Contrary to story grammars, in which text comprehension was conceptualized as the process of integration of information into a stereotypical schema or script, in more recent cognitive theories, text comprehension is viewed as the creation of "mental models." Such mental model theories derive from original work by Johnson Laird (1983) and Van Dijk and Kintsch (1983) in which understanding was not conceived as a mental representation of the text itself, but rather as a process of creation of mental or situational models of the world described in the text. In Van Dijk and Kintsch, text comprehension implied three different mental representations of the text: a verbatim representation, a semantic representation in terms of propositional content, and a situational representation. In later applications (see Zwaan and Radvansky 1998), text comprehension is related to the construction of coherent mental models. Such models are seen as complex multimodal mental representations containing spatio-temporal, causal relations, and information about objects, persons and motivations. They are continuously updated and change at different moments in time reflecting different stages in the process of text understanding. In these later developments, the interest for stories as texts has given way to a preoccupation with stories as a suitable site for the study of mental processes of understanding and of memory retrieval and storage.

These cognitive approaches have greatly influenced recent narratology. Herman (2002), for example, talks about *story world* as a concept that should replace that of *story* and equates story worlds with mental models that readers create, about who did what to whom, where, why and in what fashion in a particular story. According to him, narratives build their own possible worlds, which are different from the world in which readers live. Such worlds have their own rules so that their logic and their events make sense within them, even if they deviate from the laws of the real world. Thus, for example, in a magic realist novel such as Garcia Màrquez's *One hundred years of solitude*, it is possible for children to be born with a pigtail or for rain to last for years or for events that have not happened yet to influence the protagonists' behavior. Readers understand these possible worlds by relating them to their own experience of the natural world, and this happens through the activation of schemas and scripts that they derive from such experience.

Fludernik's approach is similar to Herman's in that she also claims that narratives are representations of possible worlds, but she argues that the primary function of narrative is communicating human experience, thus rejecting a vision of narrative as a simple recapitulation of events and downplaying the importance of action as the criterion for narrativity par excellence. In her definition:

A narrative … is a representation of a possible world in a linguistic and/or visual medium, at the centre of which there are one or more protagonists of an anthropomorphic nature who are existentially anchored in a temporal or spatial sense and who (mostly) perform goal directed actions (action and plot structure). It is the experience of these protagonists that narratives focus on, allowing readers to immerse themselves in a different world and in the life of the protagonists. (Fludernik 2009: 6)

In such a perspective, conversational and literary narratives are not as distant as they may seem, since the focus in both is not on events and actions per se but on the way humans experience and react to them.

The concept of narrativity has also undergone important changes. Narrativity can be seen as the property that defines the difference between a narrative and a non-narrative.[4] In traditional narratology, the criteria for narrativity included the features that we have discussed above, i.e. temporal ordering of events, complication, the presence of human characters, goal-directed action, etc. In more recent approaches, however, narrativity has been redefined not as a property of texts, but as something that is attributed to texts by readers. It has also been anchored to the existence of mental schemata that represent basic features of human experience. Fludernik, for example, defines narrativity as "the representation of experientiality" (1996: 20), that is, the ability to capture human reactions and emotions in the face of life events. In accordance with Prince's ideas, narrativity is also increasingly regarded as a scalar predicate, something that can be present in greater or lesser degree in a text. In this way, different narrative text-types are described in terms of high or low narrativity: e.g. "reports" are typically seen as low-narrativity texts, on account of their lack of evaluation (Fludernik 1996: 52–3). This distinction has not been devoid of evaluative judgment. It has in point of fact helped establish specific kinds of narratives as the "canon," and the natural consequence of this has been that these narratives have been researched more. We will come back to this point in Chapter 4.

Within a scalar conceptualization of narrativity, Herman (2002: 91) proposes that while "narrativehood" involves binary oppositions (either a text is a narrative or it is not), narrativity is a matter of degree such that a story may be more or less story-like. Story-likeness depends on the equilibrium between stereotypicity and breach of expectation in narratives. If a story has too many or too few stereotypical cues, its narrativity diminishes. In other words, a prototypical narrative works on expected patterns but also on their breach by creating suspense and interest.

Another strand of latest narratological research involves revisiting a longstanding preoccupation with the place of media (e.g. cinematic) and visual narratives in the remit of narratology, and even the extent to which these can be considered as narrative. The recent move away from strict textualist criteria, as we have outlined it above, has renewed this interest. For instance, in one of the few large-scale attempts to examine narrative through a comparative lens in the media, Ryan (2004a: 22) starts off with the observation that

the comparative study of media as means of expression lags behind the study of media as channels of communication; individual media have been studied with well-developed analytical tools and methodologies, but we do not have a comprehensive and widely accepted theory of the importance of the medium as material support for the form and content of message.

Ryan puts forth a program for what she calls "a transmedial narratology," which is undoubtedly a desideratum. Her vision has an obvious cognitive orientation and a lingering emphasis on narrative as defined on the basis of abstract textual criteria. That said, some of the questions that Ryan (p. 35) claims should be addressed can be adapted and extended to more socially and interactionally inclined studies of narrative too. For instance, how narrative gets transposed from one medium to another and how each medium encourages or prohibits specific ways of narration. Also, what the applicability is of concepts and analytical modes that have been developed with regard to the study of narrative in one medium across media. Ryan rightly stresses the point that the examination of such questions should "avoid the temptation to attribute features and findings to the medium solely" (p. 34). She also warns against the other extreme, that is "media blindness," which often involves an indiscriminate transfer of concepts designed for the study of narrative in one medium to narratives of another medium.

Narrative as a text-type in different media is already attracting the interest of researchers in increasing ways. Closely related to this is the focus on the interrelationships between the new ways to present stories in different media, in particular in digital media, and what these implicate for the involvement of "audiences" or "users." Above all, exactly what counts as a story, particularly in new media environments, remains a focal concern in narratology. For instance, in a comparative study of interactive drama, hypertext, computer games, web cams and text-based virtual realities (role-playing or adventure MOOs), Ryan (2004b) reports that the role of narrative in these cases differs from central to intermittent (e.g. in MOOs where dramatic action and storytelling alternate with small talk) to instrumental (e.g. computer games). The role of the user also varies in terms of how much interactivity is allowed: in computer games, for instance, the users become an integral part of the fictional world as main characters.

It is worth noting again that textual criteria, in particular the temporal ordering of events, remain as the main guiding principle in terms of what constitutes a narrative in narratological studies that are venturing out to the "transmedial" terrain. We will however revisit the issue of narrative in digital media in Chapter 4.

The evolution of narratological approaches from a rigid structuralist perspective focused on defining the abstract properties of stories toward a more flexible understanding of narrative as interaction between text and reader as well as of narrative across media has undoubtedly been positive. The recognition, within narratological studies that have traditionally focused on literary narratives, of the fact that everyday narratives may be the basis for as well as being closely related and relatable to literary narratives is also important. Within linguistic analyses too, the literary qualities of everyday narratives have often been documented (see Polanyi 1982; Tannen 1989; Wolfson 1978). Devices and strategies such as characters' reported speech, tense alternations between past and present, and performance devices are only a few amongst these. As we will see in the following chapters, questions about the stories' voice and authorship, their spatio-temporal anchoring, and the embedding of different worlds within story worlds are at the center of linguistic studies of narrative as much as of literary ones and constitute areas where interaction and enrichment between the two camps is possible and desirable. However, the problems deriving from a text-oriented vision of narrative are not easily overcome, as we will see below too. We will come back to this question in Chapter 2.

1.2   Narrative as a special text-type

As we have already suggested, one of the aims of the discussion in this chapter is to tease out certain assumptions and perspectives within the otherwise fragmented narrative studies that have had a lasting impact on socially minded linguistic approaches to storytelling, which form the main focus of this book. As we have seen so far, the attempts to delimit narrative as a text-type have been guided by the quest for clear-cut definitional criteria. Delimiting narrative has also implicated a process of setting it apart from what is *not* narrative. One notable common denominator in this respect is the inclusion of narrative in all proposed text-typologies, which, however, present a wide variation in terms of what and how many other text-types there exist, what their relative ranking is and how they are kept apart from one another, in particular from narrative. We can see this very clearly in some of the numerous attempts at such classifications: Chatman (1990) distinguishes between narrative, description and argument, while Adams (1996) distinguishes between narrative, description and expositions. Werlich's typology (1976) consists of narration, description, exposition, argumentation and instruction. In the same spirit, Longacre's (1989) text-type distinctions introduce further categories that are different from the ones above. Based on the combinations of two binary oppositions, i.e. texts with or without temporal succession and texts with or without an "agent orientation," Longacre differentiated between four text-types: narration, procedural, hortatory (cf. behavioral) and expository discourse.[5] It is notable that Longacre unusually dispensed with both description and argumentation. The use of the term *discourse* is also notable. As we have discussed so far, one of the main distinctions that approaches to narrative as text-type have worked with is that between ideal text-types and surface manifestations or linguistic realizations of those text-types. This goes hand in hand with the assumption that storytellers (or writers) manipulate in many ways and to varying degrees the "pre-linguistic" material, i.e. the events, that they have at their disposal, when expressing them in the form of a story (cf. distinction between story and discourse).

Distinguishing between text-type and discourse or discourse type is not a straightforward matter, and it is largely outside the scope of this discussion. It suffices to say though that text-types are often defined as the actual, linguistically expressed manifestations or instantiations of "discourse types," while "discourse types" tend to be posed at the pre-linguistic level, as the functions of communication that are constituted by text-types. Following this distinction, Virtanen (1992) systematizes a widely held view according to which narrative cannot be put at the same level as other text-types. Instead, it has to be seen as a "special" and fundamental text-type. A similar view is found in research on genre, where narrative has been argued to be a meta-, arch- or pre-genre, that is, an archetypal form that cannot be put on the same level as "ordinary" genres (Grabe and Kaplan 1996: 139; Swales 1990).[6] In Virtanen's terms, the narrative text-type can be used in any discourse type. For instance, one can put forth an argument by telling a story, but the opposite does not apply; that is, one cannot put forth an argument in order to tell a story. Narrative thus emerges as a versatile text-type, as, unlike other text-types, it can fulfill more than one discourse type.

As already suggested, there is not much convergence amongst text-typological approaches to narrative on exactly which and how many text-types there are. What is more, different text-types tend to be used indiscriminately: e.g. text-types covering very specific situations are placed alongside more frequent or general categorizations. And certainly, if we follow Virtanen's line, the importance and salience of narrative tends to be skewed in such typologies. Depending on how and from which standpoint one looks at these lists, they can be queried for what they have included and what they have excluded and for the reasons why a particular text is classified as X and not as Y. Furthermore, the exact number of typical features of narrative remains a controversial issue. Despite its problems, this long-standing tradition of defining narrative along with other text-types on the basis of formal, textual criteria has been instrumental in delimiting narrative as an object of inquiry, and its influence in recent socially situated linguistic approaches to narrative is undeniable. As we will see in this book, the textual features of what constitutes a story are being increasingly examined through context-sensitive approaches, and the very definitions of narrative have become much more flexible so as to include in their remit a wide range of texts.

1.3   Narrative development and socialization

One of the spin-offs of a view of stories as cognitive constructs has been the study of their development in children. The underlying assumption in this research has been that narrative possesses certain universal properties at the same time as presenting cultural specificity. One of the main aims of narrative development studies has thus been to shed (further) light on what is universal and what is culture-specific. At the same time, exactly as in other research on the development of language and communication skills amongst children and adolescents, there has been an assumption of *deficit* or *deficiency*. In other words, it has been assumed that narratives produced by children are inevitably less elaborated than the ones told by adults and that through a temporally defined progression, the former succeed in reaching the endpoint, that is the adult model, as they grow up. This perspective of non-adulthood as a transitional period marked by developing competence and judged against the normative benchmark of adulthood and its norms has been challenged from various quarters, not least within social psychology (e.g. Arnett 2004). The controversy surrounding this issue is beyond the scope of our discussion here. What is relevant, however, is that these challenges to a linear development of narrative have been connected with a shift toward the study of narrative development in context and with attention to the types of activities and social practices that the participants engage in, be they children or adults. We will discuss this in more detail in Chapter 3.

Numerous, particularly earlier, studies of narrative development have worked with elicited data. Peterson and McCabe (1983) developed, for instance, the Conversational Map Elicitation Procedure, which consisted of story prompts. Another well-known data elicitation technique involved showing children picture-based books and asking them to tell the story. The best-known in this respect is the 24-page children's book *Frog, where are you?* (Mayers 1949) and numerous studies from many languages (at least 150 studies in fifty languages) have been based on it. In particular, Berman and Slobin used it for their influential work *Relating events in narrative*: *A crosslinguistic developmental study* (1994). A number of scholars were subsequently inspired to use the same picture-based book for eliciting data and this yielded a second volume on *Relating events in narrative* (2004). As the title suggests, these studies traced in many languages the transition of children from 3 to 9 years old from the simple encoding of events as individual occurrences in a story to more complex ways of organizing them around temporal and causal interrelationships, to finally integrating them into thematically coherent plot lines.

The main finding of these studies concerns the ways in which children use forms already acquired to express new functions but also newly acquired forms to express already mastered functions. Overall, they have shown the complex interaction of universal, cognitive and linguistic forms (as shaped by the exigencies of the linguistic system of each language under investigation) in the development of narrative. In this respect, they are illustrative of a particular school of thought within narrative development that has often been criticized for basing its results on "quasi-experimental" data and for ignoring narratives as occurring naturally in everyday contexts and as part of the children's interactions with other children or with adults. There is also a question mark about what the ideal or most critical age is for looking into narrative development. Finally, as we have already suggested, the assumption underlying this approach that the mastery of narrative forms and functions develops in a linear, age-linked fashion is also debatable.

Another strand of research involves the exploration of narrative development in terms of the children's interaction with others. It has to be said here that relevant studies present considerable variation in their definitions of interaction and in the role that they assign to the context of the occurrence of narratives. A case in point is the lingering emphasis on elicited narratives in several studies despite their interest in the interactional dynamics. One of the main foci of inquiry in this respect is on the so-called adult *scaffolding*, i.e. the adult verbal support during children's storytelling. How adults' storytelling styles affect the children's own story production has also been put under scrutiny (e.g. Miller and Sperry 1988; Oppenheim, Emde and Wamboldt 1996). As a result, numerous studies have engineered storytelling situations in mother/caregiver–child dyads in research situations (e.g. mother telling child a story from a picture-based book). The results have shown that differences in the form and content of adult stories to children as well as of adult intervention in children's stories are shaped by cultural norms (e.g. McCabe 1996; Minami and McCabe 1991) and by the social identities of the adults, such as gender, social class and education (e.g. Fivush 1998; Hicks 1990).

Studies of narrative development, regardless of the kind of data they are based on, tend to focus on any of the following aspects of narrative production: event sequencing, topic maintenance or shifts, ways of referring to story characters, informativeness and evaluation of the stories. Each of these aspects is in turn associated with specific devices: for instance, event sequencing has been looked at in connection with tense choices and shifts. Evaluation has been explored in terms of how emotions are expressed but also in terms of a host of semiotic choices that have also been at the centre of interest of studies of evaluation in narrative in general (see discussion in section 2.1).

The study of cultural specificity in the narrative production of children has yielded rich and relatively consistent findings, at least in terms of where the cultural specificity seems to lie (for details, see our discussion in Chapter 3). For instance, it has shown:

- how cultural norms shape whether stories tend to be monologic or heavily interactional;
- how much emphasis is placed on sequencing events as opposed to creating more tenuous connections that are signaled by, for example, paralinguistic features such as tone of voice;
- how much telling the facts and presenting a version of events as accurate and authentic is valued;
- how explicit references to characters are and how detailed the tellings are;
- who the main characters of a story tend to be and what place the extended family network has in that;
- what the main themes of a story are;
- how children present themselves as characters in their stories.

One of the main applications of narrative development studies has been in the area of education. Two aspects have been found to be relevant here: First, narrative development in preschool children has been found to correlate with reading ability and comprehension later at school (see, for example, McCabe and Bliss 2003). Second, the narrative models and styles that children have been socialized into in their family and peer-group has been found to affect children in terms of their compliance with what is expected and valued at school (e.g. Gee 1991).

The above discussion has tried to identify certain key themes in the area of narrative development, but it needs to be stressed that the field is far from homogeneous. A case in point is Bamberg's edited collection (1997b) on narrative development in which six distinct approaches are represented on the basis of many different criteria, amongst which: the role that they attribute to the individual in development, their conception of the goal of narrative development, their methodology and the function they accord to interaction and culture. We will come back to interactional research on narrative development in Chapter 3, when we discuss how narrative styles are shaped by culture and interaction. We will see that the data on which interactional studies are based are not elicited but come from conversations and discursive practices arising in everyday contexts, either in the family or in the school settings. A more fitting description of the process studied in this type of research is that of "narrative socialization," rather than "narrative development" particularly because of the cognitive focus of the latter. Alongside the shift to the local contextual factors that shape how children tell stories, there has also been a shift of emphasis from the idea of children as passive recipients of narrative toward one in which they are active co-producers of stories (e.g. see chapters in Blum-Kulka and Snow 2002).

1.4   Narrative as mode

The study of narrative as a text-type, as discussed above, represents only one long-standing tradition. Alongside it, there is an equally long-standing cross-disciplinary tradition in which narrative is seen as a mode. Indeed, scholars such as Bruner (1986, 1990), Hymes (1996), Ricoeur (1990), MacIntyre (1981) have proposed that narrative is a mode of thought, communication and apprehension of reality which is both super-arching and fundamental to human cognitive makeup. This view of narrative has inspired many of the proponents of the *narrative turn* (see section 1.4.1 below) in the social sciences, a movement which Bruner (2010) traces back to the publication of two issues of *Critical Inquiry* devoted to Narrative in the autumn of 1980 and summer 1981. The contributors to these issues (social scientists such as Hayden White, Jacques Derrida, Frank Kermode, Nelson Goodman and others) set out to "explore the role of narrative in social and psychological formations, particularly in structures of value and cognition" (Mitchell 1980: vii, quoted in Bruner 2010: 47). Bruner himself is amongst the early proponents of narrative as mode. He sees narrative as a way of apprehending reality and as a primary means of communication. In his famous 1986 paper "Two models of thought," he opposes the narrative to the "logico-scientific" mode, which he calls "paradigmatic," arguing that although both are fundamental human paradigms, and that their products (stories and arguments, respectively) are "natural kinds" (p. 11), the logico-scientific mode has been privileged as an object of investigation and as a tool in the pursuit of knowledge. Both modes have their own objects, methods and validation criteria, but while the paradigmatic mode is based on the confirmation or rejection of hypotheses through their testing against empirical data, the narrative mode is not based on truth, but on verisimilitude. Its value does not lie in the ability to describe reality, but rather in the capacity to give meaning to human experience. In Bruner's words (1986: 13), the narrative mode "leads to good stories, gripping drama, believable (though not necessarily 'true') historical accounts ... and strives ... to locate the experience in time and space." In the narrative mode logic can be used, but it is also often violated, as many narratives bring about ruptures in expected patterns. Human intention and emotion predominate over reason and objectivity, and the worlds of action and consciousness are presented as parallel but separate universes. At the center of the narrative mode are human vicissitudes and drama, and the particularities of human existence rather than its general patterns receive the greatest attention. Thus, for example, while the play Hamlet may be instantiating the old scheme of Oedipal love, it does so in a unique way and through the mind and action of unique characters. Also, in the narrative mode, meaning is not presented in terms of definitive truths, as, for example, in scientific writings where the results of experiments are reported, but as ambiguous and open to exploration. This is particularly clear in fiction where stories lend themselves to multiple interpretations and re-readings. In that sense, according to Bruner, narratives operate through presupposition (by creating implicit meanings) and subjectification (1986: 25), i.e. by presenting events through the point of view of a character and by leaving multiple perspectives open. In sum, both modes are tools that allow humans to know the world, but also reveal the way the human mind works. As Bruner concludes (p. 43):

In the end, the narrative and the paradigmatic come to live side by side. All the more reason for us to move towards an understanding of what is involved in telling and understanding great stories, and how it is that stories create a reality of their own – in life as in art.

The idea that narrative is not merely a genre but constitutes a mode of thought and knowledge connects the work of scholars from a variety of traditions and disciplines. Hymes (1996), for example, embeds his reflections on narrative in a more general discussion about ethnography. He expresses deep concern over the loss of a tradition of narrative ability in modern societies, as for him narrative is a way of understanding and conveying experience and knowledge which maintains a sense of the particular and of the essentially human (see section 2.0). However, unlike other scholars whose interest in narrative as mode is purely academic and philosophical, Hymes is interested in the concrete social implications of the dichotomy between narrative and non-narrative forms of discourse and knowledge. He argues that oppositions such as those between narrative and scientific or scholarly discourse rest on ideological assumptions. Amongst these, for example, is the identification of the narrative mode (particularly the use of personal narratives) with oral, spontaneous, unplanned, concrete uses of language and of the scientific mode with written, carefully crafted, planned and abstract discourse. These oppositions artificially divide human communication and knowledge modes into higher and lower, prestigious and non-prestigious. Also, by associating non-narrative modes with cognitive superiority, they deny the centrality of narrative forms of understanding. Thus, such ideologically driven dichotomies end up setting the stage for social discrimination in education and other social settings. In Hymes' terms (1996: 114):

If one considers that narrative may be a mode of thought, and indeed that narrative may be an inescapable mode of thought, then its differential distribution in a society may be a clue to the distribution of other things as well – rights and privileges having to do with power and money, to be sure, but also rights and privileges having to do with fundamental functions of language itself, its cognitive and expressive uses in narrative form.

In Ricoeur's work ([1983–5] 1990), the narrative mode is connected to a philosophical reflection on the role of time and memory in human life. In his view, narrative has the fundamental role of registering human time, which he opposes to the phenomenological inner time of individual consciousness and to the cosmic time of the universe. Through the telling of stories, humans keep the memory of their experiences, the history of their communities. At the same time, the narrative mode imposes order on the heterogeneity of experience and therefore does not merely reflect it, but constructs it. The idea of narrative as a fundamental mode of knowledge also resonates with Polkinghorne's (1988 and 1991) concept of emplotment as a basic sense-making mechanism. Emplotment is defined as:

A procedure that configures temporal elements into a whole by "grasping them together" and directing them towards a conclusion or ending. Emplotment transforms a list or sequence of disconnected events into a unified story with a point and a theme. (Polkinghorne 1991: 141)

In all the above views, the narrative mode is seen as basic to human understanding of the world.

1.4.1   *Narrative as epistemology – narrative as method*

Common to the perspective on narrative as mode is the endeavor to promote the recognition and acceptance of different types of human inquiry and knowledge and to counter the predominance of scientific and empirical modes in thinking and research. As we have seen, this defense rests on a variety of arguments: one is the idea that narrative is a quintessentially human way of apprehending reality based on emotion and subjectivity (see Oatley 1999 on this point). Another argument is that stories represent the concreteness of human experience as opposed to the abstractness of experiments and general truths. Finally, there is the claim that through the mechanism of emplotment, narrative imposes order on the chaos of human experience of the world. One could conceive of these different positions as converging on a general re-evaluation of the subjective and the particular, which has been one of the driving forces behind the explosion of the narrative turn in the social sciences.

The use of narrative methods and analysis in all fields of the social sciences started gaining momentum from the 1980s onwards. The narrative turn has touched most disciplines in the social sciences. Narrative-based studies have, for example, blossomed in sociology (Bell 1999; Richardson 1992; Riessman 1991, 1993; Somers and Gibson 1994), history (Carr 1991; White 1987), psychology (Bruner, 1986, 1990; Mishler 1986; Oatley 1999; Polkinghorne 1988; Rosenwald and Ochberg 1992) and anthropology (Mattingly 1998; Rosaldo 1993). Scholars have used narratives to analyze participants' views about social issues as diverse as illness and health, social exploitation and isolation, the subordination of women to men, migration. Uniting this wide array of fields and interests is a faith in the power of storytelling as a tool for eliciting people's local knowledge and understandings of social phenomena and of narrative analysis as an instrument for analyzing them. Proponents of the narrative turn have spoken not only against quantitative methodologies that do not pay any attention to the way people generate their own understandings of social reality, but also against ethnographic methods that treat informants as mere vehicles of information (see Narajan and George 2001).

The focus of narrative turn analysts is as much on what is said as on who says it and how, and therefore there is a stated emphasis on language and discourse and greater attention to the contexts of storytelling than in previous traditions within the social sciences. Mishler's early work on interviewing and narrative (1986) was exemplary in drawing attention to the interview as a setting, to the dynamics of story elicitation and emergence within that context and to the significance of the cultural presuppositions that interviewer and interviewee brought to bear when coming face to face. He pointed to co-construction as central to storytelling in interviews and to turn-taking and other discourse mechanisms as worthy objects of attention. His work has served as a guide for much research in the design of narrative-based studies.

While attention to people's individual experience and the focus on discourse are common to social scientists that use narrative analysis, given the cross-disciplinary nature of the field, many differences can also be found in terms of specific theoretical-methodological orientations. Indeed, one finds that scholars take diverse routes in terms of the types of stories that they focus upon and the kinds of analytical toolkit that they adopt. Some analysts focus on life stories (Linde 1993; Mishler 1999), elicited through multiple interviews with informants, and study the way people construct a sense of identity through them. Others work on the different types of stories that people tell about a specific issue, for example illness (Mattingly 1998), in order to understand how people deal with such problems. Yet, others select narrative explanations of particular incidents or events in the life of their subjects, for example divorce accounts (Riessman 1990), as a lead into ways in which people make sense of turning points in their existence. Some focus on case studies and individual stories, while others try to find patterns across interviews and interviewees. Theoretical-methodological orientations vary enormously as well, since choices depend on the discipline involved and the tradition to which researchers belong. In this respect, it would be erroneous to think that the narrative turn in the social sciences has produced a specific approach to narrative.

The many elusive and diverse methodological and analytical perspectives on narrative within the narrative turn partly emanate from a lack of clarity or convergence on whether narrative is an epistemology or a method. As an epistemology, narrative becomes much more than a set of techniques and tools for collecting and analyzing data. It becomes a particular way of constructing knowledge requiring a particular commitment and even bias from the researcher in addition to a political stance. It is instructive here to turn to Blommaert's reflections on the status of ethnography, also indeterminate in its definitions, as an epistemology or a method. According to him, ethnography should be seen as an epistemology because the knowledge that it involves "is constructed by means of everyday, mundane and interpretive resources and mechanisms. Hence the frequency of the inexplicable, intuitive and autobiographical status of much of what ethnographers 'know' about their subject. Method is very often 'added' afterwards" (2001: 2). These observations are immediately applicable to much of narrative research too, which is unashamedly interpretive and subjective and problematizes preconceived ways of collecting data and notions of data categorization.

The very beginnings of the narrative turn are unquestionably epistemological in aims. Narrative, as we have already suggested, was proposed as an antidote to rationality and the quantitative measures prevalent in the social sciences at the time as well as a political tool that celebrated lay experience and lay voices and created opportunities for them to be heard and validated. It was also put forth as an alternative to modernist reality itself, which had brought about the demise of storytelling as a traditional genre thriving in close-knit groups and communities, "the decline of the value of experience" (Benjamin 1968) and the privileging of facts over personal experience. In this sense, many scholars within the narrative turn have associated it with a postmodern reaction to a modernist bias, a reaction that was generated by both a postmodern social reality and a postmodern lens of doing qualitative research (cf. Gabriel 2000: 19). As we have seen, within the narrative turn narrative was put forth as the privileged form of sense-making. Rather than this being based on hard evidence, it mostly stemmed from the simple observation that humans are storytelling organisms who, individually and collectively, lead storied lives (Connelly and Clandinin 1990). In tune with what they saw as their object of inquiry, the researchers of narrative embraced an epistemology that encourages a reflexive empathy with and understanding of the research participants.

Another shift that has been associated with the postmodernist epistemology of the narrative turn is the shift from events to experience (Andrews, Squire and Tamboukou 2008: 5). As we have seen, text-typological and narratological approaches to the definition of narrative traditionally placed emphasis on the temporal sequence of events related in a narrative as well as on the actual correspondence between the real-world events and the narrativized events. The latter were seen as expressions or representations of the former. In contrast to this, "experience-centered research stresses that such representations vary drastically over time, and across the circumstances within which one lives, so that a single phenomenon may produce very different stories, even from the same person" (Andrews, Squire and Tamboukou 2008: 5). This emphasis on the experience of the research participants has distinctly qualified the narrative turn epistemology as interpretive, meaning-seeking, subjective and particularistic, all elements which have stood in contrast to the experimentation and the core values of scientific research, such as reliability, validity and generalizability. The contrast is frequently put in terms of an anti-positivist (*sic* narrative) vs. a positivist epistemology.

The narrative turn with its research participants-driven agenda has become a pivotal perspective (often referred to as "the narrative perspective") in numerous domains such as organizational research, health research, etc. A case in point is the so-called narrative-based medicine. Set out as a patient-centered perspective, in contrast to a doctor-centered one, narrative-based medicine advocates the role and study of narrative at different levels (Greenhalgh and Hurwitz 1998: 7): the diagnostic encounter where patients should be encouraged to tell stories of their illnesses as valuable meaning-making tools and where narratives can promote understanding and empathy between clinician and patient; the therapeutic process, where narratives "encourage a holistic approach to management, are themselves intrinsically therapeutic or palliative and may suggest or precipitate additional therapeutic options" (p. 7). Finally, the level of the education of patients and professionals where "narratives are often memorable, grounded in experience and enforce reflection" (p. 7).

The narrative turn has also been instrumental in questioning the objectivity and positivist outlook of numerous social science and humanities disciplines, including that of history and historiography. In an oft-quoted paper, White (1987) suggested that writing about the past is not an objective, full-proof discourse that holds an absolute truth but a process of imposing order, structure and coherence onto the past. In doing so, historians use well-defined and culturally recognized plots such as romances, tragedies and comedies, and in this respect, they are not very different from writers of fiction. By relativizing the distinction between fact and fiction, truth and plot-making, White does not set out to undermine the validity of historical accounts but instead to put forth narrative epistemology as a legitimate way of constructing knowledge. This is far from controversial within history, and as Schwandt (1997: 97–8) puts it:

There is a long-standing controversy in the discipline of history over whether stories about past events (historical narratives) explain the occurrence of those events. The debate unfolds between defenders of formal scientific explanation on the one hand and proponents of a unique form of narrative understanding on the other, and thus the debate echoes the more general argument over... the proper goal of social inquiry. The critical issue here is epistemology, namely the nature and justification of knowledge claims ... Whether narrative explanations actually are legitimate explanations or only fictional narratives continues to be an important topic in philosophy of history.

In general, a prevalent tendency within the narrative turn is ultimately to blur clear-cut distinctions between "story and fact, story and other narratives, story and embellishment, story and interpretation" (Gabriel 2000: 17). As we suggested above, the narrative turn has been ubiquitous in the social sciences, and it has had profound implications for how social scientific qualitative methods are currently being conceived. However, as tends to be the case with all dominant paradigms, it has also been the object of intense critique. To begin with, the narrative primacy, that is the privileged position that the narrative turn has accorded to narrative, has increasingly come under scrutiny. There are two theses associated with this primacy, as Strawson suggests (2004), both of which are questionable. The first thesis claims that human beings experience their lives as narrative and in narrative form. The second, related, thesis states that experiencing one's life as narrative is essential to a well-lived life. It has to be noted that both of these theses are subscribed to in varying degrees within the narrative turn and that there are more or less moderate positions around them. At its extreme though, the position that human lives are essentially storied and that an individual cannot have true or full personhood but through the form-finding act of narration have come under fire. One of the premises of this thesis that has been viewed as methodologically problematic is that narrative is a unique form-finding and meaning-making activity. At issue here is both the privileged role accorded to narrative at the expense of other communication activities and the fact that the process of telling a story is equated with the process of imposing structure and coherence on the events (for a detailed discussion, see Chapter 6, section 2.0). Closely related to these objections is the argument that the celebratory view of narrative as a privileged mode of human communication has often lent itself to transparent or representational approaches, which treat what the tellers say as documents of life, accurate reflections of realities and thus take tellings at face value (e.g. Atkinson and Delamont 2006). These approaches are, in Josselson's terms, "animated by faith in the tellers and by the analysts' intention to record and restore as faithfully as possible the meaning addressed to them as interpreters" (2004: 3).

The problem with this tendency is that it assumes the existence of a true and given story that each teller possesses. It thus overlooks the intimate connections of what is told in a story with the here-and-now of the telling, i.e. the actual environment or context in which the story occurs. This emphasis on the context-specificity of narrative tellings is something that we will discuss in detail throughout this book.

A view of narrative as a mirror of experience is not shared by psychoanalytically inclined scholars either. Their position instead is that a "told story conceals an untold one" (Josselson 2004: 13), that what is not said or is unsayable is also a vital part of the teller's experience and that there will always be gaps and ruptures in meaning-making. So it rests upon the analyst to make the connections, decipher and discover meanings that remain "hidden within a false consciousness" (p. 5).

At a different level, analysts who seek to delimit narrative as a text-type or equally as a genre have also found the narrative primacy of the narrative turn as an unhelpfully underspecified and anything-goes position that has lent itself to presenting narrative as a deceptively homogeneous mode (for a discussion, see Georgakopoulou and Goutsos 2000: 68–9). As we have already suggested, it is true to say that there is a fair amount of variability within the narrative turn as to how narrative is defined, with more or less all-encompassing definitions at play. At its worst, this lack of specificity has hampered the development of agreed tools and frameworks of analysis, which is being increasingly deplored by leading scholars in the field. A case in point is Riessman who recently urged students of narrative

> to resist the loose talk about narrative that is common these days. The term has come to mean anything beyond a few bullet points; when someone speaks or writes more than a few lines, the outcome is now called narrative by news anchors and even some qualitative investigators. Narrative runs the danger in this usage of becoming little more than a metaphor. (2008: 152)

Having undoubtedly served as a rather revolutionary outlook within the social sciences, the narrative turn seems now to be heading toward a re-examination of its core assumptions. This is in the face not only of the existence of numerous and at times competing perspectives within its remit, but also of profound socio-cultural changes. As Savage and Burrows aptly point out, talking about qualitative methods in general, "although it was sociologists who pioneered the use of interviews in allowing popular narratives to become 'public,' the routine use of such methods in all forms of contemporary journalism, from the colour magazine to the Oprah Winfrey show marks a clear shift of expertise away from the academy" (2007: 891). They also point out that the interview as a method of eliciting narratives and in turn studying people's identities may be an important resource, but it is an insufficient one to capture the fluidity of modern lives. We will return to this big question of the place of interviews within narrative studies at various points in the book, and particularly in Chapter 6.

1.5   Analyzing narrative

Researchers who start in narrative studies are eager to find methods that can help them both define their object of investigation and study it. The reality is that there is no one-fit-for-all method of narrative analysis. Methodological choices, which are often eclectic, combine insights and conceptions that come from different disciplines.

Having said that, some very basic distinctions between orientations in narrative research can be drawn, and these largely determine the methodologies most commonly used within each tradition. In this respect, certain typologies have been proposed that describe aspects in which methodological approaches may differ. A case in point is the typology of narrative studies proposed by Mishler (1995) who distinguished between the following:

a. Studies focused on temporal ordering and reference. Within this orientation the interest is on the content of the narratives: either events or experiences are focused upon, not the act of telling per se.
b. Studies based on the analysis of coherence and structural makeup. Here the focus is on the properties that characterize narratives as opposed to other texts.
c. Studies centered on the investigation of narrative functions in social contexts. Their focus is on the interactional and social work that narrators do through stories, on the settings and on the concrete effects and consequences of narrative talk.

Further typologies have been proposed more recently by two social scientists: Jane Elliott (2005) and Catherine K. Riessman (2008). Elliott talks about the elicitation of narratives within the research interview as a qualitative method in itself. Within that method she then considers differences between what she calls a "naturalist" versus a "constructivist" approach (p.18). Naturalist approaches assume the "transparency" of the narrative data with respect to an external reality (see also Mishler's distinction between "the telling" and "the told"). Following Mishler, Riessman proposes a distinction between "thematic approaches" focused on the "what" of narrative (i.e. on the content of stories), structural analysis (focused on the way narratives are organized and therefore on how meanings are presented), and dialogic-performance analysis, i.e. an approach that draws on elements of thematic and structural analysis but makes them part of broader interpretive research agendas. In her view, while thematic and structural analyses do not pay attention to the roles of participants in the storytelling event and the local context of storytelling, dialogic performance analysis does.

Rather than representing hard-and-fast divisions between approaches, these distinctions point to parameters that may vary in research methodologies. Indeed, most researchers adopt eclectic methods, and studies can be placed on continua with respect to the amount of attention that they devote, for example, to the "what" or the "how" of narratives. However, even the broad distinction between emphasis on form and emphasis on content should by no means be taken as absolute. In fact, most investigations that focus on content, i.e. on story worlds, protagonists, events, etc. also discuss the "how," i.e. the forms in which such content is organized by narrators either by looking at temporal and causal sequences, or by looking at evaluation devices. Thus, a more productive way of differentiating methods of narrative analysis may be to look at variations in some of the research parameters adopted, for example the following:

1. Object of analysis:
   a. narratives as texts/genres
   b. events, identities, social phenomena (i.e. contexts that are external to the storytelling event)
   c. storytelling as communicative/interactional/process
2. General methodological approach:
   a. qualitative (focus on small samples, distrust of pre-existing hypotheses, emphasis on observation and analysis of participants' understandings, discovery of units of analysis)
   b. experimental/quantitative (hypothesis testing in research environments, large body of data, use of predetermined units and models of analysis)
   c. eclectic (elements of both)
3. Methods of data collection:
   a. elicited
   b. non-elicited
   c. research-independent (natural) contexts
   d. research-dependent (experimental) contexts

4. Types of data:
   a. oral/interactional
   b. written
   c. multimodal
5. Data analysis:
   a. focus on language/style (how are people narrating?)
   b. focus on content/themes (what are people narrating about?)
   c. focus on interactional processes and social practices (how do participants engage in narrative practices? Why?)

A consideration of the object of analysis allows for a first, significant distinction amongst those analysts who are interested in structure, those interested in storytelling as a way of accomplishing social action and those interested in the social phenomena, events and identities represented by and constructed through storytelling. Such distinctions in turn generally imply also specific methodological orientations. In fact, as we saw in section 1.4.1 above, many researchers (particularly within the narrative turn) refer to "narrative" as a method of inquiry per se. But this conception of narrative as a method is not shared by all narrative analysts since it rests on the assumption that narratives are tools that facilitate the understanding of some non-narrative phenomenon. Such an assumption is not shared (or only partly shared) by those who are interested, for example, in narrative as discourse or text unit, as a cognitive construct, as a kind of social practice. In addition to this, it must be noted that even among social scientists who use narrative as a method of inquiry, there is a great deal of variation in approaches to data analysis, data-gathering techniques and conceptions of narrative itself.

The list of parameters provided here can help readers better place the various models and scholars that we will present in this book. In terms of data, our emphasis will be on oral/interactional storytelling, while in terms of analysis our emphasis will be on approaches that have advocated attention to the language/ style, interactional processes and social practices of storytelling.

2   Narrative as text and structure

2.0   Introduction

As we discussed in Chapter 1, narrative is widely held as fundamental in human communication. Not only do speakers use narratives in most communicative activities, but they also seem to hold intuitive assumptions and expectations about what constitutes a ("good") story. However, the objective characterization of what counts as a story within the stream of discourse, of how it is internally organized and of how it can be separated from the talk surrounding it remains one of the most daunting tasks for linguists and discourse analysts working in the field, a preoccupation that can be traced back to Aristotle's *Poetics*. As we saw in Chapter 1, in more recent times, the definition of story units and components has been a central concern for narratology (e.g. Bal 1985; Genette 1980; Prince 1982) and for cognitive theories of text understanding such as story grammars (e.g. Mandler 1982; Mandler and Johnson 1977; Rumelhart 1975, 1980; Thorndyke 1977).The study of narrative structure across cultures and geographic areas has also occupied center stage in research about oral stories and fables in folk traditions (Propp 1968). In this chapter, we single out linguistic approaches to narrative structure that focus on ordinary storytelling and prioritize the linguistic means through which structural organization is achieved. Even though there are certain common guiding assumptions in this kind of inquiry, there have also been clear divergences amongst different perspectives. In the following sections, we will focus on differing conceptualizations of narrative structure within three approaches to narrative that have been particularly influential in linguistics: Labov's model, ethnopoetics and conversation analysis. We will take each approach separately and discuss its main assumptions and the criteria employed for identifying structural units. We will then assess their strengths and weaknesses and propose questions and avenues for future research. The discussion will highlight the difficulties involved in the definition and identification of narrative units and in keeping a balance between a focus on local phenomena and an interest in possible generalizations about the nature of narrative organization.

2.1   Labov's model

The pivotal position of narrative structure among the focal concerns of narrative analysis cannot be underestimated. Over the years, narrative structure has formed not only a powerful analytical apparatus but also a widely accepted way of thinking about and studying narrative; indeed, a hallmark of a number of diverse perspectives in both narrative analysis and narratology. It is by no means an exaggeration to suggest that one of the most influential approaches to narrative structure, and arguably the most influential within linguistics, has been the one proposed by Labov (1972; initially Labov and Waletzky 1967).

William Labov started working on oral narratives as part of a broader sociolinguistic project on vernacular language variation. Since he was interested in obtaining spontaneous vernacular forms of speech, he employed the elicitation of narratives as a technique for reducing the effects of observation and recording, thus allowing his informants to lower their monitor on speech production and to get involved in the conversation with researchers. Labov assumed that getting his informants to talk about a "sensational" key event from their past would be effective in distracting them from the formality and seriousness of the interview situation. He thus asked them if they had ever been in danger of dying, and as a result he was able to collect a great deal of narratives of personal experience told in response to this prompt. His original model of narrative analysis was elaborated in a paper written with Joshua Waletzky (Labov and Waletzky 1967) and subsequently revised on three occasions (Labov 1972, 1981 and 1997).

Labov and Waletzky defined narrative as "one verbal technique for recapitulating past experience, in particular a technique of constructing narrative units which match the temporal sequence of that experience" (1967: 13). Thus, from their perspective, not all texts that recount a past experience can be regarded as narrative. Instead, the defining property of narrative is temporal sequence, since the order in which the events are presented in the narrative is expected to match the original events as they occurred in the extra-linguistic world. There is thus an assumption that the events of the taleworld are in a referential relationship of straightforward mapping with the actual ("real life") antecedent events. This referentiality between actual and told events has puzzled many narrative analysts[1] (see our discussion in 2.1.2).

2.1.1   Narrative units

The basic narrative unit in the Labovian model is the independent clause, the smallest textual element that can convey punctual events. Labov and Waletzky noted that the relationship between clauses and events in a narrative text is not simple, since there are many types of clauses that do not appear to sequentially refer to the action in the story. Narrative clauses are those independent clauses which are ordered temporally in such a fashion that their sequence cannot be altered without changing the interpretation of events. Let us look at the following set of clauses taken from one of the narratives studied by Labov and Waletzky:

> (2.1)
> w and they was catching up to me
> x and I crossed the street
> y and I tripped, man
>
> (From Labov and Waletzky 1967: 21)

In the excerpt, x and y are defined as narrative clauses because they are temporally ordered in such a way that changing their sequence will modify our interpretation of the original events, while clause w can be moved after x or y without any change in interpretation. Labov and Waletzky distinguish between different types of clauses depending on their ability to move within the text without altering the interpretation of story world events but stress that the backbone of a narrative resides in the narrative clauses, i.e. clauses temporally ordered with respect to each other, or, in their terms, separated by "temporal juncture" (1967: 25). So, the linear succession of clauses represents the surface structure of the narrative, but the order of events is given by the sequence of the narrative clauses. Syntactically, narrative clauses are usually characterized by main verbs in the simple past or past continuous tense, while other continuous forms and more complex verbal constructions are more typical of non-narrative clauses.

Although clauses have an important role in this model, narratives cannot be reduced to strings of clauses but are characterized by the presence of higher units. The basic components of a well-formed narrative of personal experience described in Labov and Waletzky (1967) and refined in Labov (1972, 1981 and 1997) are six sections that reflect the typical progression of a narrative from the establishment of a setting to a complication, to a resolution and a return to the present. These narrative components, usually realized by clauses that have the same function as the higher unit in which they participate, are the following:

Abstract The objective of the abstract is to summarize what the story is about. Abstracts are usually represented by one or two clauses that describe the gist of a story (e.g. *did I ever tell you about the day I fell from a boat?* or *something funny happened the other day*).

Orientation The function of orientation sections is to "orient the listener in respect to person, place, time, and behavioral situation" (1967: 32). Labov recognized in the 1972 revision that much of the orientation material can be embedded into the complicating action as opposed to forming a separate pre-complicating action component.

Complicating action This section presents what happened in the narrative. It answers the question: "And then what happened?" It represents the main body (skeleton) of a narrative, i.e. the basic events around which the story revolves.

Resolution This part of the narrative is characterized as the result of the narrative, and it often coincides with the last narrative clause. The resolution relates how the complication was solved.

Coda The coda builds a bridge between the story world and the present; it can therefore be conveyed through different linguistic devices. For example, the narrator can refer to the present effects of the events told in the story, follow a character's evolution after the story has ended, or offer a moral lesson.

Evaluation The function of the evaluation is to provide the point of view of the narrator on the events and to guide the listener with regard to the significance of the narrative. In this way, it answers a possible, "So what?" question on the part of the listener. Since a story grants the speaker a long turn, the narrator needs to show that the narrative was worth the audience attention. A story without evaluation is simply a sequence of events with no point, while a good narrative is one in which the narrator is able to convey certain interpretations about the facts and an appraisal of the main characters. For this reason, evaluation is more widespread in stories of personal experience than in stories of events vicariously experienced by the narrator. While Labov and Waletzky (1967) talked about evaluation as a section, Labov (1972) recognized that evaluative devices are in fact interspersed throughout the narrative, although they often cluster toward the end of the story to provide clues on its meaning for the listener. In his 1972 paper, the author lists a great number of evaluative devices that can contribute to the point of a story and describes them in relation to their syntactic complexity. He distinguishes between *external, embedded* or *internal* evaluation. Through external evaluation devices, the narrator stops the sequence of events and steps out of the story world in order to explicitly comment on aspects of it. But the narrator does not always need to be so explicit: she or he can embed the evaluation within the story, for example by presenting her or his thoughts as occurring to her or him at the moment, or through reporting dialogue as it occurred in the story world. Labov regards internal evaluation that is deeply embedded into the complicating action as highly complex and narrators who use this kind of evaluation as communicatively skilled.

Labov postulated the following four types of internal evaluative devices:

a. **Intensifiers** are used to enhance one particular event. They are elements such as gestures, expressive phonology, quantifiers, repetition, or ritual utterances. Unlike the other three types of evaluation, intensifiers are super-imposed or added onto the basic narrative syntax without affecting the basic form of the verb phrase.

b. **Comparators** contrast what happened with what could have happened thus moving away from the actual events to consider possibilities. They can occur in the main verb of the narrative and include negatives, futures, and modals.

c. **Correlatives** bring together two events that occurred by conjoining them in a single independent clause. Among correlatives we find progressive forms of the verb, double appositives (*a knife, a long one, a dagger*) and double attributives (*a wet, cold, day*).

d. **Explicatives** suspend the narrative action to go back or forward in time. They are embedded clauses appended to the main clause, introduced by markers such as *while, though, since, because, that.*

Not all of the structural components listed above need be present for a text to be regarded as a narrative. In fact, abstracts and codas are more typical of elicited or highly ritualized narratives than of spontaneous ones. Thus, many narratives only consist of an orientation, complicating action, resolution and evaluation.

In order to exemplify Labov and Waletzky's model, we reproduce their ana-lysis of one of the stories discussed in their original paper. The story, in which a narrator relates how he almost got killed by a woman's jealous husband, is elicited through the usual danger of death question:

(2.2)
R: Were you ever in a situation where you thought you were in serious danger of getting killed?
I: I talked a man out of – Old Doc Simon I talked him out of pulling the trigger.
R: What happened?

The interviewee's answer to the question can be regarded as the abstract of the story since it summarizes the main point of the events that will be recounted in the narrative. After R's second question prompting the telling, the story begins:[2]

OR a Well, in the business I was associated at that time, the Doc was an old man...
OR b He had killed one man,
OR c or- had done time.
OR d But he had a young wife

OR e and these days I dressed well.

OR f And seemingly, she was trying to make me.

OR g I never noticed it.

OR h Fact is, I didn't like her very well, because she had – she was a nice looking girl until you saw her feet.

OR i She had big feet

OR j Jesus, God, she had big feet!

CA k Then she left a note one day
   she was going to commit suicide
   because he was always raising hell about me.

CA l He came to my hotel. Nice big 44 too.

CA m I talked him out of it,

EV n and says, "Well, we'll go look for her,

EV o   and if we can't find her, well, you
             can – go ahead, pull the trigger if you
             want to."

EV p I was maneuvering.

CA q So he took me up on it.

CA r And we went to where they found her handkerchief –
   the edge of a creek –

CA s And we followed down a little more,

CA t And we couldn't find anything.

CA u And got back –

OR v It was a tent show –

CA w she was laying on a cot with an ice bag on her
   head.

EV x She hadn't committed suicide.

RES y But – however – that settled it for the day.

CA z But that night the manager, Floyd Adams, said,
   "You better pack up

CA aa and get out,
       because that son of a bitch never forgives anything once he gets it
       in his head."

CA bb And I did.

CA cc I packed up

CA dd and got out.

CO ee that was two. (Labov and Waletzky, 1967: 35–6)

According to Labov and Waletzky, the narrative opens with a long orientation section (lines a–j) in which the narrator sets the stage for the protagonist's actions describing his associate's young wife and how she was flirting with him. Notice that through lines g–j he orients the listener toward his innocence with respect to possible accusations of complicity with the wife, since he stresses both the fact that he had not noticed the woman's behavior and the fact that he did not find her attractive. The complicating action starts in line k, with the announcement of the girl's intention to kill herself and proceeds through lines l–o depicting first the Doc's plan to shoot the protagonist and then the latter's clever defense. Line p stops the action revealing the protagonist's real intentions, while lines q–u and w bring forward the complicating action, depicting the search for the woman by Doc and the protagonist and their finding her in good conditions. Line x represents another open evaluation of the events, while line y constitutes a complicating action clause, which is in fact the resolution of the problem that initiated the narrative. Lines z–dd are also narrative clauses in that they present events separated by temporal juncture, while line ee represents the coda by bridging the listener's attention back to the present.

2.1.2   Coding issues

The story above is typical of Labov's data-set in that it is fairly monologic, it revolves around a factual complication, it is rich in evaluation devices, and it has a clear beginning and ending. However, some of the coding problems that stem from the application of a model which tries to combine a formal, syntactic characterization of narrative units with a functional definition of story constituents become immediately apparent. The main question concerns the definition of evaluation and evaluation clauses and the overlap between this coding category and the coding of other types of clauses. Labov and Waletzky clearly saw this difficulty, as demonstrated in the following text:

Not all evaluation sections have the structural feature of suspending the complicating action … In many cases, the evaluation may be present as lexical or phrasal modification of a narrative clause, or it may be itself a narrative clause, or coincide with the last narrative clause. For this reason, the fundamental definition of evaluation must be semantic, although its implications are structural. (1967: 37)

However, recognizing the semantic status of evaluation does not solve the problem of classifying clauses according to the model. For example, in the narrative presented above, many narrative clauses also have a clear evaluative function. A case in point is in lines m–o reporting the dialogue between the two men, which are designed to make the protagonist look cool and able to face a difficult situation. These clauses do not merely move the action forward; they also present the protagonist under a positive light. At the same time, the status of clauses reporting dialogue is not all that clear since Labov talks about reported speech as an embedded evaluation device. As a consequence, clauses that contain reported speech are classified sometimes as complicating action, and sometimes as evaluation. For example, lines z–aa, which report the manager's advice to the protagonist after he has been able to escape the doctor's revenge, may be regarded as embedded evaluation, since they deal with the possible consequences of events in the story, but also as complicating action, since it is as a consequence of the manager's words that the protagonist packs up and leaves. This kind of ambiguity can be seen in further analyses presented by Labov.[3]

Finally, although lines a–j represent orientation clauses (as they provide information necessary to understand the events recounted later), they are also highly evaluative since they shed a particular light on the protagonists. Thus, even though some clauses can clearly be classified as evaluative, other clauses combine different functions and therefore their status is ambiguous. As we will discuss later, these problems that are already apparent when trying to code narratives told in interviews, become even more serious with narratives that are neither monologic nor well structured.

Another problem that Labov tried to address in his later writings was the inadequacy of a purely structural approach to narrative. Labov realized that a description of narrative exclusively in terms of temporal juncture would not allow for a clear distinction between different kinds of narratives such as chronicles of past events and personal stories. Thus, he worked on *reportability* and *credibility* as important criteria for characterizing successful stories. Labov asserted that what is reportable changes according to situation and culture, but that all narrators need to demonstrate the reportability of their stories if they want to be heard. Credibility also needs to be established in order for the narrator to avoid challenges or accusations of lying. In his 1997 paper, Labov slightly revised his model by specifying and rephrasing some of the definitions presented in Labov and Waletzky (1967) and also by changing the focus from an emphasis on the construction of a formal framework for understanding narratives toward greater consideration of "reportability, credibility, objectivity, casuality, and the assignment of praise and blame" (p. 397). He thus rephrased his definition of narrative in the following terms: "A narrative of personal experience is a report of a sequence of events that have entered into the biography of the speaker by a sequence of clauses that correspond to the original events" (p. 393). This new definition emphasizes the personal significance of the events recounted as an important criterion for distinguishing stories from chronicles or simple descriptions of the past. In this way, it resonates with the importance accorded to the dynamics of experientiality as a definitional criterion of narrative, as we discussed in Chapter 1.

Overall, with his revision in 1997, Labov proposed the following changes: he specified the properties of narrative and non-narrative clauses, rephrased his definition of evaluation as information on the consequences of an event "for human needs and desires" (p. 403), and redefined reportability as "the telling of at least one event that has a great effect on the needs and desires of the participants in the narrative" (p. 406). He also related reportability to credibility. In his terms, a "serious" narrative must be credible, and in order to establish credibility the narrator needs to present logical causal relations between events. In addition, Labov analyzed other aspects that are important to the success of a story, concluding that narratives which appear to be based on objective observation and description seem to have a stronger impact than narratives that report events in a more subjective way. However, it has been pointed out by many that the possibility of narrative objectivity is in itself questionable. As Slembrouck (2003: 465) observes:

> History is not just a fabrication of the past but on the border between present and past; it is a labor of memory as left-overs in the interactional present. While narrativizations (however brief) depend on memory structures which are part of conditions of tellability, there is also the question of how the interactional moment pushes the memory to be activated in a particular direction.

Truth and the narrative reproduction of reality are often not only impossible to establish, but also, not equally relevant to all narratives, as Bauman (1986) has eloquently shown in his analysis of the function of tall tales in conversations among Texan hunters.[4]

2.1.3   Appraisal of the Labovian model

Labov succeeded in productively applying to oral storytelling a tradition that had put forth plot or thematic criteria as principles of structural organization in narrative (e.g. Propp 1968). His model was also instrumental in incorporating as part of structure what least lent itself to that, namely the affective, emotive, subjective and experiential aspects of narrative. This was done by postulating *evaluation* both as a separate structural unit and as a micro-level mechanism that can apply to an entire narrative. Evaluation thus captured a wide range of linguistic means by which a series of events could be communicated and recognized as being narratable or reportable.

In the light of the above, Labov's narrative structure encapsulates the definitional criteria of narrative on which analysts tend to converge, and its profound influence in the field has to be seen in connection with that fact. As we discussed in Chapter 1, these criteria involve (a) the presence of a change-of-state or disruption of balance (cf. complication, turning point, peripeteia, trouble) and (b) chronological ordering or more generally event sequencing. The long-standing tradition of exploring the relation between time and narrative (e.g. Ricoeur [1983–5] 1990) has implicated viewing structural organization through the lens of sequencing and disruption of balance (and its subsequent resolution or denouement, an idea which can be traced as far back as Aristotle).

Another strength of Labov's model is that it provided a general frame for understanding the narrative structure cross-culturally that questioned the traditional gulf between literary and vernacular storytelling. Indeed, he insisted on the fact that "little will be understood about the structure and function of complex narratives until the simplest and most fundamental narratives have been formally described and related to their social context" (Labov and Waletzky 1967: 12).

An often rehearsed point of critique of Labov's model relates to its dependence on (largely) monological narratives told in interviews. These data did not present cases of systematic audience participation, co-construction of the story between teller and audience and many other phenomena that characterize the telling of narratives in interaction (see Chapter 4 for a discussion). Although an effort to correct this exclusive focus on the narrator can be seen in Labov's most recent paper (1997) where the efficacy of a narrative is judged on the basis of the audience reaction to it, the model still lacks coding categories or any other means of incorporating interactional processes in the description of narrative discourse. In this way, it treats stories as largely monologic artifacts. This may be true for stories in interviews where normally a fairly attentive, non-disruptive interviewer gives the floor to the interviewee and carefully chooses prompts that ensure lengthy accounts. Nevertheless, as we will suggest below, even these specific communicative arrangements do not make up for the neglect within Labov's model of the interactional dynamics involved in the online unfolding of a story's telling that goes beyond the restrictive dyad of a teller vs. a recipient.

Lack of attention to the interactional processes at play during a storytelling event goes hand in hand with the view of a narrative as detachable from its surrounding discourse event, that is, from prior and following text; in other words, as an autonomous and free-standing text that can be analyzed in units in its own right and without reference to its co-text. Prior text can be conceived not only as the immediately preceding text(s) but also as other texts told on other occasions that may bear on the here-and-now of the storytelling event. This relationality of prior and present texts, which is often described as intertextuality, does not sit well with Labov's postulation of an autonomous narrative structure.[5] In fact, the lack of sensitivity in Labov's model to storytelling participation roles has been seen as symptomatic of a more general marginalization of the role of situational (i.e. immediate) context in shaping a story's structure. The influence of both the local context and the sociocultural variation on story structure have been well attested in studies that were inspired in the first place by Labov's model. This post-Labovian line of inquiry consists of numerous empirically based projects[6] in a wide range of settings that have documented:

- the culturally based schematic or scenario-based expectations about structure and the ways in which they shape it (e.g. Chafe 1980; Polanyi 1981; Tannen 1979);
- the sociocultural and situational variability of narrative structure;

- the dispensability of certain story sections (particularly the fragility of the abstract and coda in conversational events, Georgakopoulou 1997) and the infrequent occurrence of others (e.g. evaluation as a separate component), or equally their prominence;
- the cultural values attached to spatial organization in parallel with or as opposed to temporality resulting in the re-assessment of the role of orientation (e.g. Briggs 1997; De Fina 2003b and 2009a; Herman 2001);
- the context-specificity of audience participation during the telling of a story (e.g. Cedeborg and Aronsson 1994; Goodwin 1986); more significantly, the context-dependency of the ways in which the point of a story is shown or told (e.g. Linde 1993; Norrick 1997).

These revisions and ramifications ultimately suggest the staying power and the influence of Labov's structural components, evaluation in particular, even though his formal clausal analysis has been criticized and seen as unworkable (cf. Bruner 1997: 62). As Holmes aptly puts it, "they [the structural components] have proved remarkably robust and have had extensive use for many and varied purposes by researchers in a very wide range of disciplines" (1997: 95). Not only have they formed the basis of various elaborations and ramifications; they have also more or less directly informed the conceptual work out of which narrative analysis has taken most of its mileage in the last three decades,[7] and it is in this context of intense engagement with Labov's model and inspiration by it that any critique of it has to be seen. It is not an exaggeration in fact to suggest that narrative analysis seems unable to get away from Labov's approach. In Holmes's vivid terms, "as I proceeded I found that in whichever direction I attempted to develop the analysis, I kept inescapably returning to the need to first establish the basic structure of narratives" (1997: 95). Schegloff also notes – albeit with disapproval – that "it is striking to what degree features of the 1967 article have remained characteristic of treatments of narrative" (1997: 101).

Overall though, lack of attention to context (be it situational or sociocultural) has become the hallmark of the critique of Labov's model. The view that structural units can be postulated by the analyst a priori of local contexts and as context-free, universal elements has been criticized as too static.

2.2   Ethnopoetics, stanza and verse analysis

In contrast to Labov, ethnopoetics treats narrative structure as something that cannot be assumed a priori and independently of the context, or, more specifically, of the broader cultural environment in which storytelling occurs. The emphasis here is on the different linguistic resources that languages and peoples employ in storytelling and on the links between narratives and socioculturally mediated ways of apprehending reality. Ethnopoetic analysis (see Tedlock 1983; Woodbury 1985) aimed at the revalorization of traditional forms of verbal and visual art, particularly among societies that had been ignored by mainstream intellectual inquiry. The method was developed by Dell Hymes (1981, 1996, 1998 and 2004) within the framework of the ethnography of communication and reflected his interest in the description of Native American oral tradition.

The study of narrative traditions among Native Americans became part of a more general project that involved the investigation of principles underlying the workings of different languages, with the aim of showing that oral cultural traditions are not inferior to those that produce written genres. This line of inquiry served as an alternative to dominant linguistic models that were based on the primacy of innate biological factors in language structure and development. In ethnopoetics, the study of oral narratives was seen as intimately connected to the investigation of cultures and their specific ways of apprehending and organizing reality; also, as a means of achieving a better understanding of local forms of knowledge. Hymes' work on narrative also needs to be understood within the study of verbal art and performance in non-literate cultures that became a focus of interest amongst ethnographers and anthropologists in the 1970s and early 1980s (Bright 1982; Darnell 1974; Kirshenblatt-Gimblett 1974; Scollon and Scollon 1981; Sherzer 1983; Tedlock 1972). Narrative in this approach is a primary means of experiencing and making sense of the world but also a culturally shaped way of speaking that has a special place in the repertoire of a community's sociolinguistic genres. (See section 3.1 for a discussion of this point).

The ethnopoetic approach to narrative structure involves looking at the ways in which texts are organized as both reflecting and (re)creating a cultural tradition of meaning-making, while recognizing the uniqueness of the voice of social actors as interpreters and the potential for creativity and innovation provided by the continuous revisiting of traditional forms in new contexts. This conception of texts as interwoven with social forms of knowledge has a direct antecedent in Voloshinov (1973) and his work on language as a symbolic system based on social process through which shared meanings are constructed. Another important influence on Hymes' approach is traceable to the work of the anthropologist Franz Boas on rhythm and formal patterning in "primitive" art (1927) and to Jakobson's (1968) analyses of the formal mechanisms characterizing poetic language. These analyses involved intensive listening to texts and using existing knowledge about language and culture to find significant patterns at all levels.

The basic unit of analysis in Hymes' model is the *line*, which corresponds to one intonation unit. Some lines have sentence-like contours, but others may be equivalent to smaller units such as phrases. According to Hymes, the building blocks of narrative are *verses*, i.e. units that have sentence-like contours. Verses may be made up of more than one line and form patterns at different levels of organization. They are the basis for larger units such as *stanzas*, scenes and acts. How are these units recognized? Ethnopoetic analysis looks at systematic co-variation between (prosodic, lexical or syntactic) form and meaning, so that recurrence of the same patterns and equivalence at the same or different levels become basic guiding principles to uncover structure. Hymes (1981) found that in the Wishram Chinhook stories (as dictated by Louis Simpson), which he studied, verses were marked by couples of particles such as *now then*, or *now again* that consistently occurred in initial position. These markers provided initial cues for recognizing verses, but the most important criterion used to segment narratives was the existence of relations constituting recognizable patterns. For example, numerical patterns governing the sequencing of lines, verses, stanzas and scenes were found to be typical of specific cultures. When examining Native American texts, Hymes found patterns of two and four or three and five (present, for example, in the grouping of verses and stanzas, but also of narrative actions) that were characteristic of those storytelling traditions. He argued that verses can be recognized thanks to the existence of these numerical patterns in all languages (including English), but they are also based on the semantic relations expressed within and between units. For example, verses usually revolve around a specific action or property of a character or an object; they also present lexical repetitions or synonyms that refer to a basic concept. As mentioned, verses form higher units: stanzas, scenes and parts whose endpoints are signaled by connections between syntactic and prosodic factors and major changes at the level of semantic content, such as in the types of actions carried out in the story world, or in the relationships between actions and outcomes.

Hymes showed how close analysis of co-occurrences can reveal interesting facts about culturally specific relations of form and meaning. For example, in Chinookan texts he found a connection between four-part relations (two lines and two lines) and the foregrounding of women as actors (2004: 5). He also found that different tellers established patterns of tradition and innovation that could only be discovered through intense listening of audio-recorded data, repeated analysis and revision. Thus, his methodology involved discovering units and structure through reflection, trial and error.

Besides demonstrating the existence of an internal organization of narrative that reflects culturally specific ways of understanding reality, Hymes also drew attention to the poetic quality of verbal texts produced by oral cultures and, in particular, of traditional forms of storytelling. He specifically argued that the use of artistic patterns such as parallel structures, rhythmic repetitions and lexical oppositions attests to a high level of formal skills and cultural sophistication. In his terms, narratives are organized in ways that "make them formally poetry" and thus they embody "a rhetoric of action, that is, an implicit schema for the organization of experience" (1996: 121).[8]

Line and stanza analysis of the kind proposed by Hymes was subsequently applied by other linguistic anthropologists to the study of oral narratives in non-literate societies. For example, Scollon and Scollon (1981) analyzed Athabaskan narratives following an ethnopoetic model. They also divided stories into units characterized according to prosodic, syntactic and semantic principles, but they were more explicit than Hymes in the definition of such units. In particular, they distinguished between:

a. lines: utterances separated by pauses;
b. verses: units that correspond to complete sentences;
c. stanzas: units that share the same perspective on participants, action, time, etc.
d. scenes: units comprising at least one stanza that present major changes in location, time, actions or participants.

Scollon and Scollon argued that the action structure in stanzas mirrors interactional patterns in Athabaskan life, since Athabaskan narrators do not interpret actions but present them directly to their listeners, in the same way as interactants in everyday speech events do not encourage attempts to intervene on each other's choices and desires. Scollon and Scollon went beyond the idea that narrative structure invokes and is shaped by social forms of knowledge, in that they propose that it also (re)enacts social relations and actions.

Ethnopoetic analysis has had little application to narratives that are not the product of preliterate societies. One notable exception can be found in the work of Paul Gee (1986) who proposed an ethnopoetic reinterpretation of narratives told by a young black girl during sharing-time at a school, which had been previously studied by Michaels (1981). His aim was to show that these texts were constructed in a style typical of a culture that still had many of the characteristics of oral traditions. In line with Hymes and Scollon and Scollon, Gee regarded lines as the basic units of narrative analysis. However, he added cognitive considerations to the prosodic criteria used by previous authors for their recognition. Following a suggestion first made by Chafe (1980), he argued that lines represent basic *idea units*, i.e. contain one piece of new or focused information about a new (or already introduced) subject. Thus, line structure is signaled by initial discourse markers, by final pause or hesitation, and by the existence of different types of parallelism. In Gee's model, lines may consist of more than one intonation unit, but in written form they are generally equivalent to a sentence. In this, Gee differs from Hymes, according to whom lines do not necessarily have sentence-like contours. Gee also dispenses with verses but follows Hymes in regarding stanzas as higher narrative units. In his model, stanzas are "series of lines that have parallel structure and match each other either in content or topic" (1986: 396). Let us look at an example of a stanza taken from Gee's data:

> (2.3)
> 1. An' my mother's bakin' a cake
> 2. An' I went up to my grandmother's house while my mother's bakin' a cake
> 3. An' my mother was bakin' a cheese cake
> 4. My grandmother was bakin' a whipped cream cup cakes
>
> (From Gee 1986: 397)

In the analysis, the evidence presented for the division into lines and stanzas is prosodic, syntactic and semantic. In the stanza, every line ends with "cake" and the lines form parallel structures since 1 and 3 involve mother baking a cake, while 2 and 4 involve grandmother. At the same time, there is parallelism between the first and second line, as line 2 ends with the same words as line 1, and lines 3 and 4 end with a specification of the type of cake that is being baked. Although not all stanzas have such a clear structure, Gee argues that the existence of clearly marked stanzas is a clue to their adequacy as discourse structures. The next higher structure is what he calls an *episode*, or a section which, again, is characterized by common topic or theme, continuity in time, setting, or characters, parallelism among same-level units and certain final intonation contours.

As we have seen, in the work of Hymes, Scollon and Scollon, and Gee, the visually poetic (i.e. in stanza-like segments) arrangement of narrative structure units is not just an apparatus but also a theoretical commitment to the idea that these units reflect basic structures of human cognition and represent sociohistorically shaped forms of speaking that are common to oral cultures around the world. A narrative structure that is heavily based on prosodic patterning and repetition in oral cultures is, according to Gee (1989), related to their reliance on memory for the intergenerational transmission of and socialization into knowledge. Conversely, the relative absence of these kinds of rhythmic patterns in modern, technological cultures is due to the decrease in the relative importance of oral transmission and memory in these societies. However, according to Gee, stanza patterning does not disappear from modern Western narrative languages but rather "draws away, so to speak, more and more from the surface of language" (1989: 64) so that a stanza organization can be recovered through close processes of analysis. In fact, the formal mechanisms that distinguish poetic from non-poetic language (use of parallelism, expressive phonology, syntax and lexicon) are present across speech genres and appear in everyday language as well.

Overall, building on work by Michaels (1981; also, Michaels and Collins 1984), Gee saw the poetic patterning in the stories of black American children as part of an oral-based narrative style which avoids explicit ties and signposts in the organization of a story but instead links segments on the basis of rhythmic, recurrent patterns that exploit repetition. In Michael's terms, this sort of style can be described as topic-associating: it involves frequent shifts in spatio-temporal focus across segments to mark them out and it values implicitness in structuring. By contrast, the topic-centered style, characteristic of literate cultures and more specifically of middle-class children in the school that Michaels studied, is based on lexically and grammatically explicit connections and a clear thematic and temporal progression. The discovery of these contrastive styles did not mark the only outcome of this line of inquiry: the more significant revelation was to be found in that the oral-based or topic-associating style was not favored by the literate schooled models, with the result of disadvantaging children from ethnic and low socioeconomic backgrounds who came to school with this culturally shaped *way of speaking*. A model of narrative structure in this case became something more than a sophisticated apparatus for segmenting text: it actually documented social inequalities, differential accessibility to differentially valued storytelling styles and ultimately ideological forces at work in what had been presumed to be a universal and fundamental mode of communication.

2.2.1   Appraisal of the ethnopoetic approach

For the oral, native communities under study, ethnopoetics served as a loving act of "restoration" or "functional reconstruction" (Blommaert 2005: 8). With the help of an analytical apparatus, it re-covered an implicit form of verbal artistry that previous modes of representation (e.g. by anthropologists) had overlooked by naturalizing spoken texts when transcribing them and making them look like written. As we will see in more detail in Chapter 3, the verbal artistry involved in oral storytelling and its close links with the teller's sociocultural reality remain powerful ideas within narrative studies. That said, applications of ethnopoetic analysis to corpora or texts that are not taken from traditional preliterate cultures are rare, precisely because of the central claim that this type of structure is typical of cultures that strongly rely on verbal communication. In the spirit of Hymes' research, the few ethnopoetic analyses that have appeared since the 1980s have sought to bring to the fore under-represented, marginalized or even silenced stories, e.g. stories told by children speaking non-Western languages (Minami and McCabe 1991), stories in classroom settings (Juzwik 2004), stories in asylum seekers' interviews as part of their application (Maryns and Blommaert 2001), etc.[9]

The basic view of narrative structure as culturally shaped but also emergent in performance through linguistic and paralinguistic signals emphasizes the need to consider multiple levels (not just the syntactic plane or the plot or thematic criteria) in the identification of units of analysis. The convergence of prosodic, syntactic, semantic and pragmatic cues is an important signal of discourse organization. Its investigation in different languages and different narrative traditions has been instrumental in dispelling the supremacy of the grammatical level in narrative analysis, and in questioning the reliance on universal models. In this respect, ethnopoetics has done well to pay close attention to members' construction and interpretation of meaning (i.e. the *emic*[10] organization of text), and to the variety of resources that can be used to mark structural boundaries. However, certain claims connected with ethnopoetic analysis have raised fundamental questions, for example the status of units such as lines or stanzas. The claim that lines constitute natural units of speech is based on their correspondence with intonation boundaries. However, the recognition of prosodic contours is much more complex than it appears, and intonation units do not necessarily coincide with well-formed and complete units at other levels (such as the semantic or syntactic level).

The related claim that lines correspond not only to basic prosodic units but also to idea units and that they therefore mirror processes of apprehension and categorization of reality by the human mind is even more controversial given that it presupposes that the processing and encoding of information proceed in parallel fashion and that information sharing is central to narrative activity. In addition, the universal nature of narrative units cannot be demonstrated until enough evidence is collected from different languages and contexts. Finally, even if we accept that the line is a natural unit in human speech, the evidence for the existence of higher units such as stanzas or episodes is much thinner. The identification of such units tends to rely on the subjective interpretation of the analyst and their definition presents a certain circularity: for example, the syntactic and thematic criteria are proposed as fundamental for identifying the units in question, yet it is the analysts themselves who both decide this role and identify when, for example, a change of theme has taken place or when a unit has been syntactically complete. The lack of convergence between Hymes and Gee on the exact number of units and levels involved for instance is a telling case in point.

Despite its promise, ethnopoetic analysis has had a limited influence in narrative studies especially after the 1980s, in part because of a general decline in interest for narrative as part of folklore studies, in part because of the demands that this highly technical type of study puts on the analyst. This is without a doubt the kind of analysis that requires "skill, patience and insight in a variety of technical domains, from phonetics to grammar to discourse" and that leads to an equally technical presentation that "demands concentration and careful reading" (Blommaert 2005: 3). An examination of narrative performances in ethnopoetic terms requires not only a profound knowledge of the structures of a language, but also the ability to make connections among different levels of linguistic expression and between those and the socio-pragmatic rules and practices of a society. It is not surprising then that ethnopoetic analyses mostly come from anthropologists who have devoted themselves to the investigation of the life of specific communities. That said, the difficulties of the ethnopoetic enterprise should not detract from its value as a movement that has proposed important methodological directions and has alerted us to the ideologically laden nature of the ways in which we organize narrative. These ways, as ethnopoetics has shown, can disadvantage people who produce different patterns, however skilled, from the ones that are expected or normalized in certain environments. In this respect, ethnopoetics can be productively applied and extended to a variety of ordinary and institutional contexts for the analysis of narrative.

2.3   Narrative structure and conversation analysis

As we discussed above, Labov's model of narrative structure was heavily criticized for seeing narrative as a detached, autonomous and self-contained unit with clearly identifiable parts. The crux of the counterargument is that narrative occurs in some kind of a discourse environment, before and after other discourse activities, and is thus enmeshed in its local surroundings. This view of narrative as a sequence, in itself part of a sequentially ordered event, is in Schegloff's terms, where the work on narrative "should be redirected" in order for us to get "toward a differently targeted and more compelling grasp of vernacular storytelling" (1997: 101). What Schegloff has in mind is a conversation-analytic approach to narrative that treats narrative as talk-in-interaction. Conversation analysis grew out of ethnomethodology (e.g. Garfinkel 1967) as a sociologically oriented model that shifted emphasis away from large structures and macro-accounts and toward a locally situated micro-approach. The aim was to uncover social order and systematicity in the detail of conversations as the most basic unit of communication and as an ordinary activity.

The founding figure of conversation analysis is Harvey Sacks (e.g. 1972a; 1992a), but some of the defining directions of the area can also be found in the work of Schegloff (1968, 1979) and Jefferson (1978; also Sacks, Schegloff and Jefferson 1974). In these writings, conversations have been documented as sequentially ordered and methodical activities that both give a glimpse of and provide a platform for social actions and roles (e.g. see Sacks, Schegloff and Jefferson 1974; also chapters in Antaki and Widdicombe 1998). The basic unit of structure for conversation analysts is to be found in the turn-taking system, particularly in the adjacency pairs, which prove to be sequentially organized (i.e. produced next to each other) two-part structures, in which given first parts require particular second parts. For instance, questions and answers, greetings and return greetings, invitations and acceptances/declinations. With an almost pedantic attention to the details of naturally occurring talk as paramount for any study of it, conversation analysts have developed a systematic apparatus for a fine-grained analysis that includes a sophisticated system of transcription conventions. A discussion of this apparatus is beyond the scope of this chapter,[11] but what is notable for our purposes is how narrative is viewed within conversation analysis and more specifically how narrative structure is examined.

As already suggested, narrative in this framework is seen as an embedded unit, enmeshed in local business, as opposed to being free-standing and detached/detachable. It is then recognized that its tellings are sequentially managed and unfold online and moment by moment in the here-and-now of interactions. As such, they can be expected to be jointly drafted or co-authored by the participants involved: this theoretical shift brings into sharp focus the roles of the audience, which in previous models of narrative structure had been marginalized, and takes us away from the restrictive scheme of (active) teller vs. (passive) recipient. At the same time, the idea that storytelling is a process that raises different types of action and tasks for different interlocutors and is ultimately shaped online suggests that its tellings cannot be postulated a priori of the here-and-now of local contexts of occurrence. Instead, they *emerge* as a joint venture and as the outcome of negotiation by interlocutors. In the light of the above, a basic premise of conversation-analytic work on narrative is that recognizing structure in narrative involves an entry into the surrounding discourse activity, a development and an exit. In this respect, endpoints (e.g. preface – closing of a story) matter enormously and so does prior and upcoming talk that leads to a story and follows up from it respectively. Failing to pay attention to those and to include them in the analysis misses out on the irreducibly situational and locally occasioned aspects of storytelling as talk-in-interaction. By *local occasioning*, conversation analysts mean that "a good part of [the] meaning [of any talk] is to be found in the occasion of [their] production, in the local state of affairs that was operative at that exact moment of interactional time" (Antaki and Widdicombe 1998: 4).

As we will see in more detail in Chapter 4, by paying attention to the local occasioning of stories, conversation analysis has shed light on:

- how stories are prefaced, so that the tellers secure permission for a largely uninterrupted turn (e.g. Sacks 1974);
- how speakers display the relationship between a story and prior talk so that they can propose the appropriateness of its telling (Jefferson 1978);

- how stories can be followed up by other related stories that function as *second stories* and how entry to those stories differs from entry to stories that launch a spate of talk (Sacks 1974);
- how the participation framework in a given conversational exchange can shape a story's structure in some of the following ways: the tellers may design their stories for certain (principal) recipients, while recipients in turn may offer competing frameworks of a story's interpretation and evaluation that undercut those of the teller (e.g. Goodwin 1986; Goodwin 1997b).

One of the most influential conversation-analytic findings with regard to the sequential production of storytelling is to be found in Sacks' simple observation that "stories routinely take more than one turn to tell" ([1970b] 1992: 222). The assumption underlying this observation and running through a lot of conversation-analytic work on storytelling is that the telling of stories typically suspends turn-taking: it involves more than one turn-constructional unit and thus accords strong floor-holding rights to the teller. On the basis of this, the teller has to find ways of signaling to the interlocutors that such an extended turn is underway. It is within this sequential arrangement that Sacks places the story preface as being proposed by the teller and as raising the task of response from the recipients who have to indicate whether they wish to hear the story. The story then comes as the third part of this three-part canonical structure:

TELLER: Story Preface
RECIPIENT: Request to hear the story
TELLER: Story

Let us look at an example taken from a conversation between two mothers talking about school matters:

> (2.4)
> 1 T: By the way, did I tell you about the school trip on Thursday?
> 2 A: No you didn't (.) and I was sure to get all // the goss
> 3 T: Well, you know how I'd said I'd join in as a parent […]

We can see that in line 1, T first signals a shift of topic with the disjunct marker (Jefferson 1978) "by the way" and then introduces a story preface in the form of a question that can be seen as eliciting permission to tell the story. The "school trip on Thursday" specifically locates the telling to follow and is in some ways reminiscent of Labov's abstract. By stating that she has not been told about the trip and adding that she had somehow expected to be briefed, A is heard by T as producing a request to hear the story or at the very least as granting permission for the telling that follows.

In Sacks' analysis, the stress on the preface as an important part of a story's structure shifts the view of structure as teller-led to the interactional dynamics of the activity structuring any kind of talk. In this respect, the role of the preface is to be sought in the ways in which it aligns recipients, indicating to them what kind of activity is underway, more specifically, what kind of a story will be told. It thus raises specific tasks for the recipients, for example possible types of response appropriate to this type of story. Although these tasks are not to be seen as deterministic, as the recipients may take them up or not, what is important to note here is the intimate link of narrative structure with the ways in which stories are both launched into a conversation and exited from it. As a result of this conversation-analytic emphasis, we know more now than we ever learnt from Labov's study about how a story's endpoints can be intimately linked with its communicative context of occurrence.

A view of structure as sequentially unfolding, as outlined above, goes hand in hand with a view of structure as *emergent*.[12] In this sense, from the perspective of conversation analysts, structure cannot be postulated a priori but emerges as a joint venture and as the outcome of negotiation by interlocutors in the course of the telling. Emergence also allows us to tap into online shifts of structure, highlighting how problematic it is to assign functions to structural parts a priori of the investigation of their interactional status and on the basis of their internal semantics (cf. Edwards 1997). This shift in perspective can turn the analysis into a different enterprise altogether: from solely working with analytical and reified concepts to focusing on their interpretive reality in discourse environments as part of the speakers' own repertoires of sense-making devices.

In an influential article, Goodwin (1984) showed how the way in which a story is told, its sequential unfolding or structure, is recipient-designed: in other words, it takes into account some characteristics of the interlocutors to whom the story is addressed, and in this it makes relevant a distinction between knowing (of the story's events) vs. unknowing recipients. In similar vein, we have found that a story of shared (known) events is typically launched by a preface that aims to (re)affirm mutual reference or knowingness and/or to invite co-construction with the addressee. Specifically, in the conversations of Greek female adolescents, we found that the most salient type of entry into a story of shared events was as follows:

TELLER: Discourse Marker: "Let me tell you something" ('Shall I tell you something?' *Na su po kati*) + Recognitional question containing story abstract +/or reference to previous telling(s);
(KNOWING) RECIPIENT: Answer (confirmation) +/or Clarification question +/or Double-checking.

As shown elsewhere (Georgakopoulou 2001), the marker *na su po kati* ('shall I tell you something?') signals that the upcoming talk is going to introduce some kind of a shift in the activity underway, in this case the opening of a story. In the example below, taken from a conversation between two girls, Vivi and Tonia, we can see that this marker (line 1) is followed by an abstract ("I went through the same thing") that connects the upcoming telling with the prior talk and by a reference to a prior telling. In line 3, Tonia provides assurance or recognition of the story referred to by supplying an orientational type of information about one of the characters of the story.

> (2.5)
> 1 V(ivi): Let me tell you something (.) I went through the *same* thing as Irene's with Jannis
> 2 (..) I've told you the story=
> 3 T(onia): =The guy who was involved with your cousin=
> 4 V: =Ri:ght (.) my cousin Caterina (..) from Athens.

This process of establishing mutual reference is frequently spread over two adjacency pairs, as in cases when the addressee seems to be unsure of the events referred to, he asks a clarification question and receives a reply that jogs his memory (lines 1–4 below):

> (2.6)
> 1 V(assilis): It's like when Christos and Kostas had a row, d' you remember the story?
> 2 J(annis): When was that ma:n?
> 3 V: That time with the bill=
> 4 J: =Oh ri:ght!
> 5 V: What a story, eh? Just out of the blue really (..) as they'd gone out […]

The exploration of story prefaces in context is an example of how the study of narrative structure can move away from functionally restrictive schemes about the various structural components. For instance, rather than viewing an entry into a story as the turn that grants the teller strong telling rights or that provides the addressee with a sneak preview (Labov 1972), the analyst can explore other functions (in the sense of actions) such as that of establishing mutual reference with the addressee(s). As we have argued elsewhere (Georgakopoulou 2005a), prefaces aimed at establishing mutual reference normally do not project a long telling. Instead, they are typically followed by a mini-telling of the story, which comprises its narrative skeleton, that is, a quick reference or reminder to its events and to their resolution (if applicable). In similar vein, the analysis ought to stay alert to the systematic relations that different story openings present with the subsequent telling, in the sense of the contingencies they set up for different types of telling roles and actions by different participants. Similar considerations apply to story exit mechanisms.

Jefferson (1978) described in detail the ways in which conversational stories may be both launched into a conversation and exited from. She specifically suggested that story openings and story closings tend to be done with a set of conventionalized devices. In the case of a story opening, such devices include disjunct markers (e.g. *oh*), story prefixed phrases (e.g. *did I tell you?*, *guess who I saw*, etc.), temporal markers (e.g. *last year*) and references to characters. With the story opening, the tellers also propose to their audience how to understand the ensuing story for instance by characterizing the events that will be reported (e.g. *Something funny happened the other day*). With regard to a story's closing, Jefferson noted the importance of paying attention to the re-engagement of talk after story conclusion, as such talk demonstrates how stories are *sequentially implicative*, that is, how they can serve as a source for subsequent conversation. Participants may use a variety of techniques to display their understanding of the preceding story and to signal how their contributions follow up from that. The tellers themselves also use systematic story exit devices to signal that their story has reached an end and that turn-taking can be re-engaged; also, to elicit reactions to their story by the participants.

The study of how stories get to be told within the framework of conversation analysis has demonstrated the need to be sensitive to the variety of telling roles involved. Telling roles provide an insight into how storytelling can be negotiated moment by moment, turn by turn and thus emerge. At the same time, an integral part of the emergence of structure within a conversation-analytic approach are the actions undertaken vis-à-vis the various structural components: the possible responses or types of uptake by different participants and with regard to different structural components as these are assumed to shape a story's evolving structure (e.g. Goodwin 1984, 1986). We will discuss these in detail in Chapter 4. Here, it suffices to say that the aim of conversation analysis has not been to postulate structural components that would apply a priori and out of context. Instead, structure has been approached with the question of how tellers display the orderliness of their telling; how they manage its beginning and end; what actions they locally accomplish with it.

2.3.1   Appraisal of conversation-analytic approaches to storytelling

Narrative structure in conversation analysis is viewed as a dynamic, emergent and jointly drafted construct that is inextricably linked with the interactional dynamics of storytelling in ordinary exchanges. Thus, even if a specific telling happens to be lengthy and involving strong floor-holding rights for the teller, the interlocutors' contributions (be they verbal or non-verbal) matter and should be recorded as faithfully as possible. Bringing to the fore the intimate link of narrative structure with local contexts and the storytelling participant roles and relations has shown the difficulties involved in postulating structure as context-free and as an analytical category. Instead, orderliness and structure in this framework have been shown to lie in the ways in which tellings are managed, including the ways in which stories get to be introduced into and exited from talk.

The emphasis on endpoints of stories in this approach has implicated a neglect of the in-between part. Although conversation analysts have documented systematic trends in the introduction and closing of stories, they have paid less attention to the main body of the actual telling. In this respect, whether structural components of a Labovian kind, for example complicating action or evaluation, are generally accepted (even if redefined) by analysts in this tradition is not altogether clear; nor is what would replace them if they were dismissed. Also, the emphasis of conversation analysis on the turn as a unit has meant that what works above that unit has not been systematically or clearly studied. Goodwin (1984) characteristically works with complicating action and evaluation in his influential article discussed above in order to show their negotiability and joint fashioning (also Goodwin 1997b). The overall resonance or currency of these units though is not well explicated within conversation analysis, and there is still much scope for the analysis to turn to issues of story structure beyond the endpoints. For instance, one question that is still open is whether there is anything systematic in the relationship between different types of story openings and the structuring of the telling that follows them. Within a framework that accepts that story openings are consequential for what is going to come, we can expect to find such a systematic relationship, as has been found in our study referenced above.

The interactionist perspective of conversation analysis has often been criticized for its nose-to-data approach that does not easily abstract from local contexts and does not allow linkages between those and larger contexts and processes above and beyond single communicative events (e.g. see Wetherell 1998). This issue of navigating between micro- and macro-analysis will be discussed again in this book (see Chapters 3 and 5). In the case of structure in particular, one problem that arises is the extent to which there is anything systematic or generalizeable about it that can be abstracted from fine-grained analyses. There is also the question of how intertextuality can be taken into account in narrative structure: i.e. how the links that stories frequently establish or entertain with previous stories and indeed with storytelling events can become part of the analysis. The question is whether looking at a story in strictly here-and-now terms allows us to explore it as a trajectory that establishes connections with other tellings (through retellings, allusions, etc.), which can be developed in different settings and media and can be lifted from one discourse environment and transposed to other contexts (Bauman and Briggs 1990). As we saw earlier, Labov's insistence on looking at stories as single communicative events was criticized for its failure to incorporate intertextuality. Although coming from a different perspective, conversation analysis also finds it difficult to deal with a view of talk that involves links across time and space and norms and expectations, or any other kinds of traces that discourses bear from previous texts and occurrences.

In sum, conversation-analytic approaches to narrative have been instrumental in documenting stories as talk-in-interaction. By showing that the local context of stories matters for their structural makeup and therefore that structure is not independent of context, they have opened the way to the study of storytelling as a concrete, interactional activity in a wide variety of contexts. However, the refusal to consider the existence of any underlying structure that may go beyond the limits of local contexts also poses limitations to the application of the methodological apparatus of conversation analysis in that, as we will discuss below, narrative studies cannot give up altogether the enterprise of looking for structure in discourse phenomena.

2.4   Conclusions

Our discussion of three influential approaches to narrative structure, namely Labov's model, ethnopoetics and conversation analysis, has shown the varying degrees in which each of them sees stories as embedded into their discursive environment and the implications this has for their view of structure. It has also argued for the varying role accorded to the larger context, in particular the cultural context, in terms of how it shapes narrative organization. What the profound influence of these approaches in the field of narrative studies shows is that, although structuralist optimism is currently no less unfashionable in linguistics than in the whole of social sciences, the need for an analytical apparatus as part of the area's self-definition still holds strong (Rampton *et al.* 2005: 2). This has to be seen in the context of agreed principles within the field of linguistics, which assume that it is possible to isolate and abstract structural patterns in the ways in which people communicate and prioritize the task of establishing procedures for isolating and identifying them (Rampton *et al.* 2005: 2). There are thus good disciplinary reasons for viewing narrative as a structured activity and for employing the quest for structure as part of an analytical inquiry. More importantly, such an approach resonates with other areas in discourse analysis (see Georgakopoulou and Goutsos 2004: 11–14, 70–3). Postulating a structure can also provide a way for navigating the two often posed as irreconcilable extremes of discourse analysis: fine-grained micro-analysis that is confined to the local context and the particular, and macro-analysis that does not account for interactional contingency in local contexts (Georgakopoulou and Goutsos 2004: 189). As Hanks puts it (1996: 233ff.), it is in the dynamic interplay between the habitual, routine, rather stable and prefabricated ways of communicating on one hand and the improvised, contingent and emergent features on the other hand that we begin to gain insights into any kind of communicative practice. To put it differently, work on narrative structure can help formulate a more specific remit of the study of narrative as part of social practices, while providing methods for empirical research through specific coding categories that allow analysts to analyze narrative as an organized set of resources.

Future work on narrative structure should aim to probe more into the relationship between the type of story and narrative structure; the systematic study of telling roles (in the sense of both degree and type of contribution) vis-à-vis structural components; the integration of openings, closings and follow-ups so as to capture vital links between a story's structure and its co-text on one hand and its intertext(s) on the other (see our discussion in Chapter 4); finally, it should attempt to deepen our understanding of the nature, sequential position and relations between different structural constituents.

These directions for further research will benefit from a flexible approach to narrative structure that is amenable to synthesizing work. This involves a balanced inquiry into the interplay between socioculturally shaped regularities on the one hand, and local contingencies and individual improvisations on the other hand. As we will see in the chapter that follows, identifying and documenting the role of sociocultural dependence in the ways in which stories are told (and organized) is a focal concern of narrative analysis.

3   Narrative and sociocultural variability

3.0   Introduction

In Chapter 2 we discussed different approaches to structure in the study of narrative: our main focus was on the systematic description of the formal features that characterize narrative as a genre. In this chapter we shift our attention to research that centers on the relationships between narrative and context and on the embedding of narrative in social life. Our focus will be on the links between narrative form/content and culture, or cultures, and we will review work carried out mainly in the 1970s and 1980s that has set the basis for current thinking about the way narrative practices encode, reflect and shape communication patterns, ways of thinking and organizing social life in different cultural traditions. Implicit in the work that we discuss is the idea of sociocultural variability, i.e. the assumption that narrative activity and narrative genres are organized and conceived in very different ways amongst different peoples, and that stories vary in structure and content across cultures, thus reflecting the complexity of human experience.

The research developed within this general orientation to the social uses of narrative revolves around the investigation of narrative both as a contextually bound phenomenon and as a process that relates in specific ways to the life of linguistic and social communities. Unlike in theorizations about narrative structure, in the domain of narrative and culture, the boundaries between different approaches are not easily drawn. Indeed, in this case, narrative studies have been, in a sense, the by-product of more general theories about the relationship between language and social life as expressed in different schools of linguistic analysis such as the ethnography of communication (Hymes 1974) or interactional sociolinguistics (Gumperz 1982). However, in general terms the approaches and studies reviewed here can be grouped as follows:

a. Approaches that conceptualize the relationship between narrative and culture in terms of contexts of narrative activity
b. Approaches that see narrative as relating to culture through values and ideas
c. Approaches that focus on communicative styles

Naturally, these are not completely separable categories, as one cannot speak of cultural styles without talking about contexts of delivery. Similarly, one cannot look at narratives without considering the cultural values that are created and reproduced in those contexts. However, emphasis can be placed on different aspects of narrative leading to profound differences in the research tools and methodologies employed. There is also another distinction that can be postulated: between studies within the ethnography of communication (cf. ethnopoetics, Chapter 2) and studies inspired by Labov's model (Chapter 2), often referred to as post-Labovian. We will review the former in section 3.1 below and the latter in sections 3.2 and 3.3. In particular, we will discuss research that has developed around the investigation of speech genres and performances of traditional storytelling in non-Western communities. We will then move on to sociolinguistic research focused on sociocultural variability in story content on the one hand, and narrators' styles on the other.

In order to discuss these different ways of approaching cultural variability, we will focus on three concepts: *performance, genre* and *style*, as variously defined in different theories and approaches. These concepts have been developed in order to capture some of the ways in which narrative forms and tellings are linked to sociocultural contexts. In this sense, they can be seen as providing a mid-level conceptualization that allows analysts to make connections between the micro-level of tellings and the larger context of those tellings. This type of middle-level thinking has also been important in contextual research on language in general.

3.1   From texts to cultural contexts

The theoretical reflection on narrative and culture has been profoundly influenced by notions and methodologies that come from the areas of ethnography of communication and folklore studies. Both fields have made a significant contribution to our understanding of how narratives are embedded in the social life of communities, as in both traditions the study of narrative has been tightly connected with the study of cultural organization and expression. In these approaches then, cultural specificity has been identified with structures of social organization and modes of accumulation and transmission of knowledge. In fact, the key concept to capture the cultural embedding of storytelling has been the notion of *performance*. Before we discuss it, however, we need to briefly trace some antecedents to the ethnographic studies of narrative of the 1970s and 1980s, which will help place them in historical perspective and thereby better understand their goals and disciplinary context.

Let us start by noting that narrative has been an object of interest for anthropologists and folklorists at least since the eighteenth century because of its central role in the maintenance of tradition in non-literate societies. Stories were grouped by scholars of folklore together with other genres and regarded as fundamental to fulfilling the function of keeping traditions alive and transmitting them from one generation to the next. Thus, anthropologists studied myths, proverbs, legends and riddles that embodied the themes and values of traditional societies, and attempted to produce precise taxonomies to distinguish between each of these genres (for definitions of different genres, see Bascom 1965). The analysis of these forms of oral literature in anthropology and folklore studies traditionally disregarded most aspects of context and focused instead on structure.

This is the case with two influential narrative theories in the area of the investigation of oral traditions: the models developed by the French anthropologist Claude Lévi-Strauss and the Russian formalist Vladimir Propp. Both theories attempted to develop formal models of narrative genres considered central to our understanding of human cultures (see our discussion in section 1.1.1). Claude Lévi-Strauss devoted his attention to myths told in different parts of the world in order to show that the apparent variety in the representation and understanding of human experience that is embodied in the tales of different societies hides, in fact, an underlying homogeneity in terms of universal themes and conflicts. The method developed by Lévi-Strauss (1963, 1969) consisted in applying to the analysis of myths the structural principles of opposition and substitution that were at the time popular in structural linguistics. Lévi-Strauss argued that if one scratched beneath the surface of the linear sequence of events presented, at a deep level these stories could be reduced to fundamental constituent units called *mythemes*. Mythemes embodied basic actions or themes common to all human cultures that were related to each other in specific narratives through combinations and oppositions. For example, in his analysis of the myth of Oedipus (1969), the author proposed that the theme of the killing of monsters, which was one of the mythemes in the narrative, was related to the mytheme of the origin of man and of its status vis-à-vis other non-human creatures. This type of meaning component could be found in mythical stories all over the world.

The narrative theory proposed by Vladimir Propp (1968) was not very different in its basic principles, even though he developed it in connection with Russian folk tales instead of myths. Like Lévi-Strauss, Propp was looking for underlying structures, but unlike the French anthropologist, he did not ignore the actual ordering of events as they unfolded in the 100 tales that he studied.[1] The Russian formalist compared plots, actions and actors in his corpus of fairy tales and arrived at the conclusion that these narratives were composed of a finite number of thirty-three plot elements, or basic narrative functions, that occurred in a predictable order in all the tales. Narrative function was described as "an act of a character, defined from the point of view of its significance for the course of action" (1968: 21). So, in this scheme the constituents of a story are the actions and goals realized by the protagonists, who, in turn, incarnate general roles such as "the hero," "the helper," "the donor," etc.

As we can see, the models of narrative analysis developed by Lévi-Strauss and Propp do not incorporate any element of context and do not focus on specific cultures. Neither author set out to explore the linguistic or symbolic aspects that differentiate the realization of the same themes in different cultures, or the particularities of the telling of stories in social circumstances. Rather, they were interested in the timeless themes and conflicts that characterize human life and in the semantic universals that encode them. Their work has generated applications to the study of narrative that have been taxonomic in nature (see, for example, Thompson 1961 and Dundes 1964). In general, as these examples illustrate, it can be said that most of the research on narratives that was produced before "contextualism"[2] (Hufford 1995) emerged as a movement in linguistics and anthropology in the late sixties, was formalist[3] and, as noted by Bauman (1969), "text centered" rather than focused on the conditions of text production.

That said, it is important to emphasize that it is within the area of folklore and ethnographic studies of the late 1960s and 1970s that the roots of a context-sensitive approach to storytelling can be found. Both the formal models and the classificatory efforts of early narrative approaches ultimately focused the attention of scholars on the centrality of stories in human development and therefore generated great interest in the relationship between storytelling and human cultures. But, given that there are many ways in which stories relate to cultures, we will spell out in greater detail the elements of context that may be taken as constitutive of this relationship. It is important to note here that a precise definition of context remains a contentious issue within linguistics; however, a full discussion of this problem is beyond the scope of the present chapter.[4]

In Goodwin and Duranti's view (1992: 3), context is anything that can provide the frame of interpretation of a focal event, for example the setting, the physical orientation of participants, language itself (for instance through the structure of a genre or intertextual connections) and larger extra-situational conditions. This description can be enriched by taking into account another classification introduced by Ben-Amos, who proposes a distinction between the *context of situation* and the *context of culture* (1993: 215–16). While the context of situation includes everything that is local (for example the setting, the participation structure and the sequential organization of talk), the context of culture is a much wider frame that includes a community's shared knowledge, conventions of conduct, belief systems, language metaphors, speech genres, historical interpretations, ethical and judicial principles. One can look at contextualized studies of narrative as attempts to understand storytelling as a social activity reflecting and constructing social meanings not only within specific milieus, but also through recourse to these different aspects of local and global contexts. As noted by Schiffrin (1996: 168), when people verbalize experience in narrative form they "situate that experience globally" through recourse to cultural knowledge and expectations. However, at the same time, they also situate it locally by making it relevant to the here-and-now of participants in a social encounter. In any case, the distinction between global and local is not easy to make as the global level is always enacted, and becomes relevant, at the local level. In fact, a widely held view is that it is only by closely attending to the micro-instances of lived experience that we can tap into the global. In other words, the global does not exist a priori and outside local contexts of communication.

Another big question is what exactly global contexts mean and what the scale involved in the concept is. Some of the earlier research that we will review here works with large social and cultural groupings (e.g. ethnic or national communities) as part of the global and does not see them in pluralized terms: it is therefore culture that this research aims to look into as opposed to cultures.

3.2   Narrative as performance

One point of entry into the contextualized study of narrative has been the investigation of the way stories shape and are shaped by what Ben-Amos called the "context of culture," i.e. how narratives reflect and build upon shared knowledge, belief systems and structures of social organization that are typical of particular communities. So far, we have seen an example of this kind of approach in our discussion of the ethnopoetic movement (chapter 2.2). Specifically, we have suggested that the ethnopoetic quest for narrative organization reflects a general concern with the cultural context that generates specific discourse structures. We have also talked about the line and stanza analysis, as proposed by Hymes (1981, 1998 and 2004) and by Scollon and Scollon (1981), as a way of relating narrative organization to social and cultural specificity. But these studies also contribute to our understanding of the links between narratives and context in other ways. As we have seen, Hymes regards the study of narrative structure and form as a tool for the investigation of local forms of knowledge, particularly those related to the culture of the Native Americans. He specifically says (2004: 6):

If we refuse to consider and interpret the surprising facts of device, design and performance inherent in the words of the texts, the Indians who made the texts, and those who preserved what they made, will have worked in vain. We will be telling the texts not to speak.

Hymes argues that narrative form and modes of performance reflect both the linguistic competence of a community, i.e. the ability to build texts according to the community's poetic tradition, and the many forms of local knowledge that include certain kinds of content (for example information about natural processes and objects), and forms of apprehension and organization of reality (for example classification systems, theories about the origin of the world, etc.). Local forms of knowledge are embodied in the content of stories: what stories are about, the way in which characters act, the settings in which events take place, but also their linguistic organization, rhetorical devices and poetic power.

We have seen in Chapter 2 that a similar perspective on narrative as embodying modes of social knowledge and social organization is an underlying theme in Scollon and Scollon's (1981) ethnography of Athabaskan narrative. For these authors, Athabaskan narrative reflects its fundamental role as the main tool for the acquisition of knowledge in its poetic organization and interactional structure. Narrative organization in lines, stanzas, verses and smaller units is designed to facilitate processes of transmission of information and memorization. For example, in simple clauses, the verb (i.e. the main action) is foregrounded by means of its final position in order to signal the most important information, while the numerical distribution of verses and stanzas follows patterns that are typical of Athabaskan discourse organization and are therefore designed to aid memory. At the level of semantic patterning, Scollon and Scollon argue that the presentation of action and commentary in narrative discourse also follows patterns characteristic of the culture. Comparing the same narrative told by an Athabaskan speaker in English and in his own language, they found that while in the English version the action within a stanza follows the explanation of it given by the narrator, in the Athabaskan version the explanation follows the action. This organization reproduces patterns characteristic of the two cultures. The English ordering of explanation followed by action is consonant with the "decontextualization and non interactiveness of the modern consciousness" (p. 117) in which actions are explained, evaluated and motivated in the text before they are described. On the other hand, the Athabaskan structure in which the narrator presents actions for the audience to interpret and then proposes an explanation corresponds to the "bush consciousness" (p. 17). Thus, the stanza organization is proposed as a case of a linguistic form mirroring the interactive patterns of a society in that the lack of intervention in fictional interaction parallels, for example, the taciturnity with strangers in interethnic communication.

In general, Hymes' and Scollon and Scollon's focus was on relating narrative form to the wide cultural context by drawing parallelisms between the construction of forms and meanings in narrative and the organization of knowledge and social relations in a community. Such parallelisms were based on a methodology that involved the painstaking analysis of all details of formal organization in narrative, and it is to this careful study of forms of poetic organization that a first understanding of the importance of performance can be traced. In Hymes' work, the exact rendering of the delivery of narrative texts in Native

American cultures is part of the effort to place those texts in their cultural contexts. As a consequence, the concept of performance is closely related to the notion of the artful organization of culturally sanctioned texts. Hymes, Tedlock (1983) and other ethnographers emphasize the importance of adequately representing oral texts in written forms that closely follow their actual delivery, specifying pauses, rhythm, loudness and all kinds of details that could reveal their poetic organization. In his early writings on performance, Hymes recognized that, although concern with authentic delivery had traditionally existed in folklore studies, "the personal, situational and linguistic factors that govern authentic performance in a tradition" had "not been explicitly investigated or taken into account" (1981: 86) and that in fact there had been a conscious effort to eliminate contextual variation. Hymes insisted that, in contrast to this, variation is one of the most important aspects of performance and that realization is constitutive of tradition.

These ideas have been instrumental in precipitating a shift in the study of narratives from types of texts to types of events. Performance studies of narrative have moved the interest from the cultural context to the context of situation as an instantiation of a culture, but also as a unique encounter, by analyzing more closely the local functions of stories, the interconnections between audiences and narrators, and the strategies and devices that allow performers to make their stories interesting and enjoyable. It is in this focus on the event that we will find the bridge that allows for a methodological passage from exotic stories created within non-Western traditions to processes of everyday storytelling throughout the world.

But before delving into that connection, we need to further analyze the implications of a performance approach to narrative. Early work on narrative performance was still more concerned with types of situations than with actual events. An example of this approach is Ruth Finnegan's work on the storytelling tradition of Limba, a Northern African community. As was the case with other ethnographers and sociolinguists, Finnegan pointed to the importance of describing verbal art as literature, stating that Limba stories can be regarded as literature even if they are part of an exclusively oral tradition. In the author's view, it was precisely the oral character of Limba storytelling that called for a performance approach. As Finnegan put it: "Since performance as well as literary composition is an essential part of the art, one must also analyze the style and the techniques of storytelling, the dramatic presentation, the occasion, and the audience, in a way that is not necessary in the case of written literature" ([1966] 1981: 64).

Besides a classification of types of stories and story topics, a comprehensive description of storytelling in this community includes an account of situational occasions for tellings, settings and audiences, and an analysis of performance devices. The concept of "style of performance" encompasses the devices used to make the story more appealing, to signal story parts to the audience and to open and close the telling. Finnegan noted the use of such devices as direct speech, repetition, mimicry and onomatopoeia, alterations in tempo and tone that allow the narrator to create dramatic effects and draw the attention of her audience. In her view, stories are not tokens of a general type, nor do they belong to an established tradition in the way myths, for example, do, but instead they are delivered in individual performances whose content and form depend very much on the social occasion and on the audience. They also crucially depend on the ability of the storyteller who has the possibility of expanding on specific points and "embroidering" the narration. The teller acts the story with more or less characterization, mimicry, exaggeration and effect. Finnegan stresses that "there is no one form of any Limba story that could be called the fixed or 'correct' one, and even if some tend to recur more often than others in roughly the same form, yet even there each performance is in a sense a unique composition by the narrator" (p. 91).

As we can see, the notion of performance as used by Finnegan emphasizes the situational context in terms of the influence that occasions, topics, audiences etc. have on storytelling. As a consequence, the storyteller is no longer conceived of as a mere voice of tradition but fully enters the scene as a concrete speaker with power and ability to change the course of tradition. Ironically, Finnegan's study is not based on actual performances, but includes elicited stories that were told in situations designed to reproduce actual storytelling events, and stories dictated by informants. But this was, of course, a product of the times since tape recorders were hardly a widespread commodity, and it was partly because of their increasing popularity that researchers were able to study the actual delivery of narratives.

A similar attempt to ground the investigation of storytelling in concrete social events is found in work by Kirshenblatt-Gimblett (1974) who draws the attention of narrative researchers to the embedding of storytelling within other communicative events, including conversation. Even though this study's orientation is still fundamentally descriptive, as it lists the kinds of events in which stories can be told in the East European Jewish tradition and the types of stories that may be recounted on those occasions, it does point to important elements in the analysis of narrative as performance. In particular, it analyzes:

- the specific functions that narratives can have in relation to the more general situational context;
- the degree of integration and of saliency of narratives in the speech event;
- the strategies that narrators use to introduce their stories and make them relevant to the occasion;
- audience expectations about what counts as a good storytelling performance and about who the performer may be in a particular context;

- their possible reactions to the telling;
- the participant roles in the telling of different types of narratives, the characteristics of the performer;
- story components that define specific storytelling performances.

These elements are used to compare different kinds of storytelling events. The scope of the research is broad and far-reaching, as it describes Jewish traditions that span over a wide territory and among different communities. Kirshenblatt-Gimblett's methodology largely rests on interviews with a great number of Jewish immigrants in Canada who talk about storytelling traditions, not on spontaneous data.

The aforementioned studies by Finnegan and Kirshenblatt-Gimblett point to one way in which the notion of performance has been instrumental in the investigation of the contextualization of stories, i.e. through the foregrounding of the speech event in contrast to a previous emphasis on genre as an abstract category. Focusing on the speech event in these early approaches to performance involved talking about *storytelling* as opposed to *story*. This meant taking into account the impact of all the contextual elements constitutive of a speech event as singled out by Hymes (1974: 56–80) in his famous acronym for speaking, referred to as the *Speaking Grid*:

> *Setting and scene*: time and place and environment of the event
> *Participants*: people involved in the situation
> *Ends*: goals and objectives of the speech event
> *Act sequence*: order of speech acts
> *Key*: the tone and manner of the speech
> *Instrumentalities*: the style and forms through which the speech is delivered
> *Norms*: the rules followed in the event
> *Genre*: the type of speech event

In brief, within this tradition, variation is taken as a central element in the understanding of storytelling as a cultural act. At the same time, the methodology adopted in the investigation of performance draws attention to *emic*[5] categories, including in this case local interpretations about the relevance of contextual elements. As the speech event becomes the center of attention, the question of the authenticity of storytelling contexts also starts gaining prominence, and narrative analysts begin to reflect on their role as researchers and on the impact that this may have on the actual data collected. In addition, the emergent nature of performance becomes apparent, since informants are often not just telling stories into a tape recorder but presenting them to members of the community, and therefore innovations, reinterpretations of tradition, and local adjustments to audience reactions become apparent.[6]

Thus, the notion of performance becomes more closely associated with the idea of contextualization as a process that allows for a more dynamic view of the relations between narrators, events, speech communities and cultural contexts. In this respect, context is not a list of situational and cultural elements that determines the structure and shape of narrative, but an orchestration of those elements that come alive in specific communicative situations.

The most important work in this area comes from the anthropologist and folklorist Richard Bauman. Bauman underlines that the concept of performance is associated with a view of verbal expression as artistry and therefore with an interest in its aesthetic properties. However, unlike in classical anthropological approaches to oral expression, the artistic quality is not attributed to texts, but it is seen as emergent in a process that involves performer and audience.[7] Performance implies an assumption of responsibility on the part of the performer for the display of communicative skill and competence and an acceptance that such a display is going to be evaluated by the audience. In this sense, performance is a way of speaking, and "just as speaking itself as a cultural system (or as part of cultural systems defined in other terms) will vary from speech community to speech community, so too will the nature and extent of performance and verbal art" (Bauman 1969: 13).

Storytelling genres will accordingly vary in the degree to which they are seen as "performable" in a community and therefore also in the extent to which they are regulated.

An important point here concerns a refocusing of the event as the locus for a dynamic interplay between social rules, acts and roles underlying active processes of meaning creation and also as a site for the actual realization of genres. Performances are the sites where tradition and innovation intertwine in complex ways. In turn, performers make reference to established rules, aesthetic principles and traditions, but at the same time constantly create meanings through contextualization and re-contextualization and use conventional resources for creative manipulation. The concept of *emergence* captures this constant transformation of social realities, since every time a performer meets with an audience, conventional resources need to be adapted to the local context. In turn, the local context is continuously modified through changes in the relationships between audiences and performers. For example, a storyteller needs to keep the attention of the audience and will put into place specific strategies to ensure that this happens.

A significant consequence of the fact that stories are not told in a vacuum but by tellers to audiences in specific settings and for specific purposes is that the mechanisms through which performers contextualize meanings for their audience come to the forefront. Bauman (1969: 15) stresses the fact that performances are "keyed" in the sense that they are characterized by conventional meta-communicative framing devices (Ruesch and Bateson 1968), i.e. linguistic and paralinguistic elements that help participants interpret the meanings created within the act. Bauman lists numerous devices such as conventional formulae, stylistic elements, prosodic keys such as rhythm, tempo, stress or pitch, patterns of voice quality or vocalization. All of these help the performer guide audience interpretations. While creating social meaning, performances also bring about transformations in social roles since the performer's ability and skill will afford her or him a certain power over the listeners, thus determining changes in their mutual relationships.

The performance frame was developed in connection with verbal art in general, but the analysis of narratives figures prominently within it. As Bauman aptly put it, "oral narrative provides an especially rich focus for the investigation of the relationship between oral literature and social life because narrative is doubly anchored in human events. That is, narratives are keyed both to 'the events in which they are told and to the events that they recount'" (1986: 2).

The structure of performance events is, according to Bauman (p. 4), determined by the interplay of:

- participants' identities and roles;
- the expressive means conveyed in performance;
- social interactional rules, norms and strategies for performance and criteria for interpretation;
- the sequence of actions that make up the scenario of the event.

In the light of this, oral narratives are seen as special communicative acts in that they are based on the interplay of different dimensions: the *narrative event* (telling world), i.e. the world in which the story is told, and the *narrated events* (the story world) that make up the fabric of the story itself.[8] Both worlds are evoked and constructed through textual resources. According to Bauman, analysts may foreground one or the other of these dimensions, but ultimately, narrative performance cannot be understood without reference to these three elements: the narrative event, the narrated event and the text. This means that all aspects of storytelling are culturally variable, not just those that refer to the social event, and that they are also interdependent.

To illustrate the operation of performance mechanisms and of narrative dimensions, we present Bauman's analysis of the way one story, "The Bee Tree," a tale about a fantastic tree full of honey, told by Texan storyteller Edd Bell, changed over the years. Let us look at one of the story's episodes as told in two different versions: in 1971 and 1979.

> (3.1)
> 1971
> Well, it took quite a while to walk around it.
> Got over there

And there was ten other fellows choppin' on one side.
They'd found the bee tree too.
So we all lit in together,
Decided to pool our choppin' and get it down

(3.2)
1979
Sure enough, I got down there where they was
And there was three boys over there.
And they'd been choppin' two or three days on that tree.
And I said, "Say, fellas, y'all stealin' my bee tree?"
Well, they knew me
And they said, "No Ed," said "we are not stealin' your bee tree.
This is our bee tree."
Well, they showed me their X over there,
And one ol' boy had his initials under the X.
Well, we, uh
We didn't know which one had found it and marked it first,
'cause the other boys marked it the same day I did.
Well, I said, "Let's just chop it down and divide the honey."
Oh, they just thought that was real fine.
That was all right by th\\em.

(From Bauman 1986: 95)

These two versions of the same narrative demonstrate how different types of devices may contribute to the performance quality of a story. As Bauman notes, the first version of the episode is quite plain, it has no details and just summarizes the events. In the second version, performance devices have been added and the story is much longer. One important change consists in the addition of different passages of quoted speech. The negotiation over the cutting of the tree, for example, is re-enacted through quoted speech. The use of quoted speech makes the scene come alive but also serves to add details to the narrative. Indeed, the provision of detail is another performance device. Further details, for example, are added by the narrator on the number of boys that had been chopping the tree and the time that they had been at it. Bauman notes that the second version also exploits another performance device: syntactic parallelism, i.e. "repetition with systematic variation" (p. 97). An example of syntactic parallelism can be found in the structure "And I said" / "And they said." Finally, the narrator uses another form of parallelism in the last two lines of the second version as the last line repeats, in a different way, the content of the preceding line:

Oh, they just thought that was real fine.
That was all right by them.

In brief, the second version of the narrative has a performed quality achieved through linguistic devices such as quoted speech, detail and syntactic parallelism. Bauman also notes that in the new version of Edd Bell's narrative, there are many "meta-narration" statements, i.e. "shifts out of narrative time" that the narrator uses "to refer to himself or the audience as participants in the present storytelling events" (p. 99). These are statements that, for example, are used to comment on the believability of the story or of the narrator himself/ herself for the audience, or explanations about actions or practices referred to in the narrative. Such devices provide a bridge between the narrated events and the narrative events.

By discussing the modifications that the narrator has introduced in this traditional narrative, Bauman also shows that narrated events may be told in different ways depending on the kind of social occasion in which the storytelling happens, the participant status and, generally, the cultural norms regulating the specific interaction and broader social contexts. In this case, Edd Bell was adapting his narratives as his performance changed from events addressed to people who were familiar with the traditions he was enacting to popular events organized for wider audiences.

Bauman's analysis constitutes a powerful demonstration of the cultural variability and contextual dependence of parameters for storytelling performance. It allows for an understanding of how and why certain storytelling deliveries are more performed than others; how performance is not an all-or-nothing quality of narratives but a continuum ranging from full-fledged, sustained presentations to fleeting breakthroughs into performance modes and to more or less strategic recourse to theatricality. Analysts should stay alert to all these possibilities and their social meanings and consequentiality in local contexts. They should also recognize, as Bauman has repeatedly stressed, that the devices which key narrative tellings as performances are expected to vary cross-culturally and need to be discovered empirically. The same applies to the sociocultural meanings and values attached to performances. At the same time, it is worth noting that there is an immediate resonance between the devices that Bauman singled out as performance keys in his data and both preceding and subsequent studies of "animated" storytelling styles. As we will see below too (and in Chapter 5), the list tends to comprise historical present, animation of characters' voices, repetition, ellipsis, use of proximal deictics to refer to past events (e.g. *now* and *here* instead of *there* and *then*), use of gestures and paralinguistic features (e.g. animated tone of voice) for dramatization, etc. That said, the number of devices and the way they are used can still vary considerably from culture to culture.

3.3   Narrative as cultural grammar

While cultural elements in narrative were being explored within the framework of the ethnography of communication, another strong tradition was developing in parallel from the 1970s onwards, as an effect of the popularity of Labov's influential model of narrative structure, which we discussed in Chapter 2. Being ultimately interested in language and social variation, Labov was quick to point to certain sociolinguistic conditioning in his data: in particular, that the increased use of external evaluation characterized the narratives of middle-class participants, while a heavy reliance on internal evaluation was more typical of working-class people's narratives. These sociolinguistic insights paved the way for post-Labovian research which sought to explore the sociocultural variability of narrative structure. But cultural variability in this tradition was not anchored to social contexts and the structure of events: rather, it was related to systems of values and beliefs and therefore also to ways of judging events and actions based on moral codes. In this respect, evaluation was the most appealing among the structural components proposed in Labov's model: not only did the model allow for different positions and different types of evaluation, but it also proposed a view of evaluation that placed it on the intersection between narrative organization and narrative affectivity. Evaluation did not just bind a story together, it also showed what its point was and what the teller's involvement in it was.

The extreme context-sensitivity of evaluation, as attested by subsequent studies, did not come as a major surprise within the contextualist approach that had begun to take a strong hold in the 1980s. One of the first attempts to specify the relationship between narrative structure, in particular evaluation, and culture was Polanyi's study of American storytelling (1989). The title of the book alone, *Telling the American story: A structural and cultural analysis of conversational storytelling*, is indicative of the broad canvas that was being drawn. Culture was seen by Polanyi as a largely homogeneous entity that can be distilled into specific values which are in turn characteristic of a whole nation. She starts off with the assumption that all stories make a point about their taleworld and that that point is a reflection of cultural values and norms. In her own terms:

What stories can be about is to a very significant extent culturally constrained: stories, whether fictional or non-fictional, formal or often told or spontaneously generated can have as their point culturally salient material generally agreed upon by members of the producer's culture to be self-evidently important and true. (Polyani1989: 207)

Polanyi's analysis problematized evaluation as defined by Labov in many different ways: for instance, it suggested that evaluation can be jointly drafted in conversational stories, something that had not come out in Labov's study of largely monologic interview narratives. It also made a case for a context-specific definition of what counts as an evaluative device. For the purposes of the present discussion, what is significant about Polanyi's study is her attempt to construct a broad compendium or cultural grammar that comprised salient "American" values, starting from an analysis of the main propositions that constitute the evaluative skeleton of stories. Polanyi saw this compendium as representing a generic American story that consisted of basic truths about the nature of the world and of human relationships in it.

In brief, Polanyi's methodology was based on textual analysis and on the reduction of story evaluation to propositions about the world. Story evaluation served in fact as an anchor point in the identification of the propositions, which were expanded into the American cultural grammar, as it was basically the elements which the teller most heavily foregrounded in the telling (i.e. evaluated) that were singled out. As such, those elements were revealing of what was most interesting, worth telling or compelling about a story. The American grammar, perhaps unsurprisingly, consisted of values of an individualist or independent nature and in this way was in tune with social psychology studies which analyzed cultures in terms of broad, constitutive values. One of the distinctions drawn was, for example, that between so-called independent and interdependent cultures: the former placed emphasis on the individual's freedom of action and right to privacy as well as personal space, while the latter saw the self as being inextricably linked with the social group in which it belongs (referred to as the in-group) and placed a premium on connectedness and involvement within that group. Many studies in social psychology and anthropology have suggested a relationship between specific cultures and different kinds of personality traits (see Bourguignon 1979). Theories about the person and the self were widely seen as culturally variable, ranging from very individualistic concepts of personhood which are said to be typical of Western developed societies, to more social and impersonal conceptions in which the individual is seen as determined and constrained by a variety of forces and relationships that are culturally variable. According to cultural psychologist Matsumoto (1994), for example, one dimension of cultural difference is the opposition between individualism and collectivism, which refers to the degree to which a culture encourages individual needs, wishes, desires and values over group and collective ones. Such a dimension has been identified as basic in the differentiation of cultures (see section 3.4 for further discussion of this point). In that sense, Polanyi's hypothesis about the system of values underlying American stories resonated with the idea that cultures can be divided according to their different conceptions of the persona and that such conceptions are represented in narrative in the evaluative component of stories.

From a sociolinguistic point of view, Polanyi's study also constituted a first major step toward more contextualized definitions of Labov's narrative structure as well as a precursor to studies of conversational storytelling. From Labov's elicited narratives in research interviews, Polanyi shifted interest to audio-recorded stories that occurred naturally in casual dinnertime conversation with friends. She also showed that a careful transcription and analysis of such stories can be a valuable point of entry into the exploration of social and cultural variation. However, her notion of culture was far from refined, and rather than allowing for fragmentation, multiplicity and heterogeneity, it conceptualized it in somewhat monolithic and static terms. Although Polanyi frequently stressed that the stories were told by American-born, English-speaking, white middle-class individuals, she still went on to take them as representative of American storytellers. As already argued, Polanyi's approach was not at odds at the time the book was published with mainstream cultural analyses originating in social psychology. However, in the current climate of studies that have seriously problematized the "big" notions of culture and community, such analyses feel somewhat dated in their conceptualization. We will come back to this point below.

Using a similar definition of culture, Wallace Chafe investigated cultural variability in oral narrative in his edited volume (1980) entitled *Pear stories: Cognitive, cultural and linguistic aspects of narrative production*. Chafe's primary interest was of a cognitive nature and focused on the ways in which people articulate or verbalize memories and organize meanings when they do so. In this approach, culture was identified with value systems and ways of understanding reality and representing knowledge. However, Chafe's methodology, unlike Polanyi's, which was based on the analysis of naturally occurring data, was more experimental, and so the narratives he worked with were elicited. The study was set up so as to exclude the narration of personal experiences, since those were seen as already constructed according to specific cultural frameworks. Instead, the use of a silent (with sound effects but no words) film that showed actions and events that were universally intelligible was seen as a trigger for differences in the narration that could be attributed to linguistic and cultural differences The study subjects included native speakers of English, German, Greek, Japanese, Chinese and a Mayan Indian language. The "experiment" was simple: Subjects watched the film and were then asked to recount it to an interviewer who had supposedly not seen it. The actual film was also short (six minutes long) and simple: A man was harvesting pears which were stolen by a boy on a bicycle. While stealing the pears, however, the boy lost his hat. He subsequently gave some of the stolen pears to a group of boys who helped him find it.

The narration of this film by different participants revealed numerous differences: From the point of view of cultural influence, the most important of those were to be found in the ways in which participants named the characters of the film and referred to the events. Greek participants, for instance, opted for interpretive naming (e.g. *a thief* instead of *a boy*) that couched moral comments. More generally, social interpretations and commentary proliferated in some narratives (e.g. the Greek narratives) as opposed to mere impersonal description that characterized other narratives.

Exactly as in Polanyi's study, in the studies that are included in Chafe's volume, culture is defined in homogeneous terms and the assumption is that there is a singular and identifiable national culture, e.g. Greek, Japanese, etc. that is reflected in and shapes discourse, in this case, storytelling. In disciplinary terms, both Polanyi and Chafe appear to have been influenced by Chomsky's generative grammar, which had undoubtedly put a mark on linguistic work at the time. As a result, they were prone to conceptualizing oral narrative production as the surface manifestation of a deep system of values and propositions that could be unearthed with a careful analysis of the text. In addition, the analyst's intuition and knowledge as a "native speaker" of a language and a member of a culture were taken seriously into account (e.g. in Chafe's studies, all interviewers were native speakers of the language under study in each case). This is in sharp contrast to the privileging of emic sense-making devices and the participants' point of view that we saw in the case of ethnography of communication.

3.4   Narrative involvement and telling styles

Another way of approaching cultural variability in narrative was through the investigation of style. In most of the work that we have reviewed, the concept of style includes both narrators' choices as to the ways of telling (i.e. patterns of usage of narrative strategies revealing preferences in the presentation of events and characters) and/or interactional patterns in the relationship with co-narrators and audiences. Style is thus a general concept including both narrative devices and storytelling modes of interaction.

An important tool for the investigation of cultural variability in narrative styles has been Tannen's concept of *involvement*. Tannen investigated "stylistic devices which present the discourse in a way that shapes the listener's involvement in it" (1989: 28), which, according to her "send a meta-message of rapport between addresser and addressee by conveying the teller's attitude to events" (p. 28). Involvement, like evaluation, is aimed at capturing the linguistic ways in which discourse in general and narrative in particular encode affective processes and the teller's stance toward what is being said. Tannen contributed to Chafe's volume, *Pear stories*, looking specifically at culturally shaped elements in the narratives produced by Greek speakers. In her subsequent work, she employed involvement as the main vehicle for exploring ways in which different cultures narrativize experience and in which this culture-dependence can be tapped into by looking at the stories' expressive features. Tannen readily acknowledged the resonance between involvement and evaluation by claiming that "since the point of a narrative is directly related to the experiences of people in the culture in which it is told, it is not surprising that Labov's evaluative elements are closely related to [my] notion of involvement" (1989: 14).

However, even if the devices for involvement bear striking resemblance with the evaluative devices, the conceptualization of these two notions is different. Labov was interested in the degree and type of embedding of the point of a story in the telling, more specifically in narrative action, while Tannen's interest was less structural and more of a stylistic-rhetorical nature: Her aim was to unravel the verbal ways in which tellers attempt to keep the audience's interest alive in what is being narrated. This is evident in her distinction between *involvement through sense patterns* and *involvement through sound patterns*. The former, was aimed at "audience participation in sense-making by doing some of the work of making meaning" (1989: 17) and comprised devices such as repetition, indirectness and details.[9] As an example of Tannen's approach, we present an excerpt from a story told by a Greek woman (1989: 138–9) that she discusses. At the point where the transcript begins, the narrator is describing a man who came to her rescue when another man was harassing her:

> (3.3)
> and at the time,
> (there) enters
> enters like an act of God,
> an American
> about seventy years old,
> I'll never forget
> a, he was wearing a shirt with large checks.

According to Tannen, the detail about the American's shirt creates interpersonal involvement, since it helps the audience imagine the man and the way he looked. It also "reinforces the hearer's sense of the vividness of the memory, and therefore its reportability and authenticity" (p. 139).

Involvement strategies based on sound patterns on the other hand, in Tannen's terms "involve the audience with the speaker and with the discourse by sweeping them up in what Scollon (1982) calls rhythmic ensemble much as one is swept by music and finds oneself moving in its rhythm" (p. 17). They thus include devices such as repetition and sound-words. As we see, repetition, which was regarded by Bauman (see examples 3.1 and 3.2) as a performance device is treated by Tannen as an involvement strategy.

Tannen's study of involvement is (perhaps confusingly) both about the teller and about the audience. In terms of the actual devices described, as Tannen herself has frequently noted, the focus is on those that add vividness and dramatization to what is narrated. On the basis of her study of Greek storytelling and of East European Jews' conversations, Tannen (1980, 1984, 1989) went on to claim that sustained use in storytelling and more generally in everyday interactions of a network of features that create involvement is culturally shaped and "associated not only with Greek but also with other ethnic styles that come across as vivid" (1989: 327).

More specifically, the features that she reported as typifying the "high involvement style" of Greek narratives were: *repetition, historical present verbs, ellipsis sound-words, second person singular, minimal external evaluation* and last but not least *direct quotation in reported speech* (i.e. dialogue exchanged, characters' speech or thoughts: p. 324). Tannen referred to all instances of reported speech as *constructed dialogue* in order to stress the creative process involved in any voice animation and the impossibility of any straightforward link between what is being reported as said and what – let alone if it – was actually said. This view that the self (as teller) is more or less agentively and creatively implicated in every quotation of another voice is clearly influenced by Bakhtin's (1981) dialogical view of language.

Since Tannen's influential study, the concept of involvement has attracted a certain controversy, as it is not clear whether it applies to the actual teller, the audience and/or the story itself. Teasing those aspects apart may thus be problematic for the analysis. Although Tannen stressed the role of involvement in the audience uptake, her analysis remained more focused on the tellers and the stylistic choices they make. For the audience's role to be taken seriously into account in the analysis, a view of narrative as talk-in-interaction is required and with it attention to the local participation roles by everybody involved in a storytelling event (see our discussion in Chapter 4).

This approach is exemplified in Blum-Kulka's study (1993) of dinnertime conversations of Jewish Israeli and Jewish American families, which anchored cultural variability to interactional choices within social events. More specifically, she analyzes pragmatic socialization, or "the ways in which children are socialized to use language in context in socially and culturally appropriate ways" (p. 3). In this respect, the methodology employed by Blum-Kulka does not only consist of the analysis of story content or storytelling strategies but also focuses on participation frameworks and what narrators and audiences do in interaction with each other, including the management of turns. In fact, the study of narratives told in the course of dinner starts off from the assumption that every narrative telling constitutes an event in which three dimensions of narrativity are involved: *telling, tales* and *tellers*. Telling refers to "the act of narrating in real time, who participates in whose stories and how" (p. 363). Tale is the stuff that narratives are made of. Finally, tellers take part in the act of telling as performers, but may or may not be the persons accountable for the story. By studying narrative in general and involvement in particular in relation to these dimensions, Blum-Kulka explores questions of how authorship is culturally defined; who is entitled in each culture to tell whose stories; what the attitudes of audiences to telling, tales and tellers are; how cultures vary in the relative support granted by recipients to tellers, tellings and tales.

The results of Blum-Kulka's study suggested among other things that the children in Israeli families were given a higher chance to act as active or non-active story recipients. On the other hand, the Jewish American families tended to emphasize socialization by allowing more for the display of narrative on the part of the children. In similar vein, Jewish American families preferred largely monologic tellings while the Israeli families opted for more participatory styles. More specifically, story authorship by a single teller was highly valued in the American stories, even in cases where the tale was known to more than one participant. In terms of involvement, the Israeli families were thus more prone to high-involvement responsive strategies during a story's telling that focused on the tale and teller and showed, in Tannen's terms, "active participatory listenership" (1984: 30). In contrast, Jewish American narrative events displayed a higher proportion of low-involvement strategies which focused on the telling: for instance, the audience would signal to the story initiator that they were ready to hear the story, but they would refrain from active contributions to the tale during the telling.

The welcome fact that in Blum-Kulka's study storytelling was seen as an event means that the focus on the teller that has characterized most post-Labovian work shifted to the interactional dynamics between teller and (active) audience, and that audience contributions, be they ratifications or challenges, were factored into the analysis. The cultural aspect was also more nuanced in Blum-Kulka's study than in some of the previous works: although all participants were "Jewish," the study proved that the location and in effect the different histories of the two communities under study were instrumental in shaping their storytelling styles and norms. Blum-Kulka suggested that although the two communities shared an Eastern European background, the emphasis that the American culture places on individual rights seemed to have played a formative role in the largely monologic, teller-led storytelling style of Jewish American families. On the other hand, the Israeli storytelling style presented all the hallmarks of a culture that places emphasis on engagement and in-group involvement. It is interesting to note that in Blum-Kulka's study, too, we find echoes of the distinction between individualist and interdependent cultures and that high involvement is associated with the latter. Finally, it is notable that here too, culture is seen as a unifying, homogeneous and rather static set of values, beliefs and behaviors that are invoked in communication. This sort of definition, as we will see below too, does not allow for fluidity, heterogeneity and under-patterning in culture.

Another influential study that focused on the analysis of tellers' strategies and production formats as fundamental elements of cultural styles was the research that Barbara Johnstone conducted in Fort Wayne, a Midwestern American city. Johnstone reported that storytelling in Fort Wayne was largely monologic and teller-led. Tellers placed emphasis on situating the stories locally, in the physical and social space familiar to them and their audience. This "local color" was created through the (over)use of details about place. In the same spirit as Tannen, Johnstone views details as involvement strategies that invite audience participation in meaning-making, but she also attributes their use to the prevailing cultural attitudes toward factuality. Specifically, as Johnstone states, "for Fort Wayners, personal experience stories are taken to be iconic representations of events, as the events were experienced by the teller. They cannot appear to be fictions. Or else they will count as lies" (1990: 101). Fort Wayners thus value good stories as opposed to good storytellers. Within this cultural bias toward factually verifiable events, details in stories act as a conventional mechanism for enhancing the "reality" and "actuality" of stories, by precisely locating them in time and space.

Notions of style in storytelling have also played an important role in studies of children's socialization into narrative events and styles and of their consequences on the children's educational attainment. As we mentioned in chapter 2.2, a number of scholars such as Michaels (1981), Hicks (1990) and Gee (1989) studied the relationships between school-based literacy and children's exposure to different kinds of discourse practices and styles at home. They all focused on narrative, since they regarded it as one of the most ubiquitous and basic discourse genres in everyday life. In this area, the work of Shirley Brice Heath has been particularly influential. Heath (1983) carried out an ethnographic study of patterns of child socialization in two communities of the Piedmont Carolinas in order to investigate possible effects of different community practices on children's school performance. Even though both communities were located in the same area and had a prevalent working-class population, they were ethnically and racially different: Trackton was African American and Roadville was white. Heath devoted her attention to enculturation processes and found profound differences in the ways people regarded children's education. People in Trackton believed that small children should learn how to talk through experience and free interaction, while people in Roadville regarded the process as something that should be monitored in all aspects by adults. Heath showed how narrative practices mirrored and reinforced such differences. Specifically, she reported that, in Roadville, the criteria for acceptable stories were explicit: Children needed to tell truthful accounts of actual events, which included a moral message. In Trackton, stories were appreciated as creative endeavors and therefore fictions and lies were not rejected, as long as the narrative was witty and successfully constructed. As a consequence, while children in Trackton were encouraged to tell their stories freely and to learn storytelling skills by trial and error, children in Roadville were only allowed to speak when authorized by adults, and their performances were carefully monitored for factuality and correctness. Thus, Heath confirmed the existence of an orientation toward oral expression in African American storytelling style that clashed with the prevalent literacy-based orientation of narratives in formal education domains. This clash was being implicated in specific difficulties for minority children that were enrolled in mainstream schools.

Studying the relationships between children's socialization into narrative and culturally based storytelling styles is an important enterprise with significant pedagogical implications. Indeed attitudes to authorship of stories and entitlement rights are revealing of cultural assumptions about who can tell whose stories. Furthermore, investigating what types of stories are encouraged in socialization contexts and how children and parents are portrayed in them as characters provides a window into wide cultural values and systems. For example, Georgakopoulou (2002) and Ochs and Taylor (1995) have shown in analyses of dinnertime stories of Greek and American families respectively that stories of shared or known events are salient in these contexts as socialization tools for different objectives: for example to strengthen the co-ownership of certain experiences, to (re)affirm the family as a close-knit unit, to enact family roles and also to socialize children into knowledge systems.

3.5   Narrative and cultural values: an appraisal

Most of the studies discussed so far can be brought together on the basis of their emphasis on communication styles in storytelling as evidence for the existence of "core" cultural values more or less directly traceable to the distinction between individualist and interdependent cultures. These core values have to do with sociability (i.e. engagement, solidarity, in-group membership) on the one hand and individualism (i.e. independence, freedom of action, personal space, etc.) on the other hand. The storytelling styles that are co-terminous with sociability values are the ones that place a high premium on involvement (performance, dramatization, active participation, immediacy of events). More generally, the frequency of narrative itself is associated within this framework with interdependent cultures. The implied reasoning is that as narrative trades on the teller's and the audience's emotional and experiential engagement in the events narrated, it is prototypically more associated with processes of subjectivity. In contrast, non-narrative (e.g. expository) texts, in particular written ones, have been argued to draw more on processes of reasoning, objectivity and critical argumentation (for a discussion see Georgakopoulou and Goutsos, 2004: 40–55; see also Georgakopoulou and Goutsos 2000). It follows, then, that cultures in which storytelling is prevalent and highly valued are both more focused on involvement processes and non-literate, or primarily oral-based.

As we have seen above, studies of storytelling in cultural and social groups which fall into the interdependent end of the continuum of cultural differences have succeeded in proving the complexity and intellectual potency of their traditions, thus confirming that there are no superior languages or cultures.

In this respect, they have been instrumental in a move away from the view of cultural diversity as deficit that subscribed to notions of high and low culture toward that of cultural diversity as difference, which subscribes to the notion of multiculturalism and relativism (Harris and Rampton 2003: 7–8). Nonetheless, a number of issues of concern can be raised with regard to the conceptualization of culture underlying many of them. A central problem is related to the implicit assumption of the existence of a set of norms of a dominant culture and language, in this case "the Western world" that can be more or less explicitly used as a reference point and yardstick for comparison. A danger with this vision is that of exoticizing the object of inquiry, and therefore of reaffirming its marginal status (a similar concern has been voiced in relation to research on language and gender; see, for example, Eckert and McConnell-Ginet 1999). Another closely related issue (and one that has been intensely debated in anthropology; see Duranti 1997) involves the degree to which concepts such as involvement, performance, engagement, sociability, etc. that have often accompanied descriptions of communication in certain cultures are consistent with, make sense and have any sort of reality for the members of that culture themselves and their perspective. For instance, it is not always clear – and is sometimes even doubtful – whether the interactants that produced the data under analysis would qualify these data in terms of sociability, positive politeness, etc. (Eelen 1999). In most cases, it is fair to say that these concepts are in fact analytical, that is, etic, as opposed to indigenous or emic and, in that sense they may be amenable to an ethnocentric bias.

Thus, a problem with many cultural studies of storytelling is that they tend to take dichotomous macro-accounts of cultures for granted in linguistic research. This may lead to two methodological repercussions: linguistic differences may be exaggerated to fit the general patterns established, and conceptual links between linguistic meanings and social relations of solidarity or dominance may be made a priori and therefore interfere with the findings or interpretation of empirical research (cf. Eelen 1999; Rampton 1999), creating a circularity of accounts. For example, an accepted cultural macro-account of sociability and involvement inevitably makes the linguistic displays of power and conflict incompatible with its framework, unless they are in effect construed as sociable behavior. As our study on disagreements in the conversations (including stories) of an all-female group of Greek adolescents showed (Georgakopoulou 2001), treating disagreements as sociable and linking them with the cultural values of engagement and solidarity, as has, for instance, been the case in previous studies of Greek conversations (e.g. Tannen and Kakava 1992), runs the risk of reification of the data. Without going into the study in detail here, it suffices to mention that the analysis demonstrated that the following parameters bear on the linguistic forms and discourse functions of disagreement in the data:

a. The participants' shared interactional history and the implicitness that this history affords.

b. The participants' larger social roles and identities, such as internal hierarchical divisions amongst them that are in turn reflected in local discourse roles: e.g. who has a leading role in what, who argues more, complies more, etc.

c. The activity-type in which disagreements mostly occur (in this case, stories about the future), which defines disagreements as a process of positing, negotiating and revising alternative versions of reality for the events to take place.

Attributing the sustained use of a language choice in discourse in general and narrative in particular to one specific function or contextual parameter (e.g. culture) has by now proven to be a particularly difficult – if not impossible – enterprise. What tends to happen is that routine linguistic choices invoke and are shaped by more than one aspect of their context as well as by more than one aspect of the teller's identity at the same time. It thus becomes tricky for the analysis to tease those aspects out and to quantify, as it were, the impact of each.[10]

3.6   Locating culture: a data analysis

The data used in this section come from a corpus of narratives collected in sociolinguistic interviews for a study on the discourse construction of identity among a group of undocumented Mexican immigrants to the United States (De Fina 2003a). The researcher conducted interviews with fourteen recent immigrants (nine men and five women) to the Washington area. The immigrants mostly came from the same village in Mexico and lived in the same area. Some of them were related or knew each other. They worked in unskilled jobs such as cleaning and landscaping. Interviews were conducted by the researcher with an assistant, who was a member of the community. The questions that were asked followed a protocol that elicited socioeconomic data, such as place of origin, age, schooling, work experience, and then went on to more personal questions about the motives for migration, how the immigrants had reached the United States, their impressions about differences and similarities between the USA and their own country, and about their lifestyle in the USA and life in the neighborhood. But the log was not rigidly followed and the interviews largely developed according to the interviewees' reactions to questions. One of the issues that the research was trying to investigate was how narrators encoded and negotiated agency in their stories. Amongst the linguistic mechanisms used to convey agency, pronominal choice and switching were seen as central, and therefore an analysis of this particular aspect was conducted on thirty-five narratives of personal experience. These narratives were partly spontaneous

Table 1 *Classification of narratives according to pronominal choice*

Type of narrative	Number
"Yo" narratives	14
"Nosotros" narratives	12
Mixed pronouns narratives	9
Total	35

and partly elicited through the question, "Is there an experience that you had here in the United States that has been particularly important for you?" They related work conflicts, accidents, troublesome everyday encounters. The analysis revealed a number of interesting tendencies in the presentation of experience as having collective or individual significance in the stories. Narratives were grouped according to the prevalence of individual, collective or "depersonalized" agency based on the point of view prevalent in the story as encoded through the use of pronouns *yo* ('I'), *nosotros* ('we') or *uno* ('one'). This first, general, classification based on the prevalent use of pronouns in each narrative yielded the result shown in Table 1.

The table reveals that narratives focused on a collective perspective were almost as many as those centered on the individual, which is unusual for stories told in response to direct questions about personal experience. In addition, it was found that in almost one-third of the narratives there were significant shifts in perspectives between personalization, collectivization and depersonalization of experience. This first general analysis revealed a tendency of narrators not to emphasize either their role as protagonists in the story worlds that they evoked or the significance of the experiences told for them as individuals. Other discourse phenomena corroborated this hypothesis. First, further analyses of the narratives showed that narrators did not focus on what their actions and thoughts were in the taleworld, that even in stories where they presented themselves as protagonists they often switched the attention away from themselves as main actors. These tendencies toward collective orientation and depersonalization were confirmed by the significant presence of pronoun switches (from *yo* ('I') to *nosotros* ('we')) in interactional negotiations over the establishment of story protagonists and by the fact that the majority of story codas generalized (rather than personalized) the significance of experiences told in the narratives. Finally, this negotiation over pronoun choice in the reporting of actions was also present in the production of narratives other than Labovian stories, such as habitual narratives of life-story fragments.

In the light of the above, let us now look at one of the narratives in the corpus. The story was told by Rachel, a young woman who worked in unskilled jobs, in response to the interviewer's question about good or bad experiences in the country in the first period of her life as an immigrant to the United States.[11] Ismael, the young Mexican who accompanied the researcher to the interviews, was also present.

(3.4)
```
1  A:  Hay alguna experiencia que recuerdas, mucho de esos primeros,
2      momentos que llegaste?
3  R:  Buena o mala?
4  A:  Como tu quieras, puede ser buena o mala, cuéntame la mala, y luego me
5      cuentas la buena, o al revés.
6  R:  Uh (.) bueno la b- (.) mala, o sea es porque llegamos las tres llegamos a un
7      departamento prácticamente vacío,
8      sólo había ese sillón viejo que está allí en donde está Ismael,
9      no había televisión,
10     no había nada,
11     eso fue,
12     o sea llega uno
13     y se encuentra con todo todo vacío,
14     uh nosotras no teníamos trabajo,
15     teníamos muy poca r-
16     teníamos un sólo par de zapatos cada una,
17     no teníamos ropa,
18     no teníamos para ir a lavar la ropa,
19     teníamos que lava@rla y colgarla,
20     uh y sobre todo o sea lo que uno tiene es que extraña su familia,
21     o sea más que nada soledad y acostumbrarse.
```

Translation
```
1  A:  Is there an experience that you remember well about these first,
2      moments when you came?
3  R:  Good or bad?
4  A:  As you like, it can be good or bad, tell me a bad one and then you tell
5      me a good one, or the other way around.
6  R:  Uh (.) well the g- (.) bad one, I mean is because we came the three of us to
7      a practically empty apartment,
8      there was only this old sofa which is there where Ismael is,
9      there was no television,
10     there was nothing,
11     that was it,
12     I mean one comes
13     and one finds everything empty,
14     uh we didn't have a job,
```

15   we had very few cl-,
16   we only had a pair of shoes each,
17   we had no clothes,
18   we didn't have a place to wash our clothes,
19   we had to wa@sh them and hang them,
20   and more than anything I mean what happens to one is that one misses the family,
21   I mean more than anything else loneliness and getting used to it.

The excerpt starts with what can be characterized as a "narrative-eliciting" question on the part of the interviewer: there is reference to a specific experience, and there is the use of the verb *remember* that is so commonly associated with the act of narrating. In response to this question, Rachel asks whether she should focus on a good or bad experience (line 3). Tellers who self-select to tell a story tend to propose how they want their story to be understood by the audience right from the beginning (cf. Jefferson 1978). In this case, it is interesting to see that although asked by the interviewer to be the teller, Rachel still delimits the frame of interpretation for the story to follow with her closed question (good or bad?). It is also interesting to note at this point that the interviewer in response does not select a type of telling but she nonetheless proposes an order which prioritizes the telling of a "bad experience" (line 4). Rachel in response selects the telling of a bad experience but with some display of hesitation (see the markers "uh" and "well," the false start "well the g-" and the repair "bad one" in line 5). Below, we will come back to the implications that this interactional management of the story's beginning between the interviewer and the interviewee has for the actual telling.

The story that Rachel tells is not a canonical one in Labovian terms in that it does not have an explicit temporal juncture (see section 2.1.1 for a definition) i.e. it does not present two explicit complicating action events that are ordered in time. Nonetheless, it can still be treated as a minimal narrative because the order of at least two events that appear condensed in the same line (5) may be inferred: 1. the girls arrived at the apartment, 2. they realized that it was empty. The latter situation constitutes a complicating action with consequences: it brings about not only the aggravation of poverty, but also the psychological consequences of sadness and feelings of loneliness. In fact, the rest of the narrative is devoted to the evaluation of what this emptiness implied both materially and psychologically. The description of the apartment and of the situation in which the girls found themselves is conveyed through the evaluation clauses that follow the complicating action (lines 8 to 19), but also through performance devices. Indeed Rachel uses syntactic parallelism in her repetition of the verb *tener* ('have') in "teníamos" ('we had') and "no teníamos" ('we didn't have') at the beginning of lines 14 to 19. The lines pattern into two sets of three: lines 14–16: "no teníamos," "teníamos,"

"teníamos" ('we didn't have,' 'we had,' 'we had') and lines 17–19: "no teníamos," "no teníamos," "teníamos que" ('we didn't have,' 'we didn't have,' 'we had to'). Evaluation and performance devices contribute to convey the main point of the story: the first experience with immigration was metaphorically represented in the encounter with the emptiness of an apartment and the lack of basic commodities.

It is interesting to note that Rachel begins the narrative in the "nosotros" ('we') form, placing herself as a protagonist within a group constituted by her, her cousin and her sister, the three people with whom she arrived in the United States. This pronoun choice constitutes a shift with respect to the interviewer's question, which was formulated in the "tu" ('you') so as to elicit a "yo" ('I') answer (lines 1–5). It is also interesting to notice that Rachel directly introduces "the three of us" as a story world protagonist (line 6) without any orientation to the referents of the pronoun "us," a move that indicates how natural it is for her to talk about herself as part of a group. This way, Rachel shifts the focus of the story from "I" to "we" and maintains it throughout the narrative, as she never refers to what she specifically felt or did, but consistently keeps the attention of the listeners on the three girls seen as a unit. It is also worth noting that when she is not using the pronoun *we*, Rachel is depersonalizing the experience by shifting to *one* (Spanish 'uno') in evaluative clauses (lines 12, 13 and 20). Through these shifts to the pronoun *one*, Rachel is presenting what happened to her and to her relatives as an instance of experiences that are generalizable to other people, specifically to other immigrants. In that way, she is also depersonalizing it (on the relation between the use of pronouns and agency, see O'Connor 1994; see also chapter 6.3.1). Finding empty apartments (line 13), missing the family (20) and having to get used to loneliness (line 21) are thus discursively constructed as experiences that are not particular to Rachel (or to Rachel and her relatives), but that can be related to the immigration process. As mentioned above, both the collective focus of this narrative and the tendency to generalize experience are not exclusive to Rachel but are rather representative of many of the narratives told in this context.

Let us now relate these observations about the data to some of the questions that we have posed throughout this chapter. It has been argued in the analysis that pronominal usage and switching by narrators can be studied as strategies that encode agency. One of the main characteristics of narrative as a discursive activity is its ability to conjure a double world: the taleworld (cf. tale, narrated text) and the storytelling world (cf. telling, narrative event). Pronominal choice indexes meanings at both these levels. At one level, the teller's selection of specific pronouns indicates the type of roles that she or he assigns to herself or himself as a character in the story world. Through selection of specific pronouns, the teller may present herself or himself as an individual or as a member of a group, may stress responsibility in the performance of actions or indicate lack of participation in them. At another level, pronoun switching indexes relationships between the teller and other participants in the storytelling world since pronouns may also be used to involve the hearer in the evaluation of the action, or to take them into the story world. We have seen that in this case, the teller uses pronominal switching both to present the protagonist of the story as collective and to generalize the value of experience to other people. These strategies have been related in the literature on narrative and identity to narrators' social orientation, since pronominal choice and alternation convey particular kinds of speaker involvement but may also index particular views about the self and its role in the social world.

As we discussed in section 3.3, the connection between different conceptions of the self and specific language practices has received much attention, particularly in studies about non-Western communities. Duranti (1993), for example, argues that many non-Western cultures, including the Samoan, share an "impersonal" concept of the self, which is apparent in their treatment of responsibility in public discourse. Before him another anthropologist, Geertz (1983), had brought to the attention of scholars the existence of cultural variations in the concept of personhood. He wrote (p. 59):

> The Western conception of the person as a bounded, unique, more or less integrated motivational and cognitive universe, a dynamic center of awareness, emotion, judgment, and action organized into a distinctive whole and set contrastively both against such wholes and against its social and natural background, is, however incorrigible it may seem to us, a rather peculiar idea within the context of the world's cultures.

It has also been proposed that the construction of reference in discourse, including pronominal reference, can be regarded as a type of social practice that indexes and makes relevant implicit rules and frames having to do with the view of the persona. Hanks (1990) discussed, for example, how choice of possessives and of personal pronominal forms in Mayan reflects not only socially determined spatio-temporal frames, but also social rules about the roles of individuals in the different domains of society. He argues that the use of deictics in interaction indexes social roles. Thus, in his analysis, when a Mayan man answers the interviewer's question on how many rooms there are in his house by saying "three rooms of mine and three of my older brothers," he "links the rooms both to" their "current 'here' and to himself as owner" (p.169). According to Hanks, the pronominal choice of the interviewer pointing to himself and his brother, not the respective families, as owners, is consistent with rules of property ownership in Mayan homes. Similarly, Hanks argues that when Mayans choose to say, "we went with Manuel" as an equivalent of "I went with Manuel," they display a perspective on the event and the relationship between referents that differs from that of speakers of English.

Mülhausler and Harré (1990: 106) also reflect on how the Wintu's conception of the self as unbound and not sharply separated from others finds expression in the grammar of self-reference in their language, specifically in the use of pronominal suffixes. Hill (1989) brought a similar perspective to her studies of storytelling by Mexicano speakers in Mexico. She also explored the idea that certain cultures display a less differentiated concept of the self than developed Western cultures. From this angle, she looked at storytelling strategies on a continuum between individualistic and sociocentric views of the self. Hill characterized Mexicano speakers as "sociocentric" as opposed to "egocentric" middle-class Americans. In her work on involvement strategies used in narratives by these two groups, she found that Mexicano speakers tended to locate evaluation and self-reference within story world clauses in constructed dialogue and to use the pronoun *you* to refer to themselves, while Americans tended to locate evaluation and self reference in interactional world clauses and to use the pronoun *I* for self-reference.[12] Based on these perspectives, it would be easy to conclude that the social orientation found in the narratives analyzed is simply a reflection of a community orientation in Mexican culture.

Nonetheless, an explanation of this data based on presumed general characteristics of Mexican culture rests on the idea that Mexican culture is a kind of supra-structure with homogeneous traits that is superimposed on discourses independently of local contexts. Such a conclusion, besides being theoretically risky, would also be unwarranted unless one had access to similar interviews with Mexicans who had immigrated under different social circumstances and belonged to different social categories. More importantly, an explanation of the data based on general national traits underplays the possible role of the local context on the way identities are constructed in discourse. Thus, alternative interpretations may stem from a closer consideration of the interactional context and its possible interplay with the material characteristics of the immigrant experience and other elements of the larger social and local context as well. At the level of the material conditions of immigration, it is important to note that immigrants crucially depend on the help and support of family members, friends or acquaintances that represent their contact when they come to the United States. These relatives and friends often provide them with a place to stay and the prospect of a job. This dependence could explain the importance that they place on the group in the recounting of their experiences. At the same time, immigrants also seem to stress their relationship with the people with whom they arrived, both because sharing such an important experience creates a bond between them, and because these companions are often the only people that they see and to whom they talk, particularly in the beginning of the immigrant experience. Thus, the experience of migrating accentuates, especially in its early phases, a sense of identification with others. When immigrants respond to questions on their experience with stories that have collective protagonists, they underline the saliency of their group to them. The discursive immersion in the group could be related to some of the material and psychological aspects of migration, as immigrants often do share very difficult experiences with relatives or people they come in contact with, but they also physically share their living space with other people in multi-family homes.

In addition, the tendency to present individual experiences as non-unique, and potentially generalizable, has also been reported in other interview-based studies of immigration. Baynham (2003), for example, talks about how Moroccan immigrants to the UK often tell the story of their migration in generic form, thus presenting their individual experience as typical of their group. This kind of depersonalization can also be interpreted in the light of strategies of de-responsabilization within the local context of the interview. Immigrants in interviews are questioned about their own life choices, but the discourse that develops within the interview amongst the participants is not just a private conversation; it also responds to and echoes other voices and other discourses, circulating in society. We use the term discourses here to refer to meta-narratives involving typical scenarios, plots and stereotypical social relations that are given voice through socialization, the mass media, institutional and cultural practices (for a discussion about meta-narratives and similar constructs, see section 5.4.1). As demonstrated by studies of public discourse about immigrations (see, for example, Santa Ana 1999), mainstream discourses construct being undocumented as intentionally breaking the law, cheating and taking advantage of services and goods that should only be available to legal residents. In this sense, an interviewer who is external to the community may be seen as potentially holding some of these beliefs. A discourse of depersonalization and generalization of experience may therefore also be a strategy through which immigrants deflect personal responsibility and, ultimately, blame. By presenting immigration as a collective phenomenon and underlining that their choice to migrate is not an individual one, but was in some ways forced upon them as a community by the conditions of need that they experienced in Mexico, immigrants are able to shift responsibility away from themselves as individuals. These strategies alleviate the burden of a responsibility for breaking the law that society places on them and allow them to present migration as a social, not an individual, choice. Such differences in focus are evident in the mismatch between the interviewer's emphasis, and interest, on individual experiences, and the immigrants' responses that concentrate on the general significance of those experiences. In this respect, depersonalized narratives as a story type may also be related to the interview as a speech event. As we have seen in the analysis of the story opening, Rachel's narrative is elicited by the interviewer, and she shows some hesitation in telling it. Talking about painful memories to a quasi stranger may have been difficult for her, and she may have chosen to tell a generic narrative as a way of avoiding exposing her feelings in a relatively formal environment.

In conclusion, the analysis of the data at hand shows that relating storytelling activities and strategies to wide cultural contexts may result in oversimplification and in a neglect of the multiple ways in which local conditions shape and are shaped by narratives. As we will discuss in Chapter 6, the alternative for the analyst lies in a close ethnographic investigation of local contexts and their interplay with wider contexts and in the search for emic categories that may better reflect the way communities define themselves as opposed to predetermined labels such as national or supranational ones.

3.7   Conclusions

In this chapter we have reviewed approaches to cultural variability in narrative. We have seen that ethnographically inspired research has set the stage for a view of culture as emergent social action that is particularly evident in Bauman's work on storytelling performance. In this tradition, cultural specificity in narrative is anchored not only to story content, but also to conventional ways of telling, and to the functioning of narrative events within other social events. Most of the research here has been devoted to the study of non-Western cultures and has had limited influence on analyses of everyday storytelling in other contexts.

Sociolinguistic studies of cultural variability have focused on the definition of national and ethnic styles in storytelling and have often operated with a concept of culture that is somewhat normative, i.e. as comprising a set of values more or less homogeneously distributed within an ethnic or national group. With respect to methodologies, there is greater variability within these approaches than within the field of ethnographic studies. However, researchers in this tradition tend to concentrate more on the occurrence of certain categories in the data than to the analysis of narrative genre or narrative event.

Overall, there has been a recent move away from culture seen as the expression of large groups such as national or supranational communities and toward a more nuanced and situated approach. Within this approach, smaller groups such as communities defined in terms of profession (Cortazzi 1993), ethnicity, (De Fina 2008), gender (Coates 2005; Kiesling 2006), age (Coupland, Garret and William 2005), etc. are focused upon and seen as drawing on distinct cultural styles and resources. Similarly, there is increasing attention to the particularities of specific contexts of communication, and social and cultural identities are presented as neither fixed nor categorical entities but as emergent in the sequentiality of discourse, where they present an irreducible situational contingency (Androutsopoulos and Georgakopoulou 2003: 1). Instead of trying to identify what is culture-specific about language use, researchers tend to ask questions such as: How are cultural resources enacted and reconciled but also contested in the contingencies of situated activity? What do participants orient to in terms of their cultural identity in specific contexts? How do they draw upon it as a resource for affiliation or disaffiliation? In addition, instead of examining culture as a whole and as a distinguishable attribute that can be singled out and kept apart from other identity aspects, emphasis is placed on how culture gets co-constructed and co-articulated with other aspects of identity in discourse (e.g. gender, age, social class). We will come back to a discussion of these questions in Chapter 6.

Finally, culture has emerged in recent theorization as a less monolithic concept than in the past, as cultural theorists emphasize diversity and dissent. In Appadurai's words, an important development in recent approaches to culture is: "the recognition that the boundaries of cultural systems are leaky, and that traffic and osmosis are the norm, not the exception," as cultural theorists "foreground mixture, heterogeneity, diversity, and plurality as critical features of cultures in the era of globalization" (2004: 61–2).

This latest move toward more fine-tuned approaches to culture should not blind us to the profound impact that earlier studies of storytelling in culture such as the ones reviewed in this chapter have had. To begin, they have offered us concrete ways of analyzing language in storytelling with a view to exploring culture-sensitivity. This toolkit is in principle compatible with a more nuanced perspective too. They have also painstakingly documented the pivotal role of narrative in general and language use within narrative in particular in (re)constructing culture. Recent studies have certainly built on this, but their focus on highly contextualized analysis has made it difficult to offer generalizations about language and culture and to establish patterned relationships between storytelling styles and communities. The question that remains open is whether it is legitimate or desirable to abandon the idea that there are general cultural traits which distinguish speech communities in terms of the types of stories they tell and the way they tell them, the values that they present, etc. Abandoning the exploration of cultural specificity in narrative would certainly go against the findings of numerous studies, not least within the tradition of the ethnography of communication.

How can we then reconcile a view of narrative as the expression of sociocultural systems with the analysis of the particularities of concrete storytelling events? No easy answer is available, but some of the methodological points established in performance-based approaches may help find some solutions to this. One important point is that storytelling should be studied as a type of practice related to other practices in the culture so that narrative patterns can be connected to other kinds of social patterns. A second consideration is that we need to recognize the existence of a tension between cultural tradition and innovation in discourse, and an analysis of narrative genres based on performance provides a way of better understanding this nexus. Finally, a greater stress on emic understandings and on the participants' local theories of narrative would avoid the danger of the researchers extrapolating from data.

4   Narrative as interaction

4.0   Introduction

The study of narratives in a wide range of everyday contexts has led research-ers to challenge the focus of post-Labovian research on monologic teller-led stories that were recounted to compliant and mostly silent audiences in inter-views and instead to emphasize the complexity and variability of storytelling formats, their dependence on the local context of interaction, and the important role played by participant structures in their production and reception. In this chapter, we focus on stories as interactional achievements, and we therefore stress the significance of participation structure and of the conversational work done in the moment-by-moment unfolding of a story's telling. Our aim is to show how studies of storytelling have gradually moved from tellers to teller-ship and from story as a product to storytelling as a process. We will discuss ways in which storytellers launch, sustain and end narratives in interaction, and illustrate the role of storytellers and audiences in the unfolding of stories. In particular, we will analyze the kinds of problems that storytelling poses to tellers and audiences, the many ways in which reactions from an audience may affect storytelling, and the variability in roles that can be taken up by partici-pants in a storytelling event.

To this effect, we will engage with research that has unpacked simple notions of teller and audience, demonstrating the existence of much more complex participation frameworks in narrative events. We will also discuss the notion of *telling rights* as central to an understanding of different participant con-figurations in specific storytelling contexts. In the second part of the chapter, we will illustrate how looking at storytelling as an interactional phenomenon necessarily leads to a recognition of the variability in storytelling formats. We will therefore discuss different story types that depart from the structure of the prototypical narrative, and we will review *small stories research* as an attempt to unify efforts at broadening the scope of narrative analysis. As we will see, the questions that form the core of this chapter have been investigated mostly within the domain of conversational narratives. That said, scholars studying elicited narratives have also recognized the need to take into account their interactional characteristics (e.g. Baker and Johnson 2000; Mishler 1986; Riessman 1991) and therefore to problematize the sharp division between conversational and interview stories.

4.1   From teller to co-tellership

As we discussed in Chapter 2, conversation analysts have documented stories not as isolated texts, but rather as multi-turns units embedded in talk that are consequential for further talk. They have also emphasized that stories are not just told: they need to be introduced, developed and closed. Jefferson (1978) noted two very important characteristics of stories in interaction, i.e. their *local occasioning* and their *sequential implicativeness*. The concept of local occasioning captures the fact that narratives do not come out of the blue but, rather, emerge in relation to what is being talked about in a particular interaction and are thus made relevant to the local context. The idea of sequential implicativeness accounts for the fact that once a story is told, it will affect the way subsequent talk develops. As we will show in detail below, typical reactions to a story are evaluative comments on the characters depicted in the story, the events recounted, the moral of the story, a second story (i.e. thematically or otherwise related account that echoes and amplifies the point made by the previous story; see Norrick 1993; Ryave 1978; Sacks [1970] 1992b), or further talk on related topics. We will also see that if a narrative is treated as not sequentially implicative, i.e. it is ignored by the audience, the teller will be faced with an interactional failure that demands mending.

As noted in section 2.3, Harvey Sacks has been most influential in describing the conversational development of stories. He noted that the storytelling process is constituted by the suspension of the normal rules for turn-taking which allow for regular speaker change (see Sacks, Schegloff and Jefferson 1974). This happens because narrators need to secure longer and uninterrupted turns in order to tell a story. For this reason, "stories take more than one utterance to produce" ([1970] 1992c: 223) in that tellers need to secure the floor. As a consequence, their first utterance will usually contain hints to listeners about the fact that a story is coming, the second utterance will usually consist of a response from the audience, while the story proper will only start in the third utterance. Indeed, Sacks argues that there are three serially ordered and adjacently paired sequences in stories: a preface, a telling and a response sequence. Prefaces may be seen as similar to Labov and Waletkzy's (1967) abstract (see section 2.1) in that they usually anticipate the story content by summarizing its main point or hinting to some other detail to locate it in time and/or space. But Sacks' focus is on their interactive function more than on their structural role, since he sees them as providing an occasion for the teller to make sure that the story has not been heard before or is not going to be rejected for some other reason by the audience, while at the same time alerting the audience to what they "should do when the story is over" ([1970] 1992a: 10). Thus, if the teller announces that the story is about terrible events, the audience will look for references to terrible events in the telling in order to recognize the climax, and will also be more likely to figure out appropriate ways to react to the storytelling. Prefaces may have different components with different interactive functions. For example, an offer to tell or a request for a chance to tell is aimed at getting the floor. On the other hand, a mention of the source from which the story is taken can give recipients an idea of whether they have already heard it. Finally, an initial characterization of the story can motivate a positive or negative reply and prepare recipients for the kind of reaction that is appropriate.

Story openings and closings are among the most researched topics in the literature on stories in interaction as they clearly demonstrate the fact that storytelling involves interactional work. Story openings in conversation may take many different shapes and do not necessarily include a full-fledged preface. Jefferson (1978: 224) talks about different and more or less conventionalized ways of launching a story that themselves range from economic to elaborate story openings. She specifically discusses examples in which tellers opt for a "story-prefixed phrase" such as, *as a matter of fact* ... or *that's true now* ..., or for a disjunct marker + phrase (such as *oh that reminds me of* ....) and then start their story in the same turn (also, see section 2.3). But there are also other cases in which the teller introduces the story over a number of turns either to make sure that the recipients align as story listeners or because she or he has not been able to secure attention after the first attempt. For example, Ochs and Capps (2001: 135) note that tellers may try to get their listener's attention through "slow disclosure," i.e. by signaling through intonation that they have more to say than they have uttered. They illustrate this strategy through the following example:

> (4.1)
> Marie: Ben walked up? (and /she) handed me
>   three twenty?
> John: mhm
>   (o.6 pause)
> Marie: And I *thought* she only owed me
>   eighty....

(Ochs and Capps 2001: 136)

In the example Mary does not deliver the story immediately: she stops after raising her intonation at the end of the first utterance and goes on to tell the rest of the story only after having received a reaction from John.

Story openings appear to be less elaborated when tellers and recipients are close friends and interact regularly because in many cases stories that circulate among them are shared. As we discussed in section 2.3, Georgakopoulou

(2005a) has shown, for example, that in interactions where participants have intimate relations and interact regularly, tellers may not ask for permission to tell a story but provide the addressees with recognitional elements so as to establish mutual reference before they start the telling.

Story exit devices and story closings are as interactionally complex as openings. As Schiffrin (1984) notes, a great deal of negotiation often accompanies exit talk since tellers need to give cues to their listeners that the story has reached its climax, listeners need to show that they have understood the point of the story and, if they decide to make comments, they need to contribute topically relevant talk, including evaluations of the preceding story (cf. Jefferson 1978). Such comments also show the kind of alignments recipients take toward the story. For example, story evaluations may indicate that recipients agree with the story point made by the storyteller or that they find the story relevant to preceding talk. When ending a narrative, storytellers may opt for formulaic closings such as proverbs and clichés (Norrick 1993: 49) in order to signal both the significance of the story and the fact that they are bringing it to a close. The task of both teller and recipients is to re-engage turn-by-turn talk after the completion of a story. Jefferson (1978) showed convincingly how audience reactions that occur prematurely and before the telling has moved to an end put the onus on the teller to continue with the telling and ensure that their story has been understood in the ways in which they have proposed. Similarly, if they reach a story's closing but the audience does not respond in appropriate ways, that is, if they remain silent or if they offer tangential talk that does not show the story's implicativeness for what is to follow, tellers tend not to challenge these responses but instead to propose that the story has not ended yet and to offer a further story component until they get relevant responses (pp. 232–4)[1].

In order to illustrate how openings and closings work, let us look at a narrative told during a conversation among friends. The data come from a conversation recorded during dinner between two couples. The hosts, Amy and Ian, have prepared dinner for their close friends Bob and Sally, and they are all discussing the food.

(4.2)
Participants: Amy, Bob, Ian, Sally
1. Amy: We don't know what it's called.
2. Sally: The Koreans won't tell him.
3. Bob: White fish.
4. Amy: White fish, but that's not a-
5. Ian: But not only that but today, today it[was-
6. Bob: [well if you were in the Caribbean
7.   they would call it Grouper.
8 Amy: Grouper?

9. Ian: Today I bought it, [but I, a little Chinese came out and he was horrified=
10. Bob: [((...))
11. Ian: = that I would take this fish and with his son and everything, and he
12.   said, [well
13. Bob: [Is this the Korean fish store that is on upper East Drive?
14. Amy: [Nooo.
15. Ian: [No no.
16. Sally: This is another Korean one,
17. Bob: Ah,
18. Sally: Because people tell us that the store which is at the shop and stop in
19.   Chevy Chase is a good fish store.
20. Amy: Very good: Yeah?
21. Ian: Very very good.
22. Amy: It is, very good.
23. Ian: We go to this one because I like this particular fish,
24. Sally: You go this Korean[one,
25. Amy: [Also that one [is less expensive.
26. Sally: [This one is expensive?
27. Ian: So the guy came out, he came out with a box about this size,
28. Bob: Uhu.
29. Ian: Filled it up with ice?@, put the @fucking fish in it and then covered it
30.   with ice again and then gave me this eno@rmous box@ about this size
31. Bob: Wow!
32. Ian: He said, "fish fresh,"
33. Bob: Packaging man, it's key.
           (.)
34. Amy: He came home with this huge thing and I said what is that? (.)
35. Sally: The fish (.)
36. Ian: Apparently you cannot go out with the fish,
37. Bob: Oh he didn't tell you what kind of fish it is.

At the point where the excerpt starts, the conversation is focused on the fish
that Amy and Ian had cooked, which had been appreciated by the guests. Bob
had asked what kind of fish that was and Amy had answered that they didn't
know (line 1). In line 5, Ian tries to introduce a story centered on the fish by
producing a story-prefixed phrase, "not only that but" which links the forth-
coming story to the topic of the lack of knowledge about the name of the fish
introduced by Amy. He then tries to start the storytelling with an orientation
"today, today it was." At this point however, no one acknowledges his attempt
and he gets interrupted by Bob (line 6), who is still discussing the name of the
fish and to whose utterance Amy orients in her next turn (line 8). Ian tries to
restart the story about something that the fishmonger did, in lines 9, 11 and 12.

However, once again he gets interrupted by Bob, who inquires about the location of the shop. Thus the conversation that follows (lines 13 to 26) is focused on this question and Ian loses his chances of introducing the story. As a consequence, he has to wait for several turns in order to get another opportunity. In line 27 he tries again to continue and finally gets the audience attention. The story is about the fishmonger using a huge package for a relatively small fish. At this point members of the audience orient to the story and produce story-related utterances. In particular, Bob produces two evaluative comments (in lines 31 and 33). However, there is not much follow-up to the story that may indicate appreciation, and in fact there is a brief silence (after line 33). At this point, Amy proposes herself as co-teller by narrating her reaction to the box, and in this way she both continues talk on the story and elaborates on Ian's point about the box. Sally also intervenes projecting a fictional line of dialogue that represents what Ian might have answered in the story world (line 35). In line 36, Ian proposes a further comment that can be seen as making the point of the story more explicit since there has been little reaction to it (line 36). He says that apparently one cannot exit the shop without a box. After this, Bob produces exit talk in that he relates the conclusion of the narrative to the topic that was being discussed before the story was told, i.e. not knowing the name of the fish. As it is apparent from the transcript, however, the reaction of the audience is minimal as no further evaluation of the story is offered after Bob's line and no second story is put forth by any of the participants. This development contrasts with what has been reported about story closings above: i.e. that recipients usually engage in further talk about the narrative. Such lack of engagement is a good indication of the fact that the story has not been very successful.

This example shows both how storytelling requires conversational work, and how its development largely depends on audience reaction and participation, a topic to which we turn in the following section.

4.2   Audience participation

As we saw in Chapter 2, conversation analysts and other interactionist researchers have challenged a view of storytelling as largely teller-centered by underlining the fact that many narratives are collaboratively told by more than one teller, but also that the way stories start and develop largely depends on audience reactions. As such, stories, or parts of them, may be challenged, undercut, rejected, ignored, etc. Ochs and Capps also underline the emerging and co-constructed nature of stories, reflecting on the differences between telling a story *to* someone and telling a story *with* someone. They argue that in everyday situations, tellers often launch their narratives without having a pre-constituted message in mind and that they often use tellings as occasions for making sense of events with others in such a way that "narrative activity becomes a tool for collaboratively reflecting upon specific situations and their place in the general scheme of life" (2001: 2). In fact, narratives may be collaboratively constructed, but, as we will see in section 4.3, they can also spur confrontation and conflict. Independently of whether interlocutors collaborate with each other or not, it is important to stress that telling rights are not given but need to be established and that audiences are not compliant and undifferentiated wholes. Instead, co-tellers and audience contributions profoundly shape the course and structure of narratives.

Indeed, studies of the interactional management of narratives have shown that undifferentiated notions of teller and audience are naïve and that in storytelling events tellers and other participants align themselves to each other in complex ways, generating different types of participation frameworks. In his groundbreaking paper "Audience diversity, participation and interpretation," Goodwin (1986) discusses, for example, how in a storytelling event the structure of the talk both shapes and is shaped by the audience. He also draws attention to the complexity of the concept of audience pointing to the fact that a group of recipients becomes an audience only when they orient to the storytelling through displays of attention and engagement. He thus proposes that the "structure of attention" (p. 285) may be different, with each member of an audience variously engaged or engrossed at different points and with the status of each member changing and evolving during the storytelling. Taking inspiration from Goffman's notion of *participation frameworks* (1981), Goodwin underscores the need to distinguish between different kinds of recipients. For example, some members may be in a privileged position because they know the story (as it often happens in family interactions), or they may have been protagonists or characters in the story world of the narrative that is being told and therefore they may be called upon as co-narrators at any point in the storytelling. Thus, the audience of a telling may be composed of knowing vs. unknowing recipients, principal recipients, ratified recipients, recipients who may be promoting a teller's view or who may be delegitimating or undercutting the telling activity, offering side comments, introducing other topics, etc. As we saw in example (4.1) above, the uptake of the telling from members of the audience is also a very important factor in the development of a story, since if audiences are uninterested or challenge the story content, the teller may have to stop the telling or decisively alter it so as to incorporate any audience comments.

Goodwin (1986) illustrates the nuance of storytelling participation roles in the analysis of a story embedded in a conversation about racing cars. He shows how participants ratify each other as experts through selective audience behavior (for example, by not attending to certain utterances the way they attend to others). He demonstrates that the topic and the choice of language in which the story is told may also have an important effect on audience participation. For example, in this case, the teller talks about cars using specialized language, and these choices reveal that the intended recipients of the story are the men, not the women. Another point that Goodwin makes is that recipients are treated differentially by the teller. In this case, one of the men is designed as a focal recipient in view of his knowledge of the world of car racing that affords him special access to the story's events. Finally, the analysis demonstrates how audience participation may evolve and change in the course of storytelling. Although the women are not engrossed recipients, one of them (the teller's wife) has a special status afforded to her by having heard the story before. Interestingly, she is the one who starts the storytelling when inviting her husband to tell the story, but she then withdraws from the interaction and becomes a non-engaged participant. However, as the teller draws the narrative to a close, she becomes an active recipient again by challenging her husband's interpretation of what happened. This provokes a shift in audience participation since listeners align with her understanding of the story and distance themselves from the teller. In this way, the intervention of an audience member can change the frame of interpretation of a story and affect the telling. Indeed, although the teller still refuses to adapt to his audience reaction and continues the story, most of the listeners are now disengaged, and he has to tailor the talk to the only recipient that stays attentive. Through this analysis, Goodwin demonstrates that:

1. audience diversity may be established from the beginning of a storytelling event;
2. members of an audience can act in different ways and thus create new participation frameworks;
3. audience reactions can significantly shape the way a story is told.

Overall, audience participation has been analyzed in detail in studies of conversational storytelling. These studies have shown that recipients may react to the storytelling in many different ways. For instance, they may:

1. initiate a story by inviting someone to tell it (Lerner 1992);
2. show appreciation for the narrative through laughter (Jefferson 1979; Mandelbaum 1987) or through manifestations of empathy (e.g. emotional outbursts, repetitions, response cries, and, generally, positive back-channeling, etc., Branner 2005; Georgakopoulou 1998);
3. negotiate the meaning of a story by providing alternative evaluations (Goodwin 1984; Ochs and Capps 2001)
4. respond minimally, by just listening to the story and making occasional comments;
5. assume the much more active role of a co-teller by offering details or repairing some aspect of the storytelling (Goodwin 1979; Lerner 1992;

Mandelbaum 1987; Manzoni 2005). They may also share the telling by dueting with the teller (see Mullhohand 1996).

Last but not least, tellers have to show understanding of the point of the story, once the story has been completed. One of the most routine ways for doing so is to provide a second story, as noted by Sacks ([1970] 1992b). As the name suggests, second stories present similarities with the stories which they respond to, both on a thematic level (i.e. they are on a similar topic) and with respect to the (main) characters. What is important to note here is that this similarity is *achieved*: in other words, the assumption is that second stories are designed by their tellers so as to achieve a similarity that is recognizable by speaker A, who produced the first story and who could not have preordained or prescribed that someone would tell a second story. In this way, second stories form a procedure through which their teller displays understanding of the first story and in the process constitutes a thematic continuity backwards (see Coates 2002: 93).

Although the above perspective on second stories places the emphasis squarely on the tellers of second stories as the speakers who actually work to create the sense that their story is told in sequence with the previous one, it has also been stressed that it is the expectation of reciprocity and solidarity that is instrumental in bringing about the relation of analogy between first and second stories (Sacks [1970] 1992b: 5). This may explain the frequency of second stories in conversational interactions of intimates, as has been attested to. There, as it has been shown (e.g. see Sidnell 2003; Svennevig 1999), second stories act as a method used to display alignment and identification with a previous speaker and their story.

More specifically, Sacks' work on second stories has been drawn upon by, among others, Coates (2001) who in her study of conversational storytelling amongst male friends suggested that second stories were a frequent and powerful resource for doing friendship and displaying connectedness. As Coates put it, with second stories, tellers signaled to the teller of the previous story that "my mind is with you" (p. 81).

This demonstrable orientation to the construction of the organization of the first story is at the heart of second stories. However, exactly what thematic coherence means or what forms it takes as well as what social actions second stories perform seem to be a matter of local contexts rather than something that can be postulated in advance of specific instances of storytelling. Norrick (2000), for example, suggests that in his data, what he calls "response stories" seek either to establish common experience with the immediately foregoing story by saying "the same thing happened to me too," or to top the previous story by, for example, saying "an even funnier/scarier thing happened to me."

What the above demonstrates is that the telling of a story raises the task for the interlocutor to display understanding of the activity at hand and respond to it appropriately. That said, the actual degrees and modes of participation vary according to the relationships between interactants. Research on close-knit groups such as circles of friends (Georgakopoulou 2005a; Manzoni 2005), and families (Blum-Kulka 1993; Ochs and Taylor 1995; Tannen 1989) has shown that audience participation may be very intense within those contexts with recipients co-telling parts of the story, interrupting, repeating and punctuating the stories with laughter and response cries. The degree of audience participation may significantly vary among cultures as well. When comparing American and Israeli families, Blum-Kulka (1993) showed, for example, how co-telling and collaboration appeared to be a much more common and accepted practice among Israelis than among Americans, leading to what the author called polyphonic narration. In such an interactive style, the audience actively displays involvement with a story's telling by contributing positive feedback and/or back-channeling throughout, and particularly in the climactic event by enhancing the evaluation as proposed by the teller. On the other hand, Johnstone (1990) noted that storytelling in the Middle American community of Fort Wayne was mainly monologic and that audiences did not interfere in any way with the telling or participate in the evaluation.

Audience participation has also been investigated from the point of view of gender differences, to test the hypothesis that women's talk shows a greater degree of collaborative orientation with respect to men's talk. The idea that there exist straightforward gendered differences in talk has been a point of contention within gender studies (see Bucholtz, Liang and Sutton 1999), and comparative studies of storytelling among women and men confirm that these differences may be subtler than is commonly assumed. Indeed, it appears that contrary to widespread belief, both genders exhibit cooperative behavior, but that, for example, men may use co-construction and collaboration in more limited ways than women (see Coates 2005). It has also been found that women invite audience cooperation by presenting themselves as protagonists in stories in humorous terms (Holmes 2006; Kotthoff 2000).

4.3   Cooperation and conflict in narrative

Audience participation in storytelling is often described as essentially cooperative. Storytelling can enhance a sense of understanding and cooperation since it provides an occasion for tellers to propose their own values and for others to create and display solidarity. Mullhohand (1996) describes different categories of audience cooperation that range from full co-narration to the telling of second stories related to a previous narrative which signal a recipient's involvement.

Various linguistic devices have been found to signal co-participation both on the part of the teller and on the part of the listeners. These include:

Tags that signal or invite ratification such as, *doesn't he?*
Overt agreements
Overt requests for assistance to participants who know of the events
Ratification through repetition
Recognitional questions as part of opening stories of known events
Metalinguistic formulations that aim at creating shared assumptions such as *you know what I mean*, etc.

It should be noted that analyses of collaborative participation in storytelling have not been limited to conversational contexts, as researchers have under-scored the importance of co-construction in a variety of interactional situations including interviews and therapeutic sessions. In interview data, for example, it is becoming increasingly recognized that formal aspects of narrative are developed collaboratively with questions, comments, pauses and dysfluencies (e.g. Mishler 1986, and more recently Riessman 2002; Bell 2006; Cavallaro Johnson 2006). Narratives told within interviews are clear examples of co-constructed texts since interviewers often try to get respondents to develop certain parts of their stories either by asking for elaboration or by prompting evaluations of events and characters. At the same time, interviewees appear sensitive to the requirements of the interview and attempt to direct their nar-ratives toward the goals of the interviewer, as they perceive them (De Fina 2003b, 2009b). Narrators often change the course of their stories because of interview questions and interruptions, they provide orientation details when asked to do so, and negotiate the meaning of experiences with interviewers. In that sense, the story told cannot be seen as stemming from the tellers alone, but as co-constructed. Similar considerations apply to narratives told in therapeutic settings, since analysts follow their own agenda in trying to bring about certain changes in their patients' psychological states. Therefore, they may influence them either by directing them toward the production of narrative accounts that are acceptable to the therapist as true depictions of a patient's state (see Fasulo 1999 on this point), or they may significantly influence the kind of narrative self-construction produced by patients by altering their narrative perspective (Beran and Unoka 2005). Bercelli, Rossano and Viaro 2008 also demonstrate that therapists often are the ones who initiate patients' telling of personal stories as examples of the feelings/situations that they are describing, or elicit continuations of narratives that had been initiated in previous talk.

It must be noted, however, that storytelling is not always cooperative and that it can be, and often is, a terrain for conflict and confrontation both in the portrayal of events and characters and in the interaction with co-participants in social encounters. Indeed, narratives may generate or be integrally linked with arguments both in private interaction and in institutional contexts such as courts or asylum-seekers' interviews. In addition to this, they may themselves be employed as argumentative devices. We will thus structure our discussion below around these two axes: the uses of narratives as argumentative devices on the one hand and shifting participants' (mis)alignments in the course of storytelling on the other.

4.3.1   Narratives as argumentative devices

Narratives have often been related to argumentation, but surprisingly few studies exist on their concrete use in argumentative discourse. The scholars who have dealt with this topic underscore that there is a remarkable difference between argumentation as a formal type of reasoning and argumentation as it is actually developed in natural interaction (see Antaki 1994 on this point). In fact, in traditional logical and rhetorical approaches to reasoning, the focus is normative, as scholars look for principles underlying well-formed arguments. This is the case, for example, in formal and informal logic approaches to argumentation, which focus on how conclusions follow from premises and therefore on the assessment of arguments (see Fisher 1988). In studies based on classical rhetoric, on the other hand, the effort is taxonomic as arguments are classified into types and related to the operation of specific connectors. For this reason, the tools developed within formal approaches to reasoning are ill suited to study naturally occurring arguments. As some rhetoricians (see, for example, Perelman and Olbrechts-Tyteca 1979; Toulmin, Rieke and Janik 1979) recognize, everyday arguments are dialogical; they are designed for specific audiences and crucially depend on local contexts. Everyday reasoning is often messy, not rigorously logical and negotiated among interacting parties, thus the study of how people sustain and develop arguments needs to produce specific analytical instruments that are different from those used in logical, philosophical or rhetorical treatments of the topic. This is indeed the direction taken by research on the workings of narratives within argumentative discourse. Scholars have analyzed both ways in which whole stories are used by interactants to sustain arguments, and ways in which specific narrative sequences function within wider narratives to help storytellers make argumentative points.

Argumentative moves in discourse include proffering, backing or disputing a position, but stories are most commonly used to provide evidence for or against a position. Carranza (1998), De Fina (2000), Günthner (1995), Schiffrin (1990), among others, have shown that argumentative stories are told to back up claims that the speaker (or the addressee) proposes as controversial, or disputable. Such disputable positions are often represented by opinions, beliefs, judgments and feelings (Schiffrin 1994: 40).

There is a general agreement on the fact that the power of stories as argumentative devices comes from the fact that they provide experience-based evidence for claims, a form of evidence highly valued in everyday arguments, particularly when it is based on first-hand participation. In fact, "experiential" evidence is much more difficult to reject than rational argumentation.

Another strength of stories as argumentative devices is that they "function as eyewitness testimonials" (Müller and Di Luzio 1995). In fact, the telling of stories as backing for claims allows speakers to remove opinions from the present context of interaction and re-contextualize them by connecting them to the experience of specific characters. As a consequence, they are able to shield these opinions from challenges, given that potential contenders are turned into an "audience that vicariously participates in the narrator's experience" (Schiffrin 1990: 252). In addition, since the story world is removed from the present and, to a certain extent, from the control of the audience, narrators can construct it in ways that are supportive of their arguments, for example through the causal and temporal arrangement of events or through the voicing of opinions by characters.

As Thornborrow (2007: 1437) notes, stories (and arguments) are "discursively distinctive, that is, they are built out of analytically identifiable features both in terms of the design of individual turns within a sequence, and jointly across turns in a sequence." For example, Schiffrin (1985) shows that positions whose support is provided by narratives are often proffered at the beginning of the turn in which the story is told, and are then taken up again at the close of the argument. Müller and Di Luzio (1995) describe the typical argumentative discourse structure in which a story is embedded as following three steps:

1. Generic claim
2. Story (exemplum)
3. Re-statement of the generic evaluation as if it were derived from the story

A story functions as an exemplum when an event is used as evidence for a claim (Günthner 1995: 147). Exempla are often provided by narrators to highlight moral points and underline their moral stances. In previous work (see De Fina 2000) we have analyzed, for instance, the use of exemplary stories in the construction of moral positions about ethnicity. In order to illustrate how narratives can be used to give support to stances about ethnicity, let us consider a story told by a young Mexican immigrant in a sociolinguistic interview taken from the same corpus of narratives described in section 3.6. In the following transcribed interaction, Leo presents a story to support a negative stance about Americans, which he qualifies as racist toward other ethnic groups. Leo told this narrative during an interview focused on his experiences as an immigrant to the United States, which took place in the presence and with the collaboration of his brother (Sam) and wife (Eve). The talk preceding the story had been occasioned by a question to Leo whom the researcher (A) had asked whether he worked with Mexicans or other foreigners and how he got along with Americans. Leo had told the researcher that he didn't get along with the Americans in his work place because they seemed to think that all Hispanics are ignorant and therefore they treated them badly. His position was that Americans treat all the people who are not white badly. He then added that he had had more black friends than American friends. This is the point where the transcript starts:

```
(4.3)
 1   L:   Yo he tenido más compas [o sea-
 2   E:                           [Porque también pasan no? lo
 3        mismo, ellos pasan también[los mismos sufrimientos=
 4   L:                             [Ellos pasan lo mismo que
 5        nosotros también,
 6   E:   =que nosotros.
 7   L:   Entiendes?
 8        un este, un gabacho que trabajaba con con Rig, mi
 9        patrón,
10   A:   Uh,
11   L:   mi patrón platicó que el no quería a los hispanis,
12   A:   Uh=
13   L:   =y luego iban en el trock así y eso y veían un his-
14        una vez vio a un negro, que estaba así esperando el
15        bus,
16        y ellos iban en el trock,
17        y le escupió, pam,
18        le escupió así,
19        dice y no, "Cálmate" dice, "si hubieras venido a
20        trabajar aquí cuando tenías a Frank,"
21        se llamaba Frank ves?
22        este no: no hubieras aguantado ni un día,"
23        "El que no hubiera aguantado es él" le dije["yo creo!"
24   E:                                              [@ @
25   L:   =Ehi.
26        si y les da risa
27        o sea no no dices "ah pus pobrecito acá,"
28        les da risa,
29        los ves como que disfrutan al al acá pero ps,
30        yo si a mi me hace algo un blanco, un gabacho, a mi
31        no me importa, fuck you,
32        pus si si somos somos seres humanos porque acá?
```

Translation
(4.3)
1   L: I have had more friends [I mean-
2   E: [Because they also, right?
3   go through the same also[the same suffering=
4   L: [They go through the same
5   suffering as we do,
6   E: =as we do.
7   L: Do you understand?
8   an, well, an American who worked with with Rig,
9   my boss
10 A: Uh,
11 L: my boss said that he did not like Hispanics,
12 A: Uh=
13 L: =and then they went in the truck like that and they saw a his-
14   once he saw a black guy, who was just waiting
15   for the bus,
16   and they were in the truck,
17   and he spat at him, pam!
18   he spat, like that!
19   and he says, "Calm down" he says, "if you had come to
20   work here when Frank was here,"
21   he was called Frank, you see?
22   you would not would not have stayed one day,"
23   "He is the one who would not have stayed!" I said["I think!"
24 E: [@ @
25 L: =Right.
26   yes, and they laugh about it,
27   I mean you say "poor guy" and all that,
28   they laugh,
29   you see how they enjoy this this thing,
30   I I don't care, if a white guy, an American, does
31   something to me I don't care, fuck you
32   because we are human beings, then why?

Before the beginning of the story Leo was making the point that white Americans are racist to non-whites. He said that because some Hispanics are uneducated or do drugs, Americans extend negative judgments to all of them. Although accepting that not all Americans are racist, he had stated that there were reasons for hating them. His further point was that although he had had fights with dark-skinned people, the latter are friendlier with Hispanics than (white) Americans (line 1). His wife intervened to offer support to such a position by explaining that blacks are closer to Hispanics because they also suffer harassment by whites (line 2). Leo aligns himself with his wife by repeating her statement (line 4). Thus, the explanation for the solidarity displayed by blacks toward Hispanics – the fact that they suffer as much discrimination as Hispanics – becomes now a position that needs to be supported, and this is the point where the story is told.

The narrative starting in line 8 is intended as an example of how whites make blacks suffer the same way as they do with Hispanics. The main character is introduced in the orientation clause through an ethnic characterization: An American ("gabacho") who worked with Rig, Leo's boss. His prominence in the story is stressed by the narrator's topicalization of the noun phrase "an American who worked with ... my boss" in (lines 8–9), which is placed in subject position, although in fact it does not function as a main clause subject in the following utterance (my boss said that *he* did not like Hispanics) (line 11). The relevance of ethnic categories to the interpretation of events is signaled through the double characterization of the man as an American and as somebody who (according to Leo's boss) did not like Hispanics.

In the following orientation clause, the circumstances of the story are described: Rig and his friend were driving a truck when they saw a black man at the bus stop (lines 14–15). Then the complicating action is introduced: Frank spits at the black man (line 18) for no reason. The narrative could be read as the depiction of racist behavior by one individual, but it becomes an exemplum precisely because it is used to make generalizations about Americans, Hispanics and blacks as groups. Its force as support for the position that blacks and Hispanics are mistreated by Americans derives from the discursive strategies put in place by Leo to make the events significant beyond the individual case. At the beginning, Leo draws an implicit parallel between Frank not liking Hispanics and his not liking blacks, so that the conclusion might be drawn that if he treated blacks with hatred, he would have done the same with Hispanics. This parallel is sustained through a number of linguistic devices. In the first place, the mention of the fact that Rig's co-worker was American (line 8) and did not like Hispanics in the story orientation (line 11) creates an expectation of relevance of ethnic information to the interpretation of the action. Second, the statement that Frank didn't like Hispanics is joined to the following complicating action through the markers *and* and *then* (line 13), which suggest temporal and discourse continuity between the meanings expressed in the preceding utterance (the characterization of Frank as American) and the action described in the following ones. Moreover, the repair in line 13, where Leo was going to use the term *Hispanic* instead of the term *black* to describe the person that suffered Frank's aggression also suggests identification between the two groups.

But the narrative unfolding between lines 14 and 18 is focused on Frank's actions and could therefore be interpreted as an instance of individual behavior since both the negative feelings against Hispanics and the aggression against a black man have been attributed to Frank. However, Leo creates another, more subtle parallel between being American and disliking blacks and Hispanics. In lines 19–20, Rig is portrayed as using the incident to distance himself from his former fellow worker by telling Leo that he is lucky to have arrived after Frank had left the job. Through this statement, Rig suggests that he does not align himself with Frank in his dislike for Hispanics. But Leo rejects any distinction between the two men in the following evaluation clauses (lines 22–32) where he uses the pronoun "them" to accuse Rig and Frank (and possibly every American, since the pronoun "them" could be construed as having a more general reference) of cruelty, of laughing about their abuses. In the evaluation, Leo also stresses the parallel between Hispanics and blacks by mentioning that he would not accept any harassment from any "white guy" (line 30), and he would react because "we are human beings" (line 32). With this ending, Leo also reaffirms his moral stance and establishes himself as a champion of human values. He uses reported dialogue and the evaluation section to position himself both as a character in the story and as a person in the interactional world. In the story world he is presented as rejecting any alignment with his boss and implying that he would have fought against any attempt at discrimination. In the interactional world he is trying to present evidence supporting the fact that his statement about not liking Americans is motivated by experience. The story is opened with the collaboration of his wife. Indeed, Eva is the one who at the beginning of the transcript (line 2) introduces the argument that blacks suffer as much as Hispanics, a point that Leo takes up in the following lines. Such an argument serves as the basis for launching the narrative as an example (line 8). Leo is able to secure the floor for the telling by indicating that a narrative is coming through the introduction of a new character: his boss's friend (line 8). Once he has secured the floor, he goes on with the telling until the end when he launches the punch line (line 23), a witty response to his boss that closes the recounting of events which elicits his wife's laughter. Since there is no further response to his story, Leo adds a series of comments that are designed to emphasize his interpretation of the story and make his moral position clearer. He uses the narrative to strengthen his image as a person who does not accept discrimination by openly commenting on what he would do if somebody treated him like the black man in the story. The final evaluative comment: "we are all humans" reaffirms the parallel between treating a black man badly and treating anybody else that was in a subordinate position badly. The evaluation presents him as a moral character while offering elements of an ideology of solidarity.

It is apparent from this analysis that narratives acquire their function of exempla through careful conversational work. We have seen how Leo gradually abstracts the actions and attitudes of one character in a particular story world to present them as an instance of attitudes that can be generalized to white Americans and to blacks. At the same time, he shields the position that blacks and Hispanics suffer equally because whites treat them badly from possible criticism through recourse to his personal experience. As we have already argued, the displacement of the focus from the present interaction to the evaluation of past experience allows him to cast his interlocutors as witnesses of events and to center the evaluation on the events narrated rather than on the position itself.

A feature of this narrative that has been described as typical of argumentative narratives is the reduced role of the action component in its structure. In his analysis of racism in discourse, van Dijk (1993) noted that in narratives told to back up racist claims, the Complicating Action, i.e. the actual unfolding of story events, was very much reduced with respect to the evaluation. This particular structure was due to the fact that the focus of the narrative was not on the events per se but rather on their significance as proof for the rightness of a claim. As we can see, in the story told by Leo, the Complicating Action is brief as it is contained in lines 13–17, while most of the talk is devoted to evaluation. Because argumentative stories are used to back up claims, their focus does not usually rest on reportable events and how they developed, but rather on the significance of those events with respect to argumentative claims.

The analysis of this narrative shows how complex everyday argument is and how much discursive work goes into tying positions to previous discourse and into constructing events as relevant to the claims being made by interactants. In this sense, it illustrates the point that arguments cannot be seen as a product of certain textual format or sequences, but rather that they are constructed and negotiated in ways that crucially depend on the exchanges in which they are embedded. Ryave captures this complexity when he says that stories are fashioned in such a way as to point to certain conclusions precisely because they are contextualized by the general claims preceding their telling. He also states that through this mechanism "we have a depiction of stories of events which are progressively organized and realized so as to properly and reasonably culminate with the presentation of the preceding utterance as an integral part of the story" (1978:123).

So far, we have discussed the use of stories as support for claims, but scholars have noticed that even certain kinds of narrative sequences within stories may serve as argumentative devices. Carranza (1998) shows, for example, that storytellers may suspend the action of a story to produce a commentary through an embedded narrative. Hypothetical and counterfactual narratives may have this function as they allow the storyteller to contrast a course of events with an alternative one. An example discussed by Carranza is the case of a woman, Beatriz, who is telling a story about a supervisor who made life difficult for her at work. Beatriz argues that she did not report the supervisor to the manager and that this turned out to be a good choice because she was eventually appointed to a supervisor's position. At this moment the storyteller suspends the story to introduce a hypothetical course of events. We reproduce below the narrative sequence reported and analyzed by Carranza (1998: 292):

> (4.4)
> Beatriz: if I had gone against this woman,
>   gone to report her to the manager, to complain,
>   do you see what I mean?
>   the woman- the manager would never have given me that
>   position because she would've seen my attitude
>   that I wasn't gonna be the right person for the job
>   wasn't gonna have the calm to deal with all kinds of people

As can be observed, this hypothetical narrative functions as an evaluative comment which contributes to an argumentative position: i.e. that it pays to have a patient attitude toward other people in a work environment. In the same way, counterfactual narrative sequences can help speakers make an argumentative point by emphasizing the possible consequences of events and actions that present alternatives to what happened in a particular story world. Carranza also found habitual narratives within turns accomplishing what she called "background repair," i.e. backtracking in order to provide information in relation to discrete actions in the story line. The narratives that she analyzed were told by Salvadoran immigrants to the United States and focused on their experiences with the civil war in their country during the 1980s. The analysis illustrated how storytellers used habitual narrative sequences to strengthen certain argumentative points about the adequacy or rightness of their own or other people's reactions to social events. Habitual narratives served argumentatively by presenting events as being repeated over time, which in turn proposed an interpretation of events that is more difficult to challenge, as it is not based on individual instances. For example, presenting actions such as brutal killings and tortures by the militia not as single episodes but as repeated and usual allowed Salvadoran immigrants to the United States to make the case that it was not possible to live in El Salvador when they decided to migrate and that opposition to the regime was not an option.

Although, as we have discussed, the use of narratives or narrative sequences within argumentative discourse does not follow the strict rules of logic, this is not to say that narrators do not use logical operations to tie discourse sequences to one another. On the contrary, analyses of argumentative storytelling have shown that narrators use logical operations such as illustration, analogy, causality, both to relate their exempla to specific theses and to tie together arguments that are voiced by characters (see Carranza 1999 on this point). For example, as we saw in Leo's narrative, the story of Rig's aggression toward the African

American character was used as an example of how Americans are generally racist. In that sense, it would be erroneous to state that logic has nothing to do with everyday arguments. However, as we have seen in the discussion of example (4.3) above, narrators also build arguments through narratives thanks to their recourse to narrative strategies such as the use of constructed dialogue as a tool for exemplifying reasoning, and through the performed quality of the narratives themselves, which creates involvement in the audience. Among the devices used by narrators in argumentative storytelling, Günthner (1995) mentions, for example:

- the sequential organization of the stories that function as exempla;
- the use of linguistic elements and constructions expressing emotion;
- tension-building devices in narrative organization;
- prosodic parameters.

To sum up, narratives are powerful tools in the negotiation of everyday arguments thanks to their ability to function as evidence based on personal experience, their potential for audience involvement and their semblance of objectivity provided by the fact that claims made by narrators in the present social context can be removed from it and connected to characters and events unrelated to the situation of interaction.

4.3.2 Shifting participant (mis)alignments

As we have suggested, narratives often engender arguments amongst the participants with regard to the events reported or their interpretation. Cedeborg and Aronsson (1994) show, for example, how in family therapy complaints can be recognized as themes that form the basis of character contests which are often embedded within narratives. These narratives provide ground for negotiations and shifting of alignments among family members. Participants use a variety of strategies to display opposition toward a teller: for example, they may disqualify the teller by disaligning with her or his version of events. Shifting topic is another way of discrediting a storyteller by ignoring the story. Alignments can be traced in sequential fashion, with members ratifying or challenging each other's stories as they unfold. In addition, in family talk where stories are told and retold, their potential for becoming part of a family history increases, but repeated challenges obviously also increase the power of narratives to start conflicts. Negotiations about true and false stories indirectly concern participant status (who speaks for whom) and involve important restructuring of participant alignment. These alignments are signaled through repairs, topic shifts, ratifications, etc. However, audience members may also use participation shifts to signal their stance, for example, when they withdraw from the role of addressees, or when they assume the role of co-tellers or even main tellers.

Schiffrin suggests that stories of personal experience play a specific role in arguments and disputes since they "create participation shifts in both speaker and hearer" (1990: 249). She uses Goffman's (1981) concept of production format to illustrate this process (see also section 6.3.1 on the manipulation of participation formats for self-presentation). Goffman distinguishes between different possible positions within the notion of speaker:

- *The animator*: the person who physically produces an utterance
- *The author*: the person responsible for the utterance
- *The principal*: the person "whose position is established by the words that are spoken" (1981:144)
- *The figure*: somebody who belongs to the story world, an "aspect of the self displayed through talk … somebody who belongs to the world that is spoken about, not the world in which the speaking occurs" (Schiffrin 1990: 252).

Tellers and recipients manipulate these positions in order to present their arguments. Thus, tellers can contextualize their opinions by having characters express them and by presenting themselves simply as an animator. At the same time, they can speak as an author: i.e. someone who interprets an experience and gives her or his position about it, or as a figure, i.e. a character in the story world. These shifts allow tellers to present arguments in a more nuanced and apparently objective way, and to recruit the support of audiences. Schiffrin suggests that by creating a wider support for the teller's position, stories create "a testimony" (1990: 253) and can be used as evidence. They delegate much of the supportive work to different parts of the self (the author and the figure), to other figures (through the animator) and to the audience that becomes the evaluator of the story.

The use of stories in disputes has also been documented in M. Goodwin's (1990) and Shuman's (1986) work on interaction among urban adolescents. Goodwin illustrates how storytelling works as a fundamental tool in instigating fights based on reporting someone's words. Indeed, telling one girl that another girl has "talked behind her back" amounts to an instigation to fight because the activity of talking behind one's back is sanctioned within the community of adolescent girls that she studies. Similarly, in Shuman's data, narratives are used by high school students as tools to create animosity and confirm suspicions about others, mostly through the reporting of incidents and disputes. Shuman notes that these narratives involve complex constructions of telling and listening rights insofar as the basis for confrontation is constituted by opinions on who has the right to speak and to tell stories, and who has the right to listen. Shuman describes these rights through the concept of *entitlement*, which comprises any "claim to the authority to report on experience, to disclose, withhold, or conceal information, to be an author of events, and to repeat another's remarks" (1993: 135). She goes on to show how changes to entitlement raise questions about the ownership of experience and how in the context of stories, these serve as a way of shifting attention from issues of knowledge and accuracy of the reported events to issues of distribution and relationships between people (p. 135). In her study, telling rights are crucially a function of the ownership of experience, which as we have already seen, may be a decisive factor in who gets to tell whose story in various settings (see our discussion in sections 5.3 and 5.4). We will return to this issue of telling rights below.

4.4   Telling rights

As we have discussed in section 4.1, storytelling involves different production and reception formats. With respect to the production of the story, as we have seen, there can be one narrator, or one main narrator and one or more secondary narrators; secondary or primary narrators can in turn become audience, but not all members of the audience can become narrators and co-narrators. At the same time, audiences can consist of main and secondary ratified addressees, overhearers, bystanders (see Goffman 1981), etc. Sociocultural rules within communities may shape to a certain extent who has the right to tell a story, when and how members of the audience can intervene and what conditions have to be met for a story to be told. These rights are, however, often renegotiated in interaction. A number of authors (see, for example, Blum-Kulka 1993; Sacks [1970] 1992d; Shuman 1986) have explored the way in which tale-ownership relates to the entitlement to tell the story. Sacks ([1970] 1992d), for example, sees tellership rights as related to first-hand experience and witness status. Thus, a person who has taken part in an event, or has first-hand information about it, is in principle entitled to tell a story about it. In this sense, ownership rights are related to the access to the information contained in the story and determine in different ways the right to perform it (entitlement). However, this relationship between ownership rights and performance rights is a complicated one in that ownership rights do not necessarily determine performance rights. For example, when there is a relationship of power between interlocutors, performance rights might automatically be assigned to the most powerful speaker independently of co-ownership. This is often the case with children's stories in family interaction where telling rights are often controlled by parents. Moreover, stories may be appropriated by people who are not the original experiencers of the events told in them when they become public (see Shuman 2005). In those circumstances telling rights will also be redistributed. Processes of appropriation of stories have important social consequences as they involve social construction and reconstruction of experience.

In sum, although there are conditions that may favor individual or shared performance rights, these conditions do not automatically determine what kind of participation framework will emerge in a specific circumstance. For example, the fact that several people are in a position to tell a story does not necessarily result in joint performance. According to Blum-Kulka (1993: 384), "The reverse may be true as well: highly involved audience response to a story of personal experience (or knowledge) may turn the telling into a joint performance, implying a process of motivated claim to joint ownership. Hence ownership rights through access to the tale have no one-to-one correspondence to performance rights through access to the telling."[2]

4.5   Types of stories: beyond the prototype

As we have already discussed, interactional research on storytelling has documented stories in conversations as a collaborative enterprise. This has problematized the teller-led, heavily monologic view of narrative as emanating, for example from Labov's model, and it has also gone hand-in-hand with a gradual realization that the prototypical teller-led personal experience, past events story is far from the only or even dominant type of story told in everyday settings. In fact, there is a fascinating gamut of stories that depart from this canon. Below, we will survey some of the main forms that stories have been shown to take. We will note that there has been a proliferation of terms to describe these forms, partly as a result of the dominance of received notions about what constitutes typical narrative data. We will then present the recent move to small stories (as an umbrella term for a-typical stories) as a systematic attempt to broaden the scope of narrative analysis.

One of the first notions that have been problematized in relation to the canon of personal experience, past events stories was the idea that the events narrated were known only to the teller, that is, the distinction between the knowing teller and the non-knowing interlocutors as well as the ownership of experience rights (assumptions) that came with it. To put it differently, the emphasis started shifting from tellings of stories to retellings that recognized that one or more of the story recipients actually knew of the events told and/or had heard them before. Retold stories were first researched from a cognitive perspective, with an eye to the kinds of textual differences that they presented from first tellings and therefore with a view to exploring processes of memory and reconstruction of events over time (Chafe 1990; Ferrara 1988; Polanyi 1981). In certain cases, the data that were collected for this type of study involved a process in which the researcher asked the teller to tell the same story after a well-specified and thought-out time interval had passed from the same telling. A consistent finding that emerged was the fact that retellings were normally shorter versions than first tellings and that certain details were not included, particularly when there was no change of audience. Research subsequently shifted to the interactional dynamics of retold stories, that is, to how they get introduced and jointly told by participants in conversational contexts. For those cases, the term *retold* became somewhat restrictive and reductionist with regard to the various possibilities of more or less brief versions of previously told stories and/ or stories of known events. Norrick (1997, 2000) proposed the term *familiar tales* as an alternative that captures the gamut of possibilities, and examined the functions that the telling of such familiar tales may fulfill. He particularly drew attention to the ways in which jointly (re)fashioning known events reaffirms closeness and intimacy amongst friends and family members and helps build shared memories and a sense of belonging.

Schiffrin's study (2006) of Holocaust oral histories retold over a period of time and for different audiences that include both the interviewer and hypothesized public audiences went one step further to suggest that each retold story should be seen not just as a story but also as a meta-narrative: in other words, not only a narrative about an experience but also about prior tellings (p. 275). In this sense, Schiffrin highlights the intertextuality of retellings and their irreducible contextualization, which makes the project of documenting stylistic similarities between different versions somewhat problematic. As Schiffrin explains, even when there are striking similarities between telling and retellings, it is very difficult to claim that the same textual features carry the same social meanings in different contexts and for different audiences (p. 322).[3]

Examining familiar stories *in situ* has also taken the form of scrutinizing their relationship with participation roles. We have already mentioned how Goodwin (1984) examined the ways in which tellers recipient-design their stories to take account of the fact that some may know of the events told and others not; also, how this recipient design raises different tasks and roles for different members of the audience.

In similar vein, Georgakopoulou (2005a) demonstrated how the retellings of – in her terms – *shared stories* (i.e. stories of shared or known events) may present a continuum of forms, from full-fledged tellings to more or less elliptical and skeletal tellings, to condensed, even one-line, references. These are intricately dependent on aspects of the local context, including the participant roles and relations. The study also illustrated how the different types of initiation of a shared story both project and are shaped by different participation roles in the story's telling. These involve different tasks or types of action for different participants in the story's internal components such as action, evaluation and orientation.

Here, it is worth looking at one neglected aspect of shared stories, namely, that of *references*, as attested in Georgakopoulou's study (2005a, 2007). References (which abounded in the conversational stories of a group of Greek female adolescents) comprised a quick introduction of a shared story in the surrounding talk, mostly by means of a one-line reference to it. The latter typically consisted in a character's verbal or non-verbal reaction to the story's main events or in a punch line that encodes the words of a character and may be uttered as a formulaic impersonation (i.e. a quoted set phrase that imitates or parodies a character's speech). This extreme elliptical form of initiation seemed to attest to a process of de-narrativization or reduction that shared stories undergo, possibly after numerous retellings, until they reach a bare minimum of a reference that is as brief and elliptical as any other allusion to shared sources or texts can be.

In the excerpt below, for instance, on the basis of the ethnographic study of the group, we are in a position to know that the reference "talk to him man, talk to him" (lines 4, 61) is the punch line of one of the favorite stories from the participants' private history. These stories were labeled by the participants as "group stories" and they were included in the diary-like "Book of minutes," which recorded the exciting moments of the group's leisure activities. From thereafter, such group stories were mostly referred to by means of their punch line rather than retold. In this way, they constituted an integral part of the group's interactional history and shared assumptions, which could be drawn upon on various occasions as brief mutually intelligible comments on states of affairs, social actions and behavior, as well as third parties. For instance, the punch line "talk to him man, talk to him" forms a quick and elliptical characterization of the character talked about, Mikes, as somebody who is shy and is lacking in communication and social skills. In the original story, from which this reference was lifted, Mikes and Pavlos (a male friend of his) have gone out with a group of boys and Mikes behaves in his usual unsociable way. Having spent the evening not saying much, Mikes is staring at a friend who is chatting to him, when Pavlos in indignation tells him "Talk to him man, talk to him." Thus the punch line encodes the evaluation of Mike's personality by his friends:

(4.5)
Participants: F(otini), V(ivi)
1 F: Και πες ότι κοιτάζει αλλού
2 πώς θα του τραβήξω την προσοχή?
3 V: Θα του μιλήσεις στη γλώσσα του (.) του παιδιού
4 Μί:λα του ρε: (.) μίλα του
χα χα χα

59 F: Ωραία (.) μπαίνω μέσα τον βλέπω
60 Τι θα του πω?_
61 V: Μίλα του ρε μίλα του=
62 F: =χα χα χα
63 Έλα ρε (.) σοβαρά τώρα
64 Λοιπό:ν (.) βλέπω το Μάκη ωραί:α?

Translation
1 F: And say he's looking that way
2 how am I going to draw his attention?
3 V: You will speak to him in his language.
4 ((You'll say)) Talk to him ma:n (.. talk to him
((personation of the character talked about))
((Participants, i.e. F, T and I, laugh))

((further down))

59 F: So (.) I walk in and see him
60 What am I going to say?
61 V: Talk to him man (.) talk to him=
62 F: =hh hah hah-uh huh
63 Come on (.) we are talking seriously now.
64 So: (..) I bump into Makis right?

In this case, Mikes's negative evaluation occurs five times in the course of the telling of a story of projected events, which involves planning a meeting between the participants and two men. The reference to the shared (group) story "talk to him man, talk to him" is gradually worked up by two of the participants (Vivi and Tonia) as the main reason why Fotini should not, as a result of the planned meeting, get involved with Mikes. In other words, it is proposed as a source of character incompatibility between the two of them. In this way, a reference to shared events is drawn upon as a running commentary on and a comparison base for events that have not taken place yet.

Sequentially speaking, an initial acknowledgment and even reinforcement of the turn that encodes a reference to a shared story was found to be necessary regardless of the type of action that the reference performs locally and of the addressee's reaction to that. As can be seen in example (4.5) above, Fotini quickly acknowledges the reference "talk to him man, talk to him" by means of laughter (line 61), despite the fact that she subsequently frames it as "non-serious" talk and is quick to reintroduce the previous topical agenda (line 63).

Another prototypical feature of stories that has been questioned is their linear development from the beginning to the middle to the end and the fact that they present a closure. On closer look in conversational settings, it has transpired that stories often tend to be heavily embedded into their conversational surroundings and enmeshed in local business. As a result, the openings are not always clear or explicitly stated, and once a story is launched it is not automatic or necessary that it will be closed. Stories can be digressed from, abandoned, returned to and unfinished, sometimes quite deliberately and strategically too, for instance, when the teller wants to leave their addressees wanting for more.[4] An important point to raise before classifying a story as "unfinished" is to discuss from whose perspective the process is seen. There may be cases when abandoning a story may be integrally connected with local business and intimately linked with the exigencies of the context at hand. For instance, in a study of private email messages, Georgakopoulou (2004) found that it was commonly the case that senders were initiating a story but deferring its full telling for an offline interaction, which was seen as a more appropriate context for a full telling:

> (4.6)
> \> How are you?
> Long story that, which I am hoping to tell you face-to-face when we hopefully meet up. In any case, there are still some missing chapters, it would be good if I had something other than the Prologue.
> (34-year-old female to 40-year-old female)

In the example above, the telling of the story, as well as being explicitly constructed as narrativization-in-process, is deferred to a temporally non-specified future face-to-face interaction. In most cases, however, the anchoring in offline interactions of the stories to be told becomes specific, as we can see below, where the telling of the story is deferred till later that day:

> (4.7)
> Date: Wed, 27 Sep 2000 16:15:55 +0100 (BST)
> From: Jannis
> To: Klio
> Subject: Re: I gave Charlie (and his wife!) an earful!!
> \>I'll tell you tonight, great fun.
> Oh really? Will he come back at all – or is he history?
>
> Jannis
> ps. telepathic: we give people an earful at the same time.

As we can see above, when the full telling of the story is deferred for the near future, the initiation of stories to be told is normally done with a summarizing statement of the story's main event(s) ("I gave Charlie (and his wife) an earful!!"), and/or its point ("great fun"), reminiscent of Labov's (1972) abstract. This commonly appears in the message's subject heading.

The above examples show that deferrals or incomplete instances of tellings are not always aberrations or failed performances; they may be intimately linked with considerations of what is tellable and narratable in which context.

Another commonly attested departure from the narrative prototype involves the uniqueness or not of the reported events. The prototypical story revolves around the definition of discrete and singularly identifiable events that happened once in a specific point in the past. Nonetheless, analysts quickly noticed that even when they were attempting to elicit this kind of once tale, tellers often embarked on events that happened over and over again in their past and that those *habitual stories* were deemed by them to be as important, if not more so, as the once happenings. Riessman (1990) put forth habitual narratives as a salient story type in which tellers, when asked to produce their divorce story, narrativized their past.

In similar vein, in his study of Moroccan migrants' life stories in West London, Baynham (2003, 2005) reported the salience of a specific type of narrative which he called "generic." In this kind of telling, the reported events were presented as part of a collective, group experience adhering to a typical scenario, that of a heroic male setting off, enduring adversities in the process of his migration, overcoming them, and setting up a home and business in the host country for the rest of the family to follow. Baynham shows how this generic accounts "raises interesting questions of authority, authorization and rights to speak" (2005: 16) having to do with who has or claims the right to make generalizations since the generic story is only told by male immigrants and projects certain kinds of social roles. Baynham's study thus shows how this typifying account acts as hegemonic inasmuch as it silences, elides and/ or sidelines the migration stories of women migrants as well as other possible versions.

Finally, another aspect of storytelling that may have an impact on the type of narrative produced in context is the degree of spontaneity of the telling and its degree of dependence on an elicitation. Based on this parameter, one can draw a first, important distinction between spontaneous and elicited stories. Spontaneous and elicited stories, which may occur in both everyday and formal/ institutional contexts, are very different, particularly in terms of interactional management. However, while conversational types have been widely investigated, elicited narratives have been often lumped together in a rather simplistic way. Many erroneously identify them with the Labovian narratives of personal experience or with autobiographical tellings, and thus researchers have paid insufficient attention to different classes of elicited narratives. Among these, a kind of narrative that would deserve further study is the category of accounts (De Fina 2009b).

The notion of *account*, which has been used by sociologists to refer to "a linguistic device employed whenever an action is subjected to valuative inquiry" (Scott and Lyman 1986: 46), can be fruitfully applied to narratives (including justifications, excuses and explanations) that represent recapitulations of past events told in response to a "why" or "how" question by an interlocutor. Accounts have a strong explanatory component and are inherently "recipient designed" (Riessman 1997: 156) precisely because they are told as responses to questions. Thus, for example, typical interactional aspects of accounts are negotiations, or meta-comments, between tellers and recipients over the kind

of telling that is expected to be adequate, interventions by recipients focused
more on clarification and explanation than on evaluation per se, and well-
formed story closings that summarize the significance of the narrative. To
exemplify, let us look at an excerpt from an account on the circumstances of
migration from Mexico to the United States elicited in an interview with a
Mexican undocumented worker taken from the narrative corpus that we have
already discussed in section 3.6:

(4.8)
Participants: Interviewer, Maria
1. I: Bueno cuéntame un poco como llegaste.
2.   Cómo fue que ocurrió esto?
3. M: Cómo fue?
4.   o sea uh o sea decidimos venirnos para acá porque como estaba en
          crisis el país,
5.   eh o sea teníamos un sueldo pero ya no era lo mismo,
6.   no nos alcanzaba más que para para comer para vestir más que bien
          vestir,
7.   ya no era lo mismo.
8.   entonces un día decidimos venir para acá,
9.   *y quieres que te cuente cómo fue que pasamos la frontera?*
10. R: Lo que tu quieras.
11. M: Uh nos vinimos un veinte y cinco, veinte y seis de diciembre,

Translation
1. I: Well, tell me a bit about how you came,
2.   How did that happen?
3. M: How did that happen?
4.   well I mean we decided to come here because as the country was
          in a crisis,
5.   I mean we had a salary that was not the same,
6.   it was barely enough to to eat, to dress, more or less dress,
7.   it was not the same,
8.   therefore one day we decided to come here,
9.   *and do you want me to tell you how it was that we crossed the border?*
10. R: Whatever you like.
11. M: Uh, we came on a twenty-fifth, twenty-sixth of December,

As we can see, the elicited narrative is constructed as an answer to the interviewer's question on the circumstances of migration (lines 1–2) and is shaped
in the form of a "package" of motives for leaving Mexico. Maria briefly
describes the economic hardship that she endured in her country as an antecedent for her leaving Mexico by juxtaposing a series of past circumstances

(lines 4–8). However, we also see how, in line 9, Maria begins a negotiation with the interviewer about the kind of narrative that may appropriately follow the one just provided and, upon receiving a confirmation that she can go ahead, continues with an account of the border crossing itself (line 11). This example shows the kind of specific interactional configurations that accounts present and their possible impact on the shape and organization of the telling. It therefore indicates the importance of taking into account the nature of the interaction and the moves preceding and following storytelling in the analysis of stories.

4.6   From big stories to small stories

Many new terms and formulations have been put forth to describe different kinds of stories that depart from the prototypical narrative of personal experience that the above discussion has sampled. For instance, Fasulo and Zucchermaglio (2008) have proposed the terms "rewinds" (attempts to come up with an explanation for something that has happened by reconstructing and guessing the sequence of events that preceded the current outcome), and "templates" (condensed versions of experience providing information on unexpected outcomes or controversial occurrences) for a-typical stories that are yet typical in workplace situations, while Holmes (2006) has talked about anecdotes to describe certain types of workplace narratives. Classifications such as these are usually based on the type of events recounted or on the strategies adopted in the telling. Other classifications emphasize the communicative functions of storytelling. For example, argumentative stories is a commonly employed term to refer to stories departing from the prototypical narrative on the basis that they serve the purpose of putting forth an opinion, challenging an interlocutor's point of view, etc., as discussed in section 4.3 above. Labov himself stresses the point that these stories are bound to be different from his personal experience, past events stories and may require a different approach. As he puts it:

The narratives that form the focus of this work were normally told in the course of a sociolinguistic interview, where the interviewer formed an ideal audience: attentive, interested and responsive. Though they are fitted to some extent to the situation and often to a question posed by the interviewer, they are essentially monologues and show a degree of decontextualization. They exhibit a generality that is not to be expected from narratives that subserve an argumentative point in a highly interactive and competitive conversation. Such narratives are often highly fragmented and may require a different approach. Yet studies of spontaneous conversation also show a high frequency of monologic narratives that command the attention of the audience as fully as the narratives of the interview. (Labov 1997: 397)

Ochs and Capps (2001) have been instrumental in articulating the need for developing a different approach and going beyond the conventional narrative scholarship, which in their terms is centered on narratives with the following qualities:

> A coherent temporal progression of events that may be reordered for rhetorical purposes and that is typically located in some past time and place.
> A plotline that encompasses a beginning, a middle, and an end, conveys a particular perspective and is designed for a particular audience who apprehend and shape its meaning.

They went on to argue that "understanding narratives compels going beyond these exemplars to probe less polished, less coherent narratives that pervade ordinary social encounters and are a hallmark of human condition" (p. 57). Their book provides numerous examples of such narratives in a variety of settings, including family meal-time interactions.

Another recent systematic attempt to advance this project of putting non-canonical stories on the map can be found within the small stories perspective (Bamberg 2004, 2006a; Georgakopoulou 2005a, 2005b and 2007; Bamberg and Georgakopoulou 2008). *Small stories* was chosen as an umbrella term that captures a gamut of under-represented narrative activities, such as tellings of ongoing events, future or hypothetical events, shared (known) events, but also allusions to (previous) tellings, deferrals of tellings and refusals to tell. These tellings are typically small when compared to the pages and pages of transcripts of interview narratives. On a metaphorical level though, small stories is somewhat of an alternative formulation to a tradition of big stories (cf. "grand narratives," Lyotard 1984): the term locates a level and even an aesthetic for the identification and analysis of narrative: the smallness of talk, where fleeting moments of narrative orientation to the world (Hymes, 1996) can be easily missed out by an analytical lens which only takes full-fledged ("big") stories as the prototype from where the analytic vocabulary is supposed to emerge.

Choosing one collective term has also stemmed from the conscious attempt to shy away from the endless proliferation of terms that define departures from the prototype either in negative terms (e.g. diffuse, fragmented) or in othering terms (e.g. a-typical, non-canonical), thus making them look too heterogeneous to be collectively encompassed at the same time as making the narrative canon look deceptively homogeneous.

Small stories can be about very recent events ("this morning," "last night") or still unfolding events. In this way, their telling immediately reworks slices of experience and arises out of a need to announce and share what has just happened. They can be about small incidents that may (or may not) have actually happened, mentioned to back up or elaborate on an argumentative point occurring in an ongoing conversation. Small stories can even be about – colloquially speaking – "nothing"; and as such indirectly reflect something about the interactional engagement between the interactants, while for outsiders, the interaction is literally "about nothing."

In short, placing emphasis on small stories allows for the inclusion in the analysis of a gamut of data more or less connected with the narrative canon. Some of them fulfill prototypical definitional criteria (e.g. event sequencing, see Chapter 1) but still do not sit well with the canon (e.g. stories of projected events given that the emphasis of traditional narrative inquiry has undoubtedly been on past events). Others may fail those criteria, but if the participants themselves orient to what is going on as a story, formal (*sic* textual) criteria appear to be superfluous if not problematic. In all cases, small stories research stresses that the definition of an activity as a story should not rest exclusively and reductively on prototypical textual criteria. Instead, stories should be seen as discourse engagements that engender specific social moments and integrally connect with what gets done on particular occasions and in particular settings. The claim is that recognizing narrativity or a narrative orientation in certain activities shows regard for local and situated understandings and decisively makes social consequentiality of discourse activities part of the analysis. This is in line with more recent definitions of narrative, as we discussed them in Chapter 1, which have stressed the need for more or less rather than all-or-nothing views of what constitutes a story (e.g. see Herman 2002).

As an illustration of the kinds of narratives that may be categorized as "small stories," we can look at narratives told by adolescents in interactions. In two separate studies of storytelling among female adolescents in a small town in Greece and in a comprehensive school in London respectively, Georgakopoulou (2007: 208) found that the exchanging of small stories was common practice amongst these youngsters. She proposed the following types of small stories as being salient:

1. **Breaking news**: These involve very recent (i.e. yesterday) events, consisting of either sightings of men the participants are interested in, or reports of mediated interactions (e.g. MSN, texting, mobile phone calls) with peers. The latter are much more frequent in the London school study, which is explained by the fact that the data from the Greek adolescents were collected in the 1990s when the information and communication technologies (particularly mobile phone) had not exploded yet in youth communication. Also, the participants lived in a small town which allowed them more readily sightings of men on the street. In the classroom data from the London school, breaking news of mediated interactions was a routine activity (on average eight such stories were launched within a period).

2. **Projections**. Breaking news frequently leads to small stories of *projections*: these involve (near) future encounters with the men-talked-about and are

episodically organized interactions of "I will say – she/he will say" type. Contrary to the predominance of past events stories in conventional narrative analysis, projections were by far the most common type of storytelling in the Greek adolescents' group. The taleworld of projections, in the same vein as in stories of past events, is temporally ordered and emplotted, yet these are clearly one of the most neglected and marginalized narrative types in narrative analysis and narratology (cf. Norrick's [2000: ch. 5] discussion). The planning of the taleworld involves a turn-by-turn co-authoring and negotiation of details in the taleworld, particularly of an orientation kind. Norrick has looked at comparable cases of projections, which he terms "fantasies," as collaboratively constructed stories amongst friends. Kyratzis (2000) and Sheldon (1996) have also stressed the importance of the construction of imaginary scenarios in the children's activity of pretend play.

3. **Shared stories**. In Georgakopoulou's study (2007), breaking news and projections are often sequentially contingent, intertextually linked, interspersed with references to shared events and present thematic affinities. They also lead to chained "second" stories. They thus resonate with Goodwin's (1997a) "family of stories" which were of significance for the social group organization of pre-adolescent girls that she studied and with Schiffrin's "intertextual stories" (2000), a vehicle for meaning-making in the process of putting together a life story.

Let us now exemplify a breaking news story which we will call "The buff Stefan."[5] The story is the second of two interlocked breaking news stories told by Nadia during a mathematics period. Both involve reports of mediated interactions with two boys/suitors the day before: the first involves a reported texting communication between Nadia and Adam; the second chained story below involves an MSN communication with a web cam appearance from Stefan. When telling the stories, Nadia sits at a small table in the back corner of the classroom with her friends Lisa and Shenice.

```
(4.9)
1   N:   Anyways Shenice                              23.18
2        yeah oh m-
3        ((excited)) oh my God oh my God
4        ((muffled)) Oh my God
5        Stefan yeah? he went on web cam for me
6        ((high pitched)) he was looking so sexy
7        (     ) my man's light skin yea:h?
8        >he got cane-row and everything<
9        he IS ((excited whisper)) buff!
10       he went on web cam for me yesterday yea:h?
11       he was lookin' cris
```

12		>and I was like< blood
13		((stylized)) he was looking some kinda sexy
14		>I was like< >quack quack quack<
15	?:	((giggling))
16	N:	An' his eyes look blue you kno:w
17		cos he was wearing (.) dark blue
18		and um: (.) silver
19		and he's mixed race
20		*nice* colour mixed race >wait<
21		there's no one in our class
22		he's like (.) a little bit darker than Madeleine yeah::
23		and (.) *nice smooth skin* everything
24		*no* //spots (and like that)
25	L:	//tall- taller than you?
26	N:	No
27	L:	Smaller?
28	N:	yeah //he's
29	L:	//Taller than me?
30	N:	He's five- seven
31	L:	Taller than me ok (.) //( )
32	N:	//listen and he's and he's
33		I goes to him I goes- um=
34	L:	=if you give him my email address
35	?:	No=
36	N:	=NO:
37	L:	Why::
38	N:	He's got Madeleine's you know
39	L:	Why Madeleine's?
40	N:	((hushed)) because Madeleine's butters
41		and he doesn't like her
42	L:	Why not me?
43	N:	Cos you're too pretty
44		you'll take him away from me
45	L:	No I wo:n't
46		because I'm never online ((laughs))
47	N:	((laughing)) that's true
48		cos your sister's always on
49	L:	NO:!
50	N:	Well she's on when you wanna go on
51		and she turfs you an' things
52	L:	Oh my go:sh! I've got these leather shoes-↑
53	N:	Yeah anyways (.) and // um ((laughs))

54 S: Sha//::me=
55 N: ((laughing)) =I haven't finished
56   and then he goes-
57   and I goes to him (.) what colour are your eyes? yeah
58   cos his- cos he was wearing blue↑
59   his eyes looked blue
60   >and I was like< what colour are your eyes?
61   he was like (.) blue
62   no I'm joking ((laughs))
63   the camera just makes them look blue
64   >I was like< oh seen
65 L: (right) what colour *are* his eyes?
66 N: They're just brown
67   but he's so nice (.) I was like
68 ?:   (He::)
69 N: and I was like (.) he's like to me (.) he's like to me
70   hey beautiful when I came online
71   I was like ((high pitched)) ahh::::::
72   I don't like it when brere's say
73   you're buff or you're choong it's-
74   (.) when they say you're beautiful::
75   or you're gorgeous::
76   or you're stunning↑
77   or something like that
78   it's just better

Small stories occur in the classroom data amidst other activities, and in that respect they are in tune with people attending to many things simultaneously. They are, however, clearly marked with "generic framing devices" (Bauman 2004: 6), mostly openers, and tend to be focal topics in that they are taken up again, if momentarily exited from (e.g. when students have to orient to the classroom agenda), with minimal marking. We can see how the above story begins with a marker that signals closure of the previous topic ("anyways," line 1), an address term (Shenice), a suspense-creating exclamative phrase, uttered and repeated in an excited tone ("oh my God," lines 3–4), and with a minimal reference recognitional form that comprises the character's proper name ("Stefan yeah?" line 5). "He went on web cam for me" (line 5) is reminiscent of Labov's abstract. Subsequently, the story unfolds in the typical way of breaking news. It presents a carefully drafted description of the single most reportable event and character (i.e. Stefan going on web cam), rendered almost in slow motion, with intense focalization on the part of the teller (Mills and White 1997: 235). There seems to be a "female gaze" (Gledhill 1993) at work that scrutinizes the gazed upon man's posture, outfit, movements and physical appearance. These detailed scenes, rendered in past progressive that stresses duration (e.g. "he was wearing," line 17; "he was looking," line 13) rather than being just "description," are an integral part of eventness in breaking news. On the face of it, nothing much happens. It is, however, in the positive assessments (mostly in terms of good looks) of the character talked about and in the however fleeting encounter with them that these slices of life owe their reportability in local contexts.

We will return to these assessments and the identity work that they do in Chapter 6. Here it suffices to say that, even if departing in varying ways from the prototypical narrative, small stories in environments such as the above have been found to be of utmost importance as ways of jointly interweaving events and characters from daily experience and (re)fashioning interpretations of them, working out and through the emotional impact of them. They are also fundamental acts of sharing which thereby also reaffirm closeness in positions and viewpoints, putting them to the test, or revisiting them. What is more, in these data, small stories proved to involve the participants' focal concern at that point in their lives, namely romance and heterosexual relationships.

4.6.1   Small stories and new media

Example (4.9) above shows how a lot of the storytelling we nowadays do in our daily lives is shaped – both at the level of plot and at the level of telling – by our engagement with new media and technologies: for instance, not only do we tell stories in which the new media serve as the social settings of our experiences (as with e.g. MSN above), but the very integration of new media into our lives can shape the telling of a story. Again, Nadia, the teller of (4.9) above, was found to use her mobile phone often as an evidential resource for the story she was telling her friends: she could, for instance, show them a text-message that she had received and on which she based her story to prove the authenticity of her account. In addition to the new media shaping offline stories though, there is a wealth of online stories, particularly personal stories, which have multiplied on social networking sites and web 2.0 technologies, that have recently started attracting the attention of narrative analysts. Although this research is still in its early stages, as the phenomena examined are quite recent, it is worth noting that there seems to be convergence on the fact that stories online depart from what we have called here "canonical" or "big" stories, and in this respect they are more in tune with "small stories." In fact, small stories research is frequently noted by studies of online stories as a frame of analytical reference, as, for instance, in Heyd's (2009) study of stories in email hoaxes and in Page's (2009) study of status updates on Facebook.

Even without acknowledging research on face-to-face storytelling that has attested to the abundance of non-canonical stories in many environments, studies of online stories have also reported the salience of non-canonical stories: e.g. stories that have multiple authors and that are fragmented. These features seem to be attributable to the media-enabled possibilities for the wide circulation of a story across sites and over time – what has been labelled as a distributed story (see Walker 2004 for this term). A case in point is Hoffmann's (2008) and Hoffmann and Eisenlauer's (2010) studies of travel weblog entries, which have shown the preponderance of multilinear, multimodal, collaboratively produced and distributed narratives. These studies have argued that computer mediated communication (CMC) enables new forms of narrative interaction and authorship, ranging from the users as authors who select the telling and design of telling online and (re)shape it, to the users as "audience" who contribute to online evaluations, selecting the reading order and serializing their reading engagement with weblog narratives. As a result of medium-enabled features, Hoffmann and Eisenlauer also observe a certain fragmentation of themes and perspectives, a versatile access to the narration, a lack of closure and a semiotic flexibility. At the same time, weblog narratives are not found to form a homogeneous entity but instead to vary in size, theme, authorship and forms of interactivity. The idea that narrative tellings on the Web can be transposed (e.g. posted) in new contexts, and in that process that new meanings can be produced, is emerging as a common theme (also see Walker 2004). On the basis of that, the unprecedented potential for co-construction, versatility and intertextuality of narratives in online environments is frequently stated as the main finding (also see earlier studies of the Web and hypertext in general, e.g. Mitra 1999).

This shaping of a story by different tellers in different environments militates against a conventional structuring with a beginning, middle and an end, as described by Labov, for instance. At the same time, in many computer-mediated communication environments, it makes little sense to talk about the structure of a story in purely linguistic (verbal) terms and without taking into account the multi-semioticity or multimodality that new media offer for its role in the creation of story plots.

Another important and recurrent feature of online personal stories, from status updates on Facebook to tweets, seems to be the shortening of the distance between the narrating and the narrated world, which fits the definition of breaking news stories, as discussed above. Breaking news stories were found to be prevalent in a corpus of private email messages exchanged between friends (Georgakopoulou 2004b): their salience was found to be shaped by aspects of the mediated context at hand. In particular, the medium afforded tellers the ability to share with their friends events as they were happening to them and to receive feedback on those events from their friends very quickly. In the case of social networking sites such as Facebook and Twitter, this immediacy in sharing events, updating a story as the events are unfolding but also circulating beyond the original environment of telling has been taken to new heights. The place of breaking news stories in new media is worth assessing further. As we saw in Chapter 1, in much of the narrative theory developed so far, the deictic separation between the two worlds of telling and told or the so-called double chronology (Chatman 1990) has been a feature of major importance for the creation of the tellers' perspective or point of view as well as for their ability to reflect on the events narrated (see Freeman 2010; see also the discussion in Chapter 6). It is therefore worth scrutinizing the implications of the frequency and salience of the "breaking news" type of story in online environments for these key features of the narrative canon. More generally, the extent to which the attested forms of online stories constitute new and/or exclusively media-shaped genres needs to be explored. For instance, small stories research, which has attested to similar ways of storytelling in offline environments, is one way toward pushing forward the agenda of articulating as fully as possible what is distinctive about online stories and how that draws on or departs from other forms of storytelling.

4.7   Conclusions

In this chapter, we probed more into narrative as talk-in-interaction with the aim of providing tools for exploring audience participation and diversity in the course of storytelling as well as for doing justice to the wide range of stories told in everyday contexts. Specifically, we illustrated the importance and complexity of participant roles in interaction by showing how audience diversity and changes in the position of participants as tellers, co-tellers, knowing recipients, etc. can shape a storytelling event. These diverse roles are implicated in generating a wide range of responses and modes of participation both during the telling of the story and upon completion, some of which, as we have shown, are affiliative, and others, disaffiliative. In this respect, we also examined the role of narratives in arguments, both as devices for putting forth, supporting and challenging views and claims and as contestable resources that can be instrumental in the development of an argument. In addition, we showed how storytelling rights may be pre-assigned or negotiated during storytelling and how the distribution of such rights can have important consequences for the way in which stories develop and for the relationship amongst interlocutors in concrete social circumstances.

Finally, we discussed how the investigation of the interactional dynamics of stories has been instrumental in documenting the wide range of stories that depart from the canon of interview stories as well as how contexts generate different types of stories. This broadening of the analytic scope is bound to reveal the wide range of stories told in interview situations too, which have perhaps been so far missed out on as the focus has mainly been on monological and well-formed narratives. Similarly, the hope is that the interactional dynamics and participation roles in interview (*sic* elicited stories) will be scrutinized as much as they have been in spontaneous, conversational stories.

The findings presented in this chapter demonstrate the need for any situated analysis of storytelling to address issues of who produces particular kinds of stories in what kinds of environments, under what circumstances particular narratives are more or less accountable, and what kinds of environments encourage, nourish or equally prohibit stories. We will delve more into these questions in the following chapter.

5   Narrative power, authority and ownership

5.0   Introduction

Storytelling, particularly the kind that occurs in everyday, informal contexts, is often associated with cooperation, shared enjoyment and opportunities for the teller's display of verbal artistry. Equally important, however, is the association of stories with conflict, for example in relation to who has the right to recount a narrative, who tells the truth and who lies, and what consequences the telling of particular stories may have on the life of individuals and groups. In this respect, when we look at the use of narratives in many concrete domains of social life, we come across questions of power, credibility and authority. Indeed, narrative tellings may serve as occasions for the exercise of power and domination and for the perpetration or creation of social inequalities. It is to these aspects of the intersection between narratives and social life that we turn in this chapter.

Power is an all-encompassing concept, but in the discussion to follow, we tease specific aspects and applications of it to the study of storytelling. Thus, we illustrate how it interrelates with other pivotal concepts that have been used in narrative research within this area, namely: *control over linguistic resources, authority, telling rights, truth, ideology and ownership*. As we will discuss, power in storytelling often depends on the ability of some and the inability of others to control both the linguistic resources needed to construct narratives and the interactional mechanisms that underlie specific social encounters. Individuals and institutions that are in positions of power also need to legitimize their narratives by showing that they have the right to tell stories and that their narratives are credible depictions of events, agents, motives and circumstances. The first part of the chapter (sections 5.1, 5.2, 5.3) is devoted to the analysis of the linguistic and interactional mechanisms through which power, authority and credibility are concretely established and negotiated within storytelling practices, and to how storytelling may shape and reflect ideologically biased versions of reality. We will also consider how stories are used to provide authority and credibility to groups and individuals and/or to disseminate versions of social phenomena and events. We will therefore discuss studies of narratives in the media and in the political arena. In the second part of the chapter (section 5.4), we will focus on story ownership seen not only as a significant tool for the exercise of narrative power in the social world, but also as a crucial concept in narrative research. This will lead us into an analysis of how this largely romanticized idea of sole ownership has been gradually problematized in favor of the scrutiny of researcher–researched co-ownership.

5.1   Narrative and power

The concept of power has been of paramount importance for the definition of criteria for narrative truth, the distribution of telling rights, the allocation of telling spaces and a variety of other mechanisms that underlie storytelling in social life. However, it remains controversial and has always been at the center of heated debates in the social sciences. Understanding power is, indeed, a very complex endeavor since its forms can be varied and intricate, and its manifestations may range from direct actions (e.g. physical abuse) to subtle means of social control. Social theorists in the last twenty years have emphasized the fact that although direct coercion is still a significant aspect in the exercise of power, power struggles are ubiquitous and the processes that allow groups and individuals to establish their domination over others are subtle and multifaceted (Clegg 1993).

Modern reflections about power have a central point of reference in the work of Michael Foucault whose theorizations have focused on forms of power, their historical roots and development, and the practices and techniques of domination associated with them. Power is, in sum, at the center of Foucault's understanding of the functioning of society. Although his focus and objects of investigation changed over time, moving from the study of the relationships between power and knowledge (Foucault 1972) to the history of power forms in different stages of the development of Western societies (Foucault 1979), and ultimately to the analysis of the complex links between domination, subjectivity and agency (Foucault 1978), there is a core of ideas in his work that have been profoundly influential for social scientists in general and for discourse analysts in particular. Specifically, Foucault emphasized the important connections between power, knowledge and practices, and in so doing he shifted attention away from a conception of power as mere repression, to a focus on the multiplicity of levels and modes of exercise of power in social life. In the *Archeology of knowledge* (1972), he pointed to the association between knowledge, discourse and power, arguing that knowledge is produced through disciplines that are grounded bodies of discourse. These disciplines often develop in association with processes of domination of one group over other groups, while at the same time becoming sites for the exercise of power in that they define what can be an object of knowledge, how it can be spoken about and by whom. Foucault showed, for example, that in the eighteenth century, interest in sexuality developed as a consequence of political and social processes that had to do with population control and demographics, but that later, institutional and knowledge forming practices concurred in creating discourses about sexuality that defined the way the concept itself was viewed. Thus, knowledge is circulated and sanctioned through discursive practices that are themselves both the product and the tool of power mechanisms. These theorizations on discourse are part of Foucault's more general vision of power as a complex interrelation of both discursive and non-discursive practices that produce specific kinds of subjectivities and relationships amongst social agents. Foucault showed that a great number of the ideas and representations that circulate in societies are neither products of the free will of individuals, nor simply imposed from above, but that they are systematically related to modes of domination. In that sense,

> Foucauldian power is not something *held* but something *practised*; power is not imposed from "above" as a system or *socius*, but consists of a series of relations within such a system or *socius*; there is no "outside" of power, no place of liberation or absolute freedom from power; in the end, power *produces* desires, formations, objects of knowledge, and discourses, rather than primarily *repressing*, controlling, or canalizing the powers already held by pre-existing subjects, knowledges or formations. (Nealon 2008: 24)

Although Foucault's vision of power as embedded in the very fabric of social life appears at times too extreme and absolute, it has the merit of addressing the complexity of forms of domination and the multiplicity of levels that they involve. In that respect, his ideas have allowed for a greater understanding of the role of different kinds of discursive practices in the creation and legitimation of inequalities.

   Another significant contribution to a postmodern understanding of power comes from Pierre Bourdieu's ideas about the symbolic order. The French sociologist stresses the fact that power is not necessarily material, but can be related to the symbolic sphere of the production and reception of meaning. Within this perspective, power relationships and the existing social order are established and maintained through association and reciprocal reinforcement between material and symbolic practices. The latter, which range from rituals to sets of procedures related to the reproduction of everyday life, reflect and reinforce types of knowledge, categories and representations based on accepted and established social relations, processes and hierarchies that are perceived as natural. The internalization of mental structures and representations about social relations and social life is central to power maintenance in that it allows for the presentation of the existing order as natural.[1] In addition to arguing for a conception of power that involves both material and symbolic spheres reinforcing each other, Bourdieu also stressed the fact that in order to gain and maintain power, groups and individuals need to accumulate not only economic capital but also "symbolic capital," "a capital of honor and prestige" (1977: 179), i.e. an influence that comes from their being perceived as worthy of recognition. Such a symbolic capital is also assembled through symbolic practices, i.e. social practices involving the maintenance of relationships and of reciprocal bonds and allegiances. In that sense, as Bourdieu correctly emphasized, the social formations are never given but are renewed and modified through the concrete action and interaction of social agents, and power is not exclusively a matter of material domination, but rather of economic and symbolic domination.

These theorizations have been the basis for much of the work of narrative analysis as a source of reflection on social issues related to power and inequality (see, for example, Blommaert 2005: 83–94 and chapters in Briggs 1996a). These studies have shown the central role of discourse in general and narrative in particular in the maintenance or alteration of the social order. They have also emphasized the need to look at how discourse operates within institutions and in connection with social practices that are not discursive.

In general terms, studies of narrative and power present a concentration in the ethnographic or ethnomethodological tradition and focus on the ways in which power is imposed or negotiated within storytelling practices through detailed and interactionally based accounts. Power is not viewed as an abstract and superimposed force but as something that becomes instantiated and negotiated through concrete and local mechanisms of discursive and communicative interaction. We will see that most studies within this tradition have focused on storytelling in institutional contexts such as asylum seekers' interviews (Maryns and Blommaert 2001), police interrogations (Johnson 2008), courtrooms (Trinch and Berk 2002), etc. Other studies of narrative and power resist a neat classification as they embrace diverse methodological traditions. Nonetheless, they all tend to focus on the relationship between (mostly written) narratives and dominant ideologies (see, for example, chapters in Mumby 1993b). They also often subscribe to critical discourse analysis[2] and do not pay as much attention to local practices of meaning production, negotiation and reception, centering instead on the textual organization of stories. In these studies, the focus tends to be on narratives in the media or, more generally, in different kinds of public discourses.

5.2   Controlling stories in institutional contexts

As we mentioned, one trend in the study of the links between narratives and power has been the investigation of storytelling practices in institutional settings and the analysis of concrete ways in which the telling of stories can involve exclusion, discrimination or abuse. Indeed, although the telling of stories in informal conversations does not exclude power negotiations and struggles,[3] these aspects have been noted more in public or institutional contexts in which participants have an unequal status. People who narrate stories in a police or asylum seeker's interview, in a written appeal to an insurance company, or in a public mediation encounter usually tell their narratives to or in the presence of someone who has greater power in terms of knowledge about the functioning of the institution or organization in which the encounter is taking place; also, in terms of control over the linguistic resources that are deemed necessary or appropriate within that environment. Such resources may include the preferred language in which a narrative is told, but also the linguistic tools and structures that define the genre and style of the story that is expected in specific circumstances. On the other hand, institutional knowledge means insider understanding of the operation, practices and social roles that characterize a certain institution or organization, but also knowledge of concepts and ideas used in the specialized domain. In addition, the person who is telling the story often has less or no power of decision at all over the outcome or outcomes of the procedure in which the telling is embedded.

5.2.1 Asylum seekers' accounts

In order to illustrate how differences in the control of linguistic resources and role asymmetries may result in or intensify social inequalities, let us consider the case of asylum seekers' narratives. These stories have been studied, among others, by Maryns and Blommaert (2001) and Maryns (2005), who examined asylum seekers' interviews and procedures in Belgium. The authors emphasize the crucial role of storytelling in these institutional encounters, since asylum seekers are expected to produce narratives about the circumstances of their escape from their countries of origin in order to back up their requests for admittance in the foreign country. Such accounts are expected to be sufficiently detailed and coherent to convince officials that the narrators are telling the truth. Asylum seekers need to document their claims with precise and verifiable dates, names and events, as their stories will be used as a central piece of evidence for decisions about granting an asylum. Maryns and Blommaert (2001) and Maryns (2005) analyze two features that particularly contribute to the potential inequalities of the encounters and affect the procedures related to asylum seeking: the first is the existence of different event perspectives between tellers and officials; the second is the differential access to linguistic resources that exist both between officials and asylum seekers and among the asylum seekers themselves. The event perspective was found to constitute a potential area of conflict in expectations and interpretations, given the different roles that officials and narrators play in the interaction and their, often conflicting, objectives in terms of what they want to achieve in the communicative event. While asylum seekers are protagonists of the events they tell and regard them as highly charged lived experiences, officials may define them as collections of facts that have to eventually fit into bureaucratic categories. Having no first-hand knowledge of these experiences, officials do not necessarily empathize with the narrators; however, their interpretations of, and judgment about, asylum seekers' stories will affect the result of their pleas. In addition to these different perspectives, other institutional constraints framing the interactions may promote misunderstandings and inequalities. Officials look for patterns that will allow them to recognize typical elements in a story, while asylum seekers present themselves as individuals with unique experiences. Also, for people who have lived through shocking and bewildering events characterized by loss of orientation and control, it may be hard to produce accounts with the level of detail and orderliness solicited by officials.

In the cases studied by Maryns and Blommaert, the narrators were mostly Africans who were interviewed in a lingua franca (English, French or Dutch) that was not their mother tongue, or gave their testimonials with the mediation of an interpreter. Both the lack of proficiency in the target language and/or the lack of control over the translation of their narratives constituted evident disadvantages for the narrators and potential sources of adverse effects on the asylum-seeking procedure.

Political circumstances may profoundly affect the role that storytelling plays in different kinds of institutional events and the way the telling process relates to power and inequality. Thus, while in the case of Belgium, the asylum-seeking procedure gives officials the power to inspect narratives and judge them according to standards of truth and credibility, in other cases the institutional procedure provides gate-keepers with the power to ban storytelling altogether. This is the case documented by Jacquemet (2005) in his study of interviews set up in the United Nations High Commission on Refugees in Tirana, Albania, to decide on the granting of refugee status to Kosovars seeking UN protection during the 2000 conflicts in the former Yugoslavia. Given the existence of many documented cases in which Albanian citizens had claimed to be Kosovan refugees, the UN decided to alter the refugee interview by requiring the interviewee to answer a long list of very detailed questions on places, peoples and events. The decision resulted in a general tendency by officials to reject personal stories. Again, the differing power and expectations of the refugees on the one hand, and of the interviewers on the other, profoundly affected the way storytelling was viewed and its impact on the lives of people involved in it. As Jacquemet shows, refugees expected the interview to revolve around their past and were therefore prepared to give detailed autobiographical accounts about the events that had led to their flight from Kosovo. Officials on the other hand, having been warned about falsification, made an active effort to prevent narrative accounts and promoted a question–answer format in which they had the leading role. The decision to ban storytelling resulted, therefore, in accumulated tension between officials and refugees and in frustration on the part of those who saw their attempts to tell their stories curtailed.

5.2.2   Narratives in legal settings

These fundamental differences in power, knowledge and access to resources are not exclusive to asylum seekers' interviews. In fact, they constitute the unifying factor in a great variety of storytelling situations that are otherwise different in terms of their objectives, participation structures and discourse practices. It is important to note that in many social settings these power differences may not be absolute and may be distributed amongst different participants in a variety of ways. For example, in legal settings, attorneys, witnesses and juries may have differential access to specialized knowledge and linguistic resources, and therefore their participation in the communicative event, their power to make decisions and consequently their role in storytelling will vary as well. However, in all asymmetrical encounters, the negotiation and imposition of power in and through narrative rests in large part on interactional mechanisms and strategies deriving from the pre-established roles of the participants and the differences in their access to knowledge. The asymmetry in social roles translates into differences in telling roles that allow one party to direct and/or intervene in the storytelling performance of another party. On the other hand, the asymmetry in types of knowledge allows certain participants to manage the talk in ways that are seen as consonant with institutional objectives.

A clear illustration of the above is to be found in studies of narratives in legal settings (Harris 2001; Jacquemet 2005; Trinch and Berk-Seligson 2002). Researchers in this field have stressed that narratives told during trials and pre-trial phases cannot be understood without keeping in mind the characteristics of the trial as an institutional event. As noted by Harris (2001), the form and focus of those narratives depend on the power relations amongst participants. Thus, the telling strategies used by lawyers, defendants and witnesses need to be seen in connection with "the trial as a generic type of power-laden judicial procedure in which language plays a crucial role and which reaches beyond the legal setting to the cultural and social order" (p. 55). It has been found, for example, that the genre and style of stories produced in court depend in many ways on the direction taken by lawyers based on the phase of the trial and the development of their defense strategies. For example, many of the narratives produced by witnesses in the evidential part of the trial do not focus on significant events, but rather on what witnesses did or saw in relation to those events. Also, most narratives appear to be fragmented and non-monological because of their embedding in question–answer formats proposed by attorneys. In addition, Harris notes that, in cross-examination phases, the experiencers of the events are often stripped of their role as tellers. Instead, it is the lawyers who put forward the narrative to be confirmed by the "knower" (witness or defendant).

In similar vein, Ehrlich (2001) has shown in her study of sexual assault trials in Canada how the version of events that may emerge in a trial can be determined by the type of questions lawyers ask of witnesses and how these control the topic or selectively reformulate witnesses' responses. Ehrlich's study has thus provided further evidence for the ways in which "the institutionally sanctioned, pre-allocated role of lawyer as questioner and witness as answerer has significant implications for the co-constructed nature of courtroom narratives" (2007: 455). Ehrlich studied three trials on the same sexual assault case (2007), where the Supreme Court of Canada dramatically overturned the decision of the previous two trials and convicted the accused. Ehrlich showed how mainstream norms about gender relations were instrumental in the co-construction of versions of events between the complainant and the Crown Attorney. She also illustrated how different understandings of the events led to different *re-entextualizations* of the local talk of the speakers by powerful judges. Specifically, in the trials that acquitted the accused, the complainant and the Crown Attorney co-constructed a narrative in which the sexual activity was presented as consensual. In contrast, as Ehrlich shows, the same events and facts of the case "were interpreted by the Supreme Court in a way which was compatible with the complainant's version of events" (p. 472), and thus presented the sexual activity as coerced and not as consensual. In Ehrlich's study, as in other studies we are discussing here, the notions of *entextualization*, *contextualization* and *re-contextualization* are pivotal in the analytical toolkit, as we will explain in more detail below.

Studies such as the above have documented how, in virtue of their position within the judicial system, lawyers and other practitioners exert power through access to linguistic and interactional resources vis-à-vis the defendants and witnesses. Given their greater power in the judicial structure and their knowledge of the potential role of stories told during the trial for the acquittal or conviction of defendants, they can push the storytelling in certain directions by instructing witnesses and defendants on how to produce stories before the trial, and by managing the telling of narratives through question–answer formats, interruptions and reformulations during the trial.

The operation of these mechanisms is also evident in encounters between different types of legal practitioners and clients that precede a trial or that may constitute material for deliberation during it. These contexts partly reproduce the unequal distribution of speaking roles and of telling resources that we have described for trials. An interesting study by Trinch and Berk-Seligson (2002) illustrates, for example, how clashes in the expectations about the role of the law and the definition of guilt and innocence determine the interactional dynamics that surround narrative practices within protective order interviews.

Thus, one typical aspect of social encounters in which access to knowledge and resources is unequal is the existence of mismatches between institutionally defined expectations and actual performances. In some cases, these mismatches simply lead to different interpretations of the significance or value of stories. In other cases, such as in the legal settings that we have examined, they lead to negotiations in which those who are in a position of greater power actively try to modify aspects of the storytelling performance.

A widespread strategy used to negotiate the interpretation of a narrative or parts of it is re-contextualization, i.e. the creation of a new context of interpretation of aspects of the story that is being told. The concept of contextualization refers to the process through which participants use linguistic and paralinguistic indexes to make sense of what is being said and done through talk in a specific interactional occasion (see Goodwin and Duranti 1992). According to Bauman and Briggs (1990: 64), contextualization "involves an active process of negotiation in which participants reflexively examine the discourse as it is emerging, embedding assessments of its structure and significance in the speech itself." As Gumperz (1982) and many others have argued, contextualization crucially functions through cues such as rhythm, intonation, code or style switches, voice, etc., which provide frames for interpretations of what is going on in an interaction. Contextualization is always a negotiated and ongoing process so that meanings are constructed and reconstructed as the interaction unfolds. This process implies the possibility of continuously introducing changes in the frame of understanding of discourse and therefore of re-contextualizing meanings. Re-contextualization is therefore a significant strategy of negotiation in the kinds of storytelling contexts that we are examining in that it allows one party to point to elements of form or content that are required for a narrative to be acceptable in the context at hand, and/or to revisit its significance within it.

Among re-contextualization processes, one that has attracted particular attention is entextualization. Bauman and Briggs define it as: "the process of rendering discourse extractable, or making a stretch of linguistic production into a unit – a text – that can be lifted out of its interactional setting" (1990: 71). Entextualization involves lifting a piece of discourse out of its context of production and inserting it into new contexts in which it receives a new interpretation. This discursive process can be seen as lying at the heart of negotiations over story content, format and interpretation in institutional practices where participants are on an unequal footing. Indeed, stories get formulated, reformulated, lifted from their occasions of production and inserted into new contexts in a continuous process that is often regulated by the more powerful parties. The original story told by a defendant, for example, gets transformed not only through its negotiation between teller and legal practitioner, but through its transformation into a written record, its reformulation across documents and contexts, its reproduction within quotes and references by parties who may or may not have listened to its original production (see Carranza 2010). Re-contextualization in general and entextualization in particular are thus significant processes in the configuration of the genre and scope of narratives and are central tools in the transformation of everyday narratives into other kinds of texts with a specific functionality within social practices.

Examples of these strategies of negotiation can be found in Johnson (2008) who describes them in detail using another type of legal context of storytelling: police interviews with suspects. She argues (pp. 327–8) that:

The suspect's story, first couched in lay terms and often unevaluated in terms of culpability and responsibility, is reshaped and transformed through negotiating wording, meaning, additional detail and stance that make it more valuable as evidence in relation to the crime for which the suspect may be charged and later tried.

In a similar vein to lawyers in trials, police interrogators manipulate turn-taking by interrupting the teller in order to obtain details that they think are missing from the story, or to deviate tellers from the course they are taking. They also reformulate lay descriptions in terms that are acceptable within the legal context and put pressure on tellers in order to transform their point of view in relation to the events. In the case of suspects, these reformulations often result in a shift from promoting an identity as an innocent person to accepting an identity as a guilty individual. Let us look at a specific example of negotiations over the interpretation of events and of discursive re-contextualization in storytelling. The excerpt (Johnson 2008: 331–2) is taken from an interrogation of an individual suspected of an assault against his girlfriend that nearly ended in her death. The police interrogator (POL) is trying to assess the state of the suspect (SUS) before the onset of the incident with the girlfriend:

(5.1)

1	POL:	Can I can I just perhaps interrupt you there for a moment
2		just so I can get a full picture. What sort of a state were
3		both of you in I mean were you drunk, happy?
4	SUS:	Well I was pretty happy.
5	POL:	Drunk I'm talking about.
6	SUS:	Well it's quite true to say that I had been drinking. I was
7		not paralytic. I was tired. I was wondering why why she
8		was shouting and screaming and hitting me because I did
9		not understand that. I knew [victim's name] was stoned
10		as well as pissed. I knew that she'd drunk quite a fair
11		amount and I knew that she was stoned.
12	POL:	You're you're saying to me that you knew that she was
13		drunk and high on drugs. Is that what you're –
14	SUS:	-Yes
15	POL:	I'm sorry you- everybody must understand exactly what

16		you're saying er ok then. So she's banging your head
17		against the wall did you say?
18	SUS:	Yea I kept trying to walk away.
19	POL:	Yes.
20	SUS:	And she's there shouting at me, don't walk away
21		from me. And she was repeatedly like pushing me against the
22		wall.

At the beginning of the excerpt, the police interrogator is taking advantage of his position as an evaluator to interrupt the storytelling. When explaining his interruption of the suspect, "just so I can get a full picture" (line 2), he simultaneously indexes his role as someone who is evaluating the telling and the role of the teller as someone who is required to produce a clear reconstruction of events. The police interrogator also provides the suspect with possible descriptors of his state at the time of the events, attempting to transform what in the suspect's previous narrative was a vague orientation into a more precise description of such condition ("What sort of a state were both of you in I mean were you drunk, happy?" lines 2–3) But, interestingly, when the suspect uses an evaluative term provided in the previous line by his interlocutor ("I was pretty happy," line 4), the interrogator pressurizes him into reformulating his utterance (line 5). The reformulation of the description from "happy" to "drunk" also achieves a transformation of the orientation from a description of a state: happiness, into a potential admission of a cause for criminal behavior, drunkenness. Thus the suspect's description of his behavior is re-contextualized as having a new meaning in the legal frame and in fact the suspect's reaction is that of taking a defensive stance, "Well, it's quite true to say that I had been drinking" (line 6), which implies that he accepts that the reformulation of his state as being drunk is a potential basis for legal responsibility. He then goes back to the narrative describing his girlfriend's behavior as derived from her being "stoned" (line 9) and "pissed" (line 10). The police interrogator intervenes again to propose a reformulation of the words "pissed and stoned" into more precise and legally acceptable terms: "You're you're saying to me that you knew that she was *drunk* and *high on drugs*" (lines 12–13). When the suspect agrees, the police interrogator goes on to explain his requests for clarification with the following, "I'm sorry you- everybody must understand exactly what you're saying" (lines 15–16). This is an important move in the exchange in that the police interrogator is hinting at the fact that the narrative will be used in the legal procedure and that therefore it will be read and judged by other people who are not present in the room. Through this intervention, the interrogator points to the process of entextualization of the narrative into a potential legal text and therefore proposes a different frame of understanding and production for it.

5.3   Authority and telling rights

As we can see in the above discussion, the discursive workings of power go hand in hand with the "powerful" parties' more or less explicit claims to authority, which comprises their right not only to propose narrative versions of events that can be regarded as more influential than other versions, but also to evaluate and reformulate other peoples' narratives. However, authority can also be analyzed in connection with processes of self-legitimation. Such processes of (re) affirmation of the teller's or the tale's legitimacy within storytelling have been discussed at length by Briggs (1996a), who claims that authoritative discourse is in large part based on the successful management of rhetorical and linguistic structures by the people in positions of power. He points, for example, to the use of specialized lexicon, such as the recourse to words and expressions that belong to a specific field of knowledge to which only individuals in a position of power have access, as a means of indexing authority. He also discusses control of the turn-taking system, such as in the framing of narratives within question and answer formats, strategies that we have already analyzed in connection with legal interviews.

Briggs points to other ways in which authority can be indexed[4] in storytelling. An important mechanism is speech style, since the authoritative voice is often achieved not only through the use of technical terms, but also through rhetorical structures used within the narrative itself or within the discursive practice in which the narrative is embedded, which also point to the special social status of the people practicing them. Analysts of power-laden negotiations between plaintiffs and mediators in traditional communities, which hold public meetings to resolve such questions, have described some of these highly complex patterns. Haviland (1996) illustrates, for example, how in publicly mediated disputes over marital contrasts amongst the Tzotzil in Zinancatán, Mexico, the elderly members of the community assert their authority by producing a highly ritualized discourse of exhortation and admonition in response to the plaintiffs' narrative accounts of their problems, which in contrast are told in everyday informal language. At the same time, these authoritative figures are able to restore order by selectively incorporating the plaintiffs' voices into their own reconstructions of events. In this way, authority is both indexed in the kind of rhetorical structures used in discourse, and constructed through the management of the turn-taking system in which the elders have power to direct the flow of speech. People in a position of authority regulate telling turns not only by selectively assigning the floor to different participants, but also by intervening with their own reformulations of stories.

Haviland also showed how authority can be encoded through the inclusion in stories of a variety of voices, not only those of the litigants, but also those of other characters.[5] In particular, he discussed instances of constructed dialogue or reported speech (see section 3.3 on this point) as devices that allow narrators and mediators to back up claims, to provide evidence for their interpretations of events, and/or to present themselves as morally authoritative and their enemies in an unfavorable light.[6]

Up to this point, we have considered authority and the strategies used to exercise it only in institutional storytelling contexts. However, authority can be invoked, accepted and contested in everyday storytelling as well. In educational contexts, for example, teachers may implicitly draw on their authority to accept or reject stories uttered by children if these do not fit the parameters set by educational standards (Michaels 1981) (see section 3.3 on this point). Similar mechanisms are often found in family narrative activities as well. Ochs and Taylor (1995) studied dinnertime interaction in American families and found that there were significant differences in the storytelling roles played by children, mothers and fathers, in that fathers were implicitly or explicitly granted a privileged position in eliciting and evaluating narratives. Ochs and Taylor found that mothers either directed children to tell narratives to their fathers, or initiated narratives that had the father as the primary recipient. They also found that fathers were the main "problematizers" in evaluating the stories, i.e. that they were those who more often criticized the behavior of the family members as figures in the story world. These special prerogatives assigned to fathers point to their privileged role in the family as well as to an implicit acceptance of their authority as judges of other family members. These findings suggest that there are subtle ways in which authority may be enacted in everyday life, but also that authority may be exercised in storytelling without much negotiation when the differences in social roles are tacitly accepted.

5.3.1   Truth, credibility and persuasion

So far, we have discussed how institutionally pre-allocated power asymmetries may shape the telling of stories. This discussion has highlighted the vulnerability of stories to institutional processes. Below, we will shift our focus to the power of the stories themselves in propagating institutionally and publicly shaped ideological projects. To do so, we will tackle questions of truth and credibility. Credibility, i.e. the possibility for a story or a narrator to be accepted as truthful, is often based on the idea of the primacy of personal experience over other forms of experience and knowledge, hence the widely held view of narrative as a privileged genre for communicating personal experience. When investigating the role of narrative in fact construction, Edwards and Potter (1992) noted, for example, that embedding narratives into accounts increases their plausibility and that people gain credibility through narratives because these contain many details and give particular vividness to the reconstruction of facts. Narratives are widely seen as conveying experience in an unmediated fashion, and thus questions about evidence and truth are less likely to be asked of narrators. In this sense, a subtle link is established between authenticity and the narrative of experience. Labov's (1972) famous definition of narrative as "recapitulation of past experience" is a clear example of this link. While Labov merely claimed that narratives present a straightforward relationship with reality, other scholars advocated a much more idealized view of the relationship between storytelling and experience. Summarizing some of these positions, Amy Shuman (2005: 9) notes:

For some (Atkinson, 1995: xii, Schank, 1990: xi), storytelling has the status of "natural" communication, a fundamental and universal way of documenting and describing experience (Coles, 1989). Sometimes, especially in the popular literature, storytelling is asserted to be a representation of either the human soul or the human brain.

Echoes of this view of narrative can be found in the celebration of narrative as a more authentic mode of knowledge and organization of experience than the "logico-scientific mode" (see section 1.2 for a thorough discussion of this point). In Bruner's words: "It is only in the narrative mode that one can construct an identity and find a place in one's culture. Schools must cultivate it, nurture it, cease taking it for granted" (1996: 42). Social philosophers such as Taylor (1989) and MacIntyre (1981) have also underscored this point by arguing that in order to develop a moral sense, individuals need to understand and experience their lives narratively. Finally, White (1987: 215) has gone as far as to suggest that narrative can be equated with knowledge. These views of narrative as representing real experience and as providing more authentic forms of knowledge find an echo in popular culture. Murray (1997) argues that we live in a storytelling society, where narrative has become a dominant mode of communication. Media studies in general have shown a variety of ways in which such popularity is exploited. Abell, Stokoe and Billig (2000) discuss, for example, how celebrities and popular figures use narratives in interviews to make claims to identity. Analysts of TV news reporting have emphasized that TV journalism is strongly oriented toward storytelling as a central tool to attract public attention on everyday events that would otherwise go unnoticed (Berger 1996; Dahlgren 1992). According to Ekström (2000: 474):

Stories have a potential to involve the audience in ways only this mode of communication can achieve. First, they elicit empathy, identification and excitement and a desire to find out how the story ends ... Second, stories perhaps more than other modes, offer models which help us understand reality, other people and ourselves. Clear-cut plots and well-defined characters help viewers create order in reality and reinforce established interpretations of real-life phenomena and relationships.

It is not surprising then that narratives are ubiquitous in communicative events which revolve around the persuasion of the public and/or its recruitment for a cause, such as political discourses and advertising. Shuman (2005) analyzed, for example, the use of individual stories in what she calls "promotional junk mail," in which advertisers present the case of an individual or a family to attract people's attention to a cause and elicit their donations. She argues that it is the apparent immediacy of the personal story, even when this narrative is carefully orchestrated by those who create the message, that helps get the advertiser's message across by appealing to the reader's empathy.

Similar mechanisms of empathy creation are exploited by politicians, who tell stories to provide supposedly "true accounts" about aspects of their life and experience and to give an aura of trustworthiness about them. All this is done by virtue of the popular conceptions about storytelling described above. By telling stories, politicians can show that their ideas are based on every-day experience (both theirs and other people's) rather than on logical reasoning, and such experience is often constructed as "more real" than words and speeches. A clear example of this can be found in the "biography tour" initiated by the Republican candidate to the 2008 Presidential elections in the United States, John McCain, as a way of introducing himself to the public in a region of the country where he was not well known. Let us look at ways in which this tour is described in an extract from a press article on the topic published on the CNN website:[7]

McCain tells his story to voters

(**CNN**) – Sen. John McCain on Monday recalled his family history and patriotic roots as he kicked off a tour to introduce himself to the general electorate.

"I have lived a blessed life, and the first of my blessings was the family I was born into," McCain said.

The presumptive Republican presidential nominee, speaking in Meridian, Mississippi, focused on how his upbringing and his family's military history shaped his views for the future.

"By all accounts, the McCains of Carroll County were devoted to one another and their traditions; a lively, proud and happy family on the Mississippi Delta," McCain said, describing the area considered his "ancestral home."

McCain is on a weeklong biography tour, which will take him through five states that he says were part of his "formative experiences."

In addition to recounting memories from his childhood, McCain described some of the most influential people in his life. He recalled growing up under the care of his mother, the "formidable Roberta McCain," her identical twin sister and his grandmothers.

Roberta McCain, 96, is often seen on the campaign trail with her son.

McCain said his family instilled in him the values of duty, honor and sacrifice at an early age.

"The family I was born into – the family I am blessed with now – made me the man I am," he said.

The beginning of the article presents McCain's use of his family history and roots as a means to "introduce himself to the general electorate." In that sense, personal narrative is implicitly seen as a window to self-disclosure. McCain is reported to have characterized his family as "lively, proud and happy," a description aimed at legitimizing his upbringing as having taken place in a socially healthy environment. Such a first step, the depiction of a good family environment, is used as a basis for the following move, the grounding of his current vision of the world in his upbringing. Thus, the values "of duty, honor and sacrifice" that he holds are presented as having being instilled early in his childhood by his mother and other "influential people in the family." These narrative elements allow the presentation of McCain to tap into generally shared images of close-knit families producing happy and morally strong individuals, and of true values coming from experience, not from abstract reasoning, and having been acquired early and maintained through time. This notion of steadfast convictions is typically evaluated in political debates as superior to recent or suddenly acquired positions, which tend to be seen as the product of political convenience. In fact, many a politician has suffered defeat because of accusations of "flip-flopping," or changing their views.

As we can see above, McCain's personal narrative is organized around the central theme of tradition and of how values are passed from one generation to the other and is thus designed to give credibility to the candidate by demonstrating his sincerity and the moral authenticity of his convictions. Beyond this referential content, there is also the fact that in putting the telling of personal stories at the center of his tour, the McCain campaign emphasized the use of narrative as a particularly effective means for reaching out to his electorate. This strategic choice of storytelling is based on the conception of narrative as an "authentic" mode of communication and feeds into views of trustworthiness that are popular in the United States. Speaking informally, through personal stories, rather than more formally through a political speech, makes a politician look more like a "regular guy." In point of fact, the myth of the "regular guy" is one of the most successful ones in the political inventory of the Republican Party (see Frank 2004; Greenwald 2008[8]). It invokes the idea that an average person is better than an intellectual or a politician because she or he has life experience and can talk about it in a straightforward manner. Thus, a politician has to present herself/himself as a regular guy in order to attract people to her/his party. Regular guys do not talk in abstract terms, but speak everyday language and tell stories instead of delivering formal addresses. All these ideological elements were present both in the reporting (as presuppositions) and in the storytelling that McCain delivered as part of his "biography tour" in an effort to promote him as a candidate for the people.

This example shows how credibility and trustworthiness are related to narrative both through the construction of experience as a highly legitimate basis for the formation of ideas and through the recounting of personal experience as one of the most authentic modes of communication. Behind these views, there is an implicit acceptance of storytelling as a way of realistically reproducing lived experience, not as a process of more or less strategically manipulating it or even constructing it. Thus, when McCain talked about his upbringing through a story, he was trying to focus the attention of the public on the details of his biography, but not on their accuracy or truth.

5.3.2   Truth and ideology

The role of storytelling in relation to truth is particularly significant when we examine it in the context of hegemonic cultural processes. Social theorists such as Gramsci (1971) and Bourdieu (1977) have argued that in order for groups to impose their power, they have to win at a symbolic level, that is, they need to achieve consensus on cultural values, practices and frames of understanding of reality. In these theories, domination is achieved through the inculcation of beliefs and values. In Bourdieu's terms, they become internalized in people's consciousness as *habitus*, defined simply as "a set of dispositions" (1977: 72) rather than a fixed and rigid system of beliefs. The concepts of hegemony and symbolic domination are both useful for describing ideologies as sets of integrated beliefs, values and principles of social action that allow social systems (and groups) to impose and hold power by providing a cultural basis for their institutions and forms of social organization.

The nature and functioning of ideologies have been the subject of heated debates among social scientists (see Blommaert 2005:161–75).[9] An exhaustive discussion of this issue is beyond the scope of this chapter, but it can be assumed that social and political systems need to rely on the symbolic sphere in order to establish and maintain control over society and that cultural practices are imbued with images, metaphors and narratives that form the basis of mainstream understandings of reality. How are these ideologies or ideological elements disseminated and inculcated? Discourse analysts and other social scientists emphasize that discourse practices play a central role in the creation of consensus (Fairclough 1989). They have also argued that storytelling holds a special ideological power in the range of discourse practices (Jacobs 2000). Some attribute this power to the very nature of stories as dramatizations of experience. Witten states, for example, that narrative is "a singularly potent discursive form through which control can be dramatized, because it compels belief while at the same time it shields truth claims from testing and debate" (1993: 100). Mumby claims that narrative as a social "symbolic act" has the ability to play "a role in the construction of a social text as a site of meaning within which social actors are implicated" (1993a: 5). Stories are widely held to be significant sites of ideological construction and transmission both because of their ability to become virtual stages for conflict and resolution and because of their emotional appeal.

The role of stories in the (re)affirmation of ideologies has mainly been examined in relation to public contexts and discourses about socially significant events. In such cases, truth becomes a complex matter since the relation between events and their recounting is mediated by institutional mechanisms of production and reception and by expectations about narrative content and narrators' attitudes. Blommaert (2005: 84–95) describes, for example, the conditions of production of narrative testimonies presented during the hearings of the Truth and Reconciliation Commission. The hearings took place in South Africa, starting in 1996, to give voice to the victims of human rights violations perpetrated during apartheid. As Blommaert notes, these hearings established the legitimacy and the right to be heard for thousands of victims who had never before been allowed to tell their stories, but at the same time they also created certain conditions of tellability and certain expectations. Among these conditions, there was the idea that victims' narratives needed to conform to an "overarching topic" (p. 85) of suffering. Such a motif was explicitly thematized by the hearing commissioners, emphasized in the accounts of witnesses, and directly invoked in the questions addressed to them. Blommaert discusses the case of a narrator whose testimony did not explicitly present suffering as a central motif in order to argue that he was not heard in the same way as those who had given emotional renditions because his story did not follow the expected patterns. This study shows how institutions create specific rules for narrative performance that largely determine the ways in which facts and experiences will be discursively organized, and therefore they inevitably mediate between events and their perception by audiences.

A similar idea about the ideological functions of overarching themes in public narratives is proposed by Ehrenhaus (1993) in his analysis of the construction of a hegemonic version of the Vietnam War in the US press and media. The author claims that the public discourse on the Vietnam War in the United States uses a

> therapeutic motif which casts all issues and questions of relationships in matters related to Vietnam – be they personal, cultural, or political, – in terms of healing and recovery. The body is ravaged by war; the wounded must make peace with what remains. The mind is haunted by images, aromas and sounds; veterans must learn to face their demons. (Ehrenhaus 1993: 81)

According to Ehrenhaus, this motif can be conceived of in narrative terms, in the sense that it constitutes a certain kind of story template that circulates and gets enacted through different texts and in different contexts. There is a basic breach in social harmony represented by the war and a reaction to it: the shock that the war creates in public consciousness. Then there is a resolution, the healing that leads to recovery and reintegration.

In both examples discussed above, narrative is related to ideology and power through the construction of narrative frames and motifs as semiotic structures capable on the one hand of organizing experience in a unified way, and on the other, of effectively preventing different voices to emerge or to be heard. However, it is not altogether clear what a motif or theme is and how it is realized in different narratives. Ehrenhaus' discussion of the Vietnam "therapeutic motif" in particular can be seen as representative of a tendency amongst some narrative analysts to equate ideology with narrative by describing ideologies as sets of wide cultural themes that are organized in narrative patterns. This approach (cf. White 1978) espouses the idea that hegemonic discourses are based on the ability to impose *meta- or master narratives*, which we will discuss in section 5.4.1. Hence the proliferation in the social sciences of writings in which the term narrative is loosely used to refer variously to dominant discourses, metaphors, ideas and/or images.[10] The association between meta- (or master) narratives and ideologies has gained ground partly thanks to work by the philosopher Jean François Lyotard (1984), who contrasted modern to postmodern culture in terms of the latter's resistance to overarching myths, totalizing cultural schemata or systems of beliefs.

5.3.3   Narrative, power and the media

An important area of research in the study of connections between narratives, power and ideology has been the analysis of constructions of events in the media. As we discussed in section 5.3.1, narratives are seen as a powerful genre in the media, particularly the press, for the constitution of social knowledge and consensus. As news stories largely define the events that are worth talking about and the way they are talked about, they are an important source for the social construction of everyday experience. Questions of narrative truth are significant in this domain given the historical importance of objectivity in journalism. According to Tuchman (1972, quoted in Richardson 2004: 45), journalists follow four strategies in realizing their goal of objectivity: they use sources that provide alternative versions; they present supporting evidence for their claims; they use quotation marks to distance themselves from claims; they structure information in a way as to depict conflicting facts. Thus, journalists can claim that by continuously switching between points of view, they are able to present an impassioned picture of events and opinions. However, studies of narratives in the media, particularly those inspired by critical discourse analysis,[11] contend that news stories are biased, usually in favor of mainstream ideologies both because of the presence in them of socially shared and preconceived assumptions about the social world and because their production and circulation are to a great extent dictated by the economic and political interests of those who control the media. The importance of conventional images and positions in news stories was stressed by Hall *et al.* (1978: 54) as follows:

An event only makes sense if it can be located within a range of known social and cultural identifications. If newsmen did not have available in a routine way such cultural maps of the social world, they could not make sense for their audiences of the unusual, unexpected and unpredicted events which form the basic content of what is newsworthy. Things are newsworthy because they represent the changefulness, the unpredictability and the conflictual nature of the world. But such events cannot be allowed to remain in the limbo of the random, they must be brought within the horizon of the meaningful.

The argument seems to be that the ideological bias of the news consists in this reduction of what is unknown to shared and accepted patterns of meaning, to commonsensical views about identities and patterns of social action which, in virtue of being widespread, largely reflect mainstream understandings and stereotypes. Hence, Hall *et al.* (1978) argued, for example, that the way the British press reported muggings in the 1970s was based on a preconceived fear of crime which was not backed by facts but instead conformed to and strengthened the stereotype of members of minority groups as crime perpetrators. Others (e.g. van Dijk 1991, 1998) have proposed a similar idea stressing that journalists present events within largely implicit mental models (cf. scripts, frames) that usually reflect tacit assumptions about, and shared understandings of, the world. In this way, news stories can frequently contribute to the perpetuation of ideological assumptions and values that have become naturalized, i.e. widely circulated, commonplace and by extension unquestioned.

Early critical discourse analytic studies of news stories (see Fowler 1991) focused on how the choice of lexical terms in titles and in the body of the story reflects mainstream meaning associations or cultural concepts. They also focused on how syntactic processes, such as active and passive constructions, reflect levels of agency attributed to different social actors. Matheson (2005: 21) showed, for example, how the use of military terms in press briefings during the 2003 invasion of Iraq reflected a vision of the war that was biased toward the interpretation of events that the British and American military wanted to push for. Thus, calling journalists that followed troops "embedded" or employing euphemistic expressions such as "blue on blue attacks" for errors that had resulted in the killing of allied soldiers contributed to painting a picture of the war that was deeply influenced by the way it was depicted by the military. In sum, proponents of critical discourse analysis have drawn attention to the ways in which news stories may be ideologically oriented, through close analyses of word choice, word collocations (the way words are combined) and intertextual connections between words (the way words are used across news stories).

However, when considering how stories build interpretations of events and identities, it is also important to attend to the level of textual organization, i.e. the way stories are put together to construct meanings. In this respect, many studies have stressed the role of emplotment (see section 1. 4) in the creation of a story as a particular version of an event or series of events. As Young (1987) argued, emplotting events by taking their ending or their consequences as a beginning allows for the building of a frame of interpretation that connects random events into a unified whole. When applied to news stories, emplotment allows for an analysis of how narratives create particular frameworks for the interpretation of events. In a study of the reporting of different episodes of racial rioting in the American press, Jakobs (2000: 21) notes, for example:

It is plot, more than anything else that encourages the public concentration of attention on to specific events. Processes of emplotment encourage what Umberto Eco (1979; 1994) has called "narrative lingering," where narrative time slows down to encourage the reader to take inferential walks: relating the story to one's own life, deepening the narrative to consider its relationship to events in the past and possible events in the future. As Abbott (1988) has argued, plot is the best way to study the "time-horizon problem," where events can differ in their speed and duration. A focus on which events are selected for narration (and which events are not selected), as well as which events produce the effect of narrative lingering, provides important clues about how a given individual, group or collectivity understands the past, present and future.

The analysis of the discourse organization of news stories is very important to understand how emplotment is achieved. In his groundbreaking work on press discourse, van Dijk (1998) proposed that the discourse structure of news in the press can be described in terms of a set of semantic/functional categories reminiscent of those proposed by Labov (1972) for narratives of personal experience. Although his model was devised to account for news discourse in general, it treated stories as a fundamental component of such discourse. The categories proposed by van Dijk (1998: 52–7) are organized in a tree-like schema, such that some are hierarchically ordered with respect to each other, while others may either be combined with each other or correspond to possible alternatives. The categories described are not all necessary components of a news text. They represent functional elements that describe the particular discourse structure of this textual genre. The proposed higher categories are Summary and Story. The Summary, which is concretely expressed in the headline and lead paragraph, presents the main topics of the news story. The Story is composed of two main components: Situation and Comments. The category Situation includes Episodes (Main event and Consequences) and Background (including Context, History, Circumstances, Previous events). The category Comments, includes Verbal reactions and Conclusions. In Figure 1 we present a visual representation of van Dijk's schema.

According to van Dijk, although the categories tend to appear in a top-down order, i.e. with the main categories carrying the most information appearing before the embedded categories, the way they are actually realized depends on principles of relevance. So, for example, Comments may appear early in a

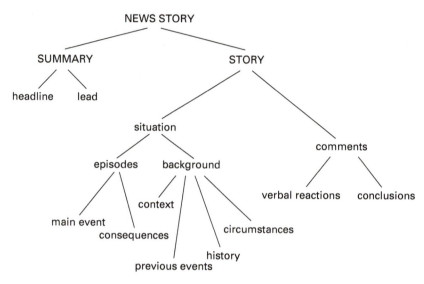

Figure 1

news article, although in most cases they will tend to be presented at the end. Thus, van Dijk underlines that in news stories, as opposed to everyday stories, events are not presented in chronological order since "important information comes first" (1998: 65).

One may query van Dijk's view of the centrality of temporal ordering in everyday narratives, or the sharp opposition between everyday and news narratives, but the important point that he makes is that news stories exhibit a specific textual organization that often results in the privileging of certain types of information over others. Subsequent research has somewhat problematized this model showing that news stories may exhibit less linear structures (Ungerer 2000) or minimal structures represented in one-sentence stories (Bell 1998). That said, scholars agree on the fact that news stories are highly selective in that they focus on what may be considered (or presented as) newsworthy. They also point to the existence of a top-down direction in the construction of the news story such that the title and lead dominate the telling and thus heavily guide its interpretation. The imperative for newsworthiness has been found to influence the kinds of facts that are at the center of news stories, in the sense that either there is a preference for sensational events or an attempt to sensationalize them. As Ungerer discusses, reporters topicalize certain events rather than others, by "extracting them" (2000: 190). Besides topicalizing events in specific stories, newspapers and newscasters may topicalize social issues by printing or telling a great deal of stories on a specific event and/or by talking about events in certain ways.[12]

Recent studies of the role of news stories in shaping public opinion have broadened the field of investigation by focusing on processes of intertextuality and entextualization, for example by looking at how news stories are created from other texts such as research reports, interviews or press releases, and what their patterns of circulation are (Pander Maat 2008; Van Hout and Jacobs 2008).

5.4   "My story": stories as "wholly owned" by their tellers

Issues of truth and authority, as discussed above, also relate to narrative ownership. Who owns the story is in this sense very closely connected with who owns the *experience* reported in the story. As Harvey Sacks points out, however, "our experiences are just about the only thing that we can say truly belongs to us, and at the same time, ownership of experience is often a contested category" (quoted in Shuman 2005: 161). On one level, ownership of the experience and by extension of the story has been closely linked with authenticity both in lay discourses and within the narrative analysis scholarship. The very fact that the narrative turn in the social sciences started off as an anti-positivist move that sought to let the lay voices be heard, and the people's experiences to find a forum and to be legitimated like any other source of evidence, attests to this link. Authenticity is thus connected with personal experience and in turn with ownership. This has given personal experience stories a privileged place in narrative studies. Tellingly, Labov (1972) stresses the point that what he calls *vicarious* experience stories do not present the same evaluation and degree of involvement on the part of the teller as personal experience stories. Shuman's (1986) study of adolescents' interactions, which we have already discussed (see section 4.3.2), also shows how speaking on behalf of another, in this case reporting what other people said, raises issues of entitlement (i.e. who has the right to tell whose story?) and can be contested on the grounds of lack of ownership. In her more recent study (2005, also see section 5.3), she argues that questions of entitlement also occur when personal stories are used to represent a collective experience and are taken out of their context, to act as "allegories." These transitions from the personal to the collective "push storytelling to its limits" raising "ethical questions of ownership" such as the extent to which the representation is a sufficient, adequate, legitimate or appropriate rendering of the original experience (p. 3). We will return to this question of narrative ownership between the personal and the collective in section 5.4.1.

In public life and in popular culture, personal stories have been increasingly appropriated and eulogized on the basis of the widely held idea that they are owned by their tellers and as such can serve as powerful testimonies. This can be attested to in many arenas, amongst which in the recent fascination with reality shows and the increased use of personal stories as part of documentaries on

TV. In these settings, stories are recruited and included in order to "lend cred-ibility to an interpretation of an event," to authenticate and provide an insider's perspective "on what might appear to be exotic, grotesque and unbelievable events," and even to "offer a subversive and potentially emancipatory alterna-tive" to dominant interpretations and views (Shuman 2005: 9).

As already suggested, in these uses of storytelling and in widespread con-ceptions of it, the close link between stories and (ownership of) experience has been frequently essentialized and seen in realist terms. Put differently, stories have been seen as a transparent record of what has "really" happened and as such a point of entry into establishing the truth. This vision has had import-ant analytical consequences, as analysts have often shied away from a critical appraisal of their data: put crudely, the assumption has been that if the stories under analysis are owned by their tellers, then they should not be questioned, reviewed or reflected upon. Josselson (2004) talks about the "hermeneutics of faith" to describe this tendency of the analysts to essentially believe the teller's story, taking it at face value, trying to record it as faithfully as possible and in the end viewing it in representational terms (cf. Atkinson and Delamont 2006). In contrast to this, we have seen on numerous occasions in this book how stories are no more true or real records than any other discourse but are rather resources for more or less strategically creating authenticity in different contexts and for different purposes. More importantly, every telling is locally occasioned and ultimately shaped by the teller's current perspective and their relationships with the storytelling participants. While discussing Labov's (2003) quest for truth in relation to stories told as part of the South African Truth and Reconciliation Commission, Slembrouck (2003) stresses that the kind of "forensic" approach represented in Labov's work is mainly aimed at inferring "responsibility claims" and "what really happened" from the study of "linguistic structure." And he goes on (p. 467):

It corresponds with a view of narrative analysis as oriented to rather strictly polar read-ings which must distinguish truth from untruth. It seems then that the present era is faced with two strands of narrative inquiry: one in which subjective orientations ... yield an experiential truth – fragmented, identity enabling, invested with point of view, subjectifying – and another type of reading in which narratives of experiences are being scanned to establish a narrator-independent version of what happened – transpersonal, objectifying, oriented to prevailing notions of history and institutional truth.

The two strands that Slembrouck refers to above owe their existence to the complex interplay that all stories present between personal ownership and localized experience on the one hand and widely circulating, shared, general-ized stories on the other hand. They represent a conflict between looking at truth versus looking at construction (social and personal) as central in stories. Below, we will try to unravel some of the implications of this conflict for nar-rative research.

5.4.1   Story ownership between the personal and the collective in narrative analysis

Experience and story ownership essentially accord tellers an agentive status: they become the authors of their lived experience. At the same time, narrative analysts have been fascinated and puzzled by how every story we tell is both personal and social in that it reflects and builds upon familiar narrative plots (Bamberg 2006b). Bruner (2001: 29–30) puts this "balancing act" in terms of a "dual function of autobiography":

On the one hand it is an act of entrenchment ... That is to say, we wish to present ourselves to others (and to ourselves) as typical or characteristic or "culture conforming" in some way ... [But] to assure individuality ... we focus upon what, in the light of some folk psychology, is exceptional (and, therefore, worthy of telling) in our lives.

Bruner also stresses the fact that this requirement for something extraordinary to have happened is culturally mediated and not necessarily applicable beyond the Western culture. Furthermore, he highlights that even if we draw on a "core" cultural story when telling "our" story, the discursive environment in which this story will be told will ultimately shape it. However, in Bruner's work as in that of numerous narrative scholars (see, for example, chapters in Brockmeier and Carbaugh 2001; McAdams 1993), narrative ownership is essentially seen as partly biographical and individual and partly social and cultural. In turn, what counts as reportable experience and a tellable story is seen as wholly dependent on normative, culturally shaped ideas of what a life is, or is supposed to be (see Freeman and Brockmeier 2001). There are proliferating ways of referring to these cultural plots from which we draw on when putting together "our own" story. These are by and large under-specified categories and tend to be either overlapping or interchangeable in use: e.g. *scenarios, plots, core stories, genres* (in the sense of knowledge of schematic types of stories), *archetypal narratives, master narratives* (sometimes referred to as master discourses), *dominant* (cultural) *narratives,* (root) *metaphors,* etc. There is also some convergence on the importance of certain master narratives and character types in the telling of (at least Western) autobiographies: e.g. the narrative of growth and transformation, the narrative of redemption; the romantic hero, the martyr, etc. Certain plot features have also been found to be important markers of shared plots, for example the inclusion of turning points in the putting together of one's autobiography (Bruner 2001; Mishler 1999).

   At the same time, studies have increasingly stressed the need to shift attention away from more or less static reproduction of such master narratives toward the tellers' agentive resistance and lack of compliance with them. The project of documenting people's counter-narratives has been ideological and political in essence. It has sought to legitimate silenced, under-represented or

untold stories and explore their potential for challenge, subversion and conflict (see Baynham and De Fina 2005 on this point).[13] In Langellier's terms,
"narrative performance refers to a site of struggle over personal and social
identity and as such the analysis of narrative is not only semantic, engaging the
interpretation of meanings, but must also be pragmatic: analyzing the struggle over meanings and the conditions and consequences of telling a story in a
particular way" (2001: 151). Langellier makes two points that are relevant to
our discussion here: the first is that the analysis should seek to determine the
transgressive potential of narrative meaning-making, and the second is that
this cannot be done "based upon the text alone or the performer's experience,
outside its conditions of performance" (p. 175). This position implies that narrative inquiry should not privilege the referential and representational aspects
of narrative. Indeed, a commonly voiced critique in relation to the inquiry
into master narratives and to deviations from them (e.g. by means of *counter-
narratives*) is the focus in this kind of research on issues of representation. In
addition, the very definition of master narratives (and such terms) has been put
under scrutiny too. As Kölbl asks, "how do we know that [something] is the/a
master narrative, especially when considering that 'we' in the western world
live in different and internally highly differentiated societies with numerous
coexisting and interacting (and often also conflicting) life-forms?" (2002: 30).
And he continues with more questions (p. 30):

I would like to ask what we mean by master narrative. Is it a narrative version (or rather
discourse) that is most commonly spread within a particular population, in the sense
that we could empirically test it? Or is it a particular discourse or ideology that is most
dominant in the public sector, e.g., in such cultural artefacts such as books, films, newspaper articles, etc.? Or is it an ideology or way of talking that constrains the actions of a
particular population in very specific ways? Or, last but not least, is it a particular way of
talking that impacts (only) on how people tell their stories, but has no, or only limited,
consequences on how people think and how they act?

As Kölbl concedes, these questions are not aimed at negating the interplay
between the individual and the social in narrative meaning-making, but they do
stress the need for analysts to "spell out [their] theoretical assumptions about
the connection between ... master narratives at the cultural and social level ...
and individuals telling stories ..." (p. 31).

There are no fast and easy answers to such questions, which continue to
polarize analysts between those who opt for macro-accounts of narratives
in networks of ideology and power and those who refrain from big claims
and attend to the level of fine-grained micro-analysis of storytellings in local
contexts. For the purposes of our discussion, however, it is important to note
that studies of master narratives have provided further evidence for the fact
that issues of narrative ownership are navigated between the personal and the
collective with more, or less, success and tension. When tellers do not see

their experience as fitting into a cultural plot, or when their story departs from a widely available plot, this tension may become unsolvable and may even delegitimate certain accounts. At the same time, as Shuman claims (2005), stories are powerful resources for re-categorizations of experience, and therefore the telling of counter-narratives can "expose the construction of a dominant story by suggesting how else it could be told" (Harris *et al.* quoted in Andrews 2002: 3). In this sense, master narratives can be re-owned and reappropriated by tellers' individual accounts, but also personal tellings can contribute to the opening up and redefinition of the available inventories of plots.

5.4.2   *Researcher-researched story co-ownership*

The above discussion is revealing of a long-standing preoccupation within narrative studies with "who owns the story" and with the tendency to accord a certain primacy to experiential ownership (i.e. the teller being the experiencer and the main character in the tale). This goes hand in hand with the stated aim of narrative inquiry, right from its inception, of legitimating lay experience within scholarly research. This anti-positivist epistemology has at times romanticized ownership issues and to some extent shielded them from the researcher's presence. The fact that the story was "likely to be the product of an interactive situation (an interview dialogue, for instance) [was] largely effaced in the telling, thereby creating the illusion that the resultant story is self-sufficient, wholly 'one's own', surging up from the depths of Being" (Freeman 2006: 133). The question of where the researcher stood in the process of the teller's soul-searching and piecing together of her or his life story has thus only recently been seriously addressed. As a result, there has been some criticism about the realism of interview narrative data, and more precisely about the tendency to treat interview stories as expressions of the teller's self, instead of narratives embedded in interactional events ultimately shaped by the local context of the interview and by the role and agenda of the researcher in it (for a detailed discussion, see section 6.2).

Looking into the researcher–researched relationships has thus refocused the issue of teller ownership to the idea of co-ownership and co-authorship with the researcher. Interview stories have thus been increasingly viewed as co-productions: told in face-to-face interaction with a researcher, for her or him and in response to her or his questions. In addition, the analysts' very act of interpreting interview stories inevitably involves some kind of "rewriting" or of "re-owning." The original – largely idealistic – mission of narrative scholars to let the voices of their subjects be heard can never be a completely unmediated experience. As Andrews points out, "our lives are never only our own; others interpret and reinterpret the meaning (or lack thereof) contained within them" (2008: 2). What is more, any attempt to make sense of the lives of others will be connected with "the vantage point" from which a researcher "views the world" (p. 1). This makes any interpretation both a provisional, incomplete act and an act of active meaning-making of somebody else's story through the researcher's own story and life experiences. "New experiences, and new understanding of old experiences, bring with them a new perspective not only on our own lives – our present, as well as our pasts – but on the way in which we make sense of the lives of others" (p. 1).

If the act of interpretation of somebody else's story is inevitably a never-ending, partial act of (re)appropriation by the researcher, then the master narratives that we found to play a pivotal role in the telling of a story are bound to be instrumental in this process. Indeed, the "shared" plots that the researcher will be bringing in to interpret the stories under analysis will ultimately (re)shape them, making them speak to her or his own concerns and frameworks of interpretation. Many researchers have recognized this hermeneutic circle (i.e. the researcher (re)constructing and (re)writing the researched) and have opted for various reflexive accounts of their narrative data to try and redress it or, at the very least, acknowledge it (see Cavallaro Johnson 2008; De Fina 2009b, 2011). One way, increasingly gaining ground, has been to revisit narrative data many years after their initial collection and interpretation and rework and reinterpret them on the basis of the researcher's current life story projects and concerns but also, and perhaps equally importantly, on the basis of the researcher's current engagements with developments in narrative studies and other related disciplinary work. In these reflexive journeys, Andrews (2002), for instance, has been astonished to find that stories that she had read earlier as stories by elderly female political activists, would be "re-read" as stories about various models of motherhood. Thus, she acknowledges the role played by her being a mother in this data revisiting. Riessman (2002, 2004) has also gone back to data collected twenty years before with a focus on divorce and gender and reflected on the reasons for her different reading second and third time round. To begin, she reflects on how in her initial analysis, carried out at a time at which the researcher-researched relationships had not been problematized as much as they have been recently, she "left major aspects of [her] positioning out of the representation, referring to [herself] as an anonymous 'interviewer'" (2002: 200). In a reanalysis of a divorce narrative told by Tessa, the author acknowledges that her original reading of her story as a story of "survival" did not do justice to other, running in parallel, emotions in Tessa's account: that of insecurity and fear of an abusive husband. As Riessman (2002: 200) claims:

I am not suggesting that my representation was false – only partial and incomplete, in part because of an over-identification, but also because Tessa was one of many research participants in a study of the divorcing process. I read her account in the context of other women's, where freedom from limiting and abusive relationships was a central theme.

I took strength from Tessa's talk about surviving and edited from awareness the hardships of her life and vulnerability.

Riessman's and others' revisitings of narrative data cast serious doubt on stories collected for research purposes, as being able to "stand on their own" and "speak for themselves" (p. 209). They thus move the issue of narrative ownership from the naïve representational view of stories as being owned by their tellers to the murkier and more complex questions of stories as being complex products of the observer's and observed subject's shifting voices and subjectivities. We will return to such reflexive accounts of researcher–researched relationships in section 6.3.4.

5.5   Conclusions

In this chapter we have probed into questions of narrative power, authority and truth in institutional contexts as well as into issues of story ownership and representational power in the domain of narrative inquiry itself. In the process, we put under scrutiny the main concepts that, in our view, have allowed analysts to understand how stories can contribute to social inequality and shape cultural struggles. In particular, we have reviewed research that has uncovered

- the role of stories in access to and control over social processes;
- the interactional and rhetorical strategies used in storytelling to encode/construct power, authority and credibility;
- the role of contextualization and re-contextualization as mechanisms that allow people in positions of power to dominate less powerful partners in storytelling events.

Thus, we have shown, for example, that narrative inequality lies in, among other things: the ability or inability of tellers and recipients to use storytelling as a resource; their possessing (or not) the tools to shape their narratives as acceptable textual genres in the social contexts in which their telling occur; their having (or not) the power to interrupt, redirect and to re-contextualize a story; being able or unable to draw on a privileged social position or on restricted fields of knowledge to legitimize their constructions and interpretations of reality.

We have argued in favor of research approaches that link the close analysis of very local meaning-making processes with the operation of wider social mechanisms of power, control and inequality without abandoning the inquiry into the specificity of the discursive and social practices that characterize social encounters or domains of communication. In that respect, it is hoped that these kinds of investigations will cover further ground by extending the domain of research to a greater variety of institutional and social contexts.

We have also discussed how storytellers shape, in various ways, the versions of reality that are to be presented to audiences by emphasizing the trustworthiness and credibility of their accounts, by building them on the foundations of a variety of shared cultural constructs, but also by separating those events that are seen as tellable from the untellable ones. In this area, particularly in research dealing with ideology and truth, we have found a predominance of critical discourse analytic studies. Researchers operating within this tradition have done well in documenting storytelling in public discourse and in the media as a crucial site for the (re)construction of cultural hegemony and therefore also as a crucial area of investigation into power and inequality. That said, as we have argued, a common pitfall in some of these studies is the lack of close textual analysis, and the reliance on all-encompassing categories such as the construct of meta-narratives that obliterate the specific nature of storytelling as a type of discourse practice. Some of these problems may be overcome through a greater integration of ethnographic approaches with critical discourse analytic methodologies. It is also important to emphasize the need to avoid the temptation, still lingering in some critical discourse analyses, to reduce power and domination to the mere imposition of ideologically biased interpretations of events; also to overlook the variability and contradictions that exist in stances and ideological positions even within the same media outlet and the same news reporting. Such a critical awareness would imply placing greater emphasis on the processes that lead to the production and circulation of narratives in the media as well as opening up research to different kinds of media narratives and their intertextual connections.

Finally, we discussed how researchers' views of collective and private ownership may determine the focus of their investigation, and how a decision about who owns the story often determines how a story is understood. The same critical awareness that we have advocated for in research on storytelling, power and inequality needs to illuminate the researcher's own methods and premises. For this reason analysts need to look more closely at how constructs such as authority, ownership and truth are applied in their own collection, analysis and interpretation of narrative data.

6   Narrative and identities

6.0   Introduction

In this chapter, we will discuss the multiple relationships that exist between narrative and identities, how links between the two have been conceptualized within different paradigms and what questions are raised by research in this field. In particular, we will look at biographical, sociolinguistic and conversation-analytic work on identity and explore similarities and differences amongst them, with the help of key concepts such as positioning, categorization, self-presentation and indexicality. Our general aim is to document and evaluate a shift in the field from psychologically based conceptions of identity largely centered on the individual self and its expressions in language to more recent views in which identity is seen as a process firmly grounded in interaction.

The first problem that every analyst is faced with when attempting to study the interactions between narrative and identity is the difficulty of defining identity itself. Although the latter has become one of the most important concepts not only in linguistics but in a variety of disciplines within the social sciences, it is surprisingly hard to find precise definitions and a basic agreement on them. This is because characterizations of identity vary according to the basic theoretical assumptions inspiring the researchers who have proposed them. In any case, definitions and choices of terms reflect the fundamental oppositions around which the debate over identity has evolved in the social sciences in general. Identity can be seen and defined as a property of the individual or as something that emerges through social interaction; it can be regarded as residing in the mind or in concrete social behavior; or it can be anchored to the individual or to the group. Furthermore, identity can be conceived of as existing independently of and above the concrete contexts in which it is manifested or as totally determined by them. Finally, it can be regarded as substantially personal or as relational. The methods for studying identities in language have been profoundly influenced by these alternative views.

A further problem is that the area of inquiry concerned with the study of interconnections between language, narrative and identity does not constitute a unified field. Research has developed in and across a variety of disciplines, such as social psychology, linguistics, anthropology, history, just to name a few, and studies belong to different traditions and employ a variety of methodologies. That said, the so-called biographical studies of narrative exhibit many commonalities in terms of how they view the self and its constitution through narrative. As we will discuss, such studies have become canonical in the field, but there has also been a parallel, even if more recent, move toward views of identity that place interactional processes in the constitution of the self at the center of attention, and that stress the social nature of identity, its plurality and its interdependence on different levels of contextualization.

Below, we will consider what has contributed to the formation of this interactionist paradigm in identity studies, namely the movement toward a non-essentialist view of the self, the conception of identity as a social construction, and the emphasis on relationality as central characteristics to identity processes. We will subsequently structure our discussion around studies that are derived from biographical approaches (section 6.2), and studies that are inspired by the interactionist paradigm (section 6.3). This separation should not be taken as marking clear-cut boundaries in so far as interactionist trends exist within biographical approaches (see, for example, section 6.2.1 on positioning), while autobiographical narratives often constitute the data of many interactionally oriented studies.

6.1   The interactionist paradigm

6.1.1   De-essentializing the self

Identity is traditionally associated with the self. For this reason, most recent theorization on identity rests on a re-conceptualization of the self as a category, in particular on a critique against the view of the self as unitary and continuous, residing in the individual mind or spirit, and often also characterized by rationality and free will. From this perspective, the self is an essence that can be grasped and described and its characteristics can be isolated and do not essentially vary through time. In his excursus on the historical development of personality theories, McAdams (1996: 297) argues that an open reflection on the crisis of the self as an autonomous and well-constituted entity dates back to the nineteenth century, when a substantial number of Westerners started writing about the problems in experiencing themselves as unique and integrated persons. However, modern psychology, particularly in the United States, has been, and to a certain extent still is, dominated by a paradigm in which the self is seen as a property of the individual, firmly located within the mind and abstracted from experience and interaction with others. In her fascinating review of psychological theories of the person, Vivien Burr (2002: 4–5) notes that the modern conception of the individual as a rational and moral being, defined by a fixed set of traits constituting her or his personality, is in fact relatively recent, and typical of the Western world. It is traceable to the rise of individualism between the Renaissance and the seventeenth century when it culminated in the Cartesian ideal of the individual as an essentially rational creature. Central to this conception was a separation between individual and social and between mind and body and a view of subjectivity as firmly situated in the mind. This notion of the self also underlies dominant trends in psychology; for example, the quest for the essential traits that describe different types of individuals and can serve as behavior predictors. It has, however, also given rise to a pervasive dualism in which oppositions are set between the individual and the group, the personal and the social, intellect and action and which has infiltrated theories of personality, determining a never-resolved fluctuation between behaviorism and cognitivism.

The tendency to essentialize and abstract the self from its social environment has come under growing attack in the last forty years thanks to a mounting awareness of the changes that have occurred in social life in postmodern societies. Observers of contemporary societies, such as Anthony Giddens (1991) and Zygmut Bauman (2005), note that postmodern life is characterized by uncertainty, fracture, physical and social displacement and by the experience of flow and disunity. Modern men and women have lost their certainties and their allegiance to systems of beliefs and traditional structures of social organization and have become much more aware of the lack of continuity and permanence both in their personal life and in the environment.

6.1.2   *Identity as social construction*

The rise of social constructionist thinking in different areas of knowledge has been an important influence in the shift toward de-essentializing self. In it, the basic idea is that social reality does not exist as an independent entity. In their groundbreaking work *The social construction of reality*, sociologists Berger and Luckman argue that the social world, even if it appears to stand as an objective entity, is in fact built by human action and interaction and is not independent of it. Individuals continuously constitute social reality and are constituted by it in a dialectical process. In their words: "Society is a human product. Society is an objective reality. Man is a social product" (1966: 79). Two principles are apparent here: (i) all social categories are created and negotiated through processes of communication amongst human beings; (ii) the individual and the social do not stand in opposition to each other and cannot be conceived of as separate.

Social constructionism has become the dominant paradigm in linguistic theorization about identity. Linguistic anthropologists, ethnomethodologists and sociolinguists alike have also found in it a strong theoretical basis for the

claim that processes of identity construction are closely connected to linguistic and communicative processes. Indeed, if the self is not seen as pre-existing
social interaction, but as constituted through it, and if identities are bound to
social contexts, then language has an extraordinarily important role in this constitution, since it is at the center of most of the social practices in which human
beings are engaged. Identity is, therefore, a process, not an entity, something
that does not belong to individuals but rather emerges in interaction and within
concrete social practices and is achieved through discursive and communicative
work (Zimmerman and Wieder 1970). As we will see, this fundamental idea
underlies very different approaches to identity in narrative, such as positioning
theories (Davies and Harré 1990), studies of identity as performance (Bauman
2004) and talk-in-interaction approaches (Antaki and Widdicombe 1998).

6.1.3   Identity as a relational phenomenon

The growing awareness, within linguistics and related disciplines, of the role of
interaction as a fundamental site for the constitution of identities has posed further challenges to essentialist conceptions of the self. Interaction is relational
in that the feelings, behavior and ideas of one person are constituted within the
flow of communication, a flow that implies a constant work of mutual understanding and reacting. Language is the main tool for this (re)fashioning, and
its role as well as the constant presence of "the other" in any process of self-
recognition and expression have long been recognized. In his early work on
subjectivity, Emile Benveniste ([1966] 1971), for example, equated the subject with the subject of speech, but he also pointed to the act of speaking as
involving a dual role as a speaker and as a listener and a continuous alternation
between the "I" and the "you."

Similarly, Bakhtin (1981) emphasized relationality and multivocality in his
influential conception of language and communication as essentially dialogic
and multivocal, insofar as the voice of the individual is inextricably tied to the
voice of others.

Another angle on relationality comes from symbolic interactionism in
psychology and sociology. Symbolic interactionists see the individual as a
fundamentally social being and propose role taking as an essential process
of identity management and negotiation. This conception is clear in Mead's
construct of the "generalized other" (1956: 110), according to which a person
always acts based on social rules that she or he expects to be shared by others
and therefore that both acting and interpreting action always involve indexing
and understanding social processes. From this perspective, people construct
themselves using others' interpretation of their behavior as a fundamental
point of reference; therefore, identity can never be seen as a process originating in a solitary ego. Similar views are implicit in Erving Goffman's influential

work on the interaction order and on self-presentation. Goffman believed that human beings always need to manage themselves in social situations and that self-presentation is at the core of social interaction. He saw participants in an interaction as continuously defining and redefining their roles in order to maintain control over the situation. This role play and the management of self-presentation are major enterprises in social life. His notion of "face" embodies such a vision in that it represents identity as managed and negotiated, not as internally construed. "Face," says Goffman (1967: 5),

may be defined as the positive social value a person effectively claims for himself by the lines others assume he has taken during a particular context. Face is an image of self delineated in terms of approved social attributes – albeit an image that others may share, as when a person makes a good showing for his profession or religion by making a good showing of himself.

Here, too, identity is stripped of all essentialist qualities to become an entirely social process, and attention is directed to the mechanisms that allow individuals to manage and negotiate their selves in social circumstances. A pivotal notion in this respect is that of *footing* defined as "the alignment we take up to ourselves and the others present as expressed in the way we manage the production or reception of an utterance" (1981: 128), which as we will see, is central to a great deal of work on narrative and identity.

6.2   The storied self: identities within biographical approaches

Narrative has served as a major methodological tool for researching people's identities in a variety of disciplines within the social sciences. It is important, however, to emphasize that only a particular type of narrative has mainly served as the object of this inquiry, namely the life story and less frequently the so-called short range stories of landmark events (e.g. stories of pregnancy, marriage, divorce, illness, etc.). The latter are reminiscent of Labov's narratives of personal experience which, as we saw in Chapter 2, were collected as a response to the question "Were you ever in danger of dying?" Common to both types of stories is that they are routinely elicited in research interviews. Also, both involve personal past experience from which the teller has sufficient distance to be able to reflect on them. Such narratives have been employed as heuristics for the inquiry into tellers' representations of past events, and into their ways of making sense of themselves in light of these past events. The guiding assumption has been that the telling of stories allows the teller to bring the coordinates of time, space and personhood into a unitary frame so that the sources "behind" these representations can be made empirically visible for further analytical scrutiny in the form of "identity analysis."

The study of narrative as a point of entry into the teller's personal, social and cultural identities has undoubtedly been the main focus within studies inspired by the narrative turn which we discussed in Chapter 1 (e.g. McAdams 1988, 1993; MacIntyre 1981; Polkinghorne 1988; Sarbin 1986). Most of those studies are often grouped together as proposing a "biographical" approach to identity. It is also common to talk about identities in biographical approaches as "narrative identities": the assumption here is that narrative uniquely affords the analyst a glimpse of how people construct a sense of self; also, that narrative is so closely linked with life and experience that it is the prime way of making sense of them in the form of stories about "self." In McAdams' oft-quoted terms: "Identity is a life story. A life story is a personal myth that an individual begins working on in late adolescence and young adulthood in order to provide his or her life with a purpose" (1993: 5). Similarly, Bruner claims that "in the end, we become the autobiographical narratives by which we 'tell about' our lives" (1994: 53). We can see in both views a sort of developmental and temporal perspective: with living comes the telling and retelling of the life story and in that process comes unity, coherence and a stable and continuous sense of self across time and space.

This definition of one's identity as the crux of the interconnection between life as a whole and narrative has fundamentally incorporated the idea of one ideally coherent life story. In Strawson's view, this interconnection can be rephrased in the form of two normative and dominant ideas: The "narrativity thesis" according to which life is experienced as a narrative, and the "ethical narrativity thesis" according to which "experiencing or conceiving one's life as a narrative is a good thing; a richly narrative outlook is essential to a well-lived life, to true or full personhood" (2004: 427). It is thus fair to say that research on narrative and identity within biographical studies has privileged both a certain kind of subjectivity and certain kinds of identities. More specifically, there has been a focus on the project of "storying" oneself as intrinsically oriented toward coherence and authenticity. In this respect, most studies have focused on how, even though through a dynamic process, tellers gradually move to a unified and rather stable account of self that is interwoven into their life story (e.g. Brockmeier and Carbaugh 2001; Daiute and Lightfoot 2004). The ethical narrativity thesis is lurking behind this view: the point is that "the unity of a narrative embodied in a single life" is equated with "the unity of an individual life" and in turn with "a good life" (MacIntyre 1981: 203). Put more succinctly, a good life is seen as one that has narrative unity. This idea has indelibly marked the methods of biographical researchers. Not only have their data for exploring the teller's self almost exclusively consisted of life stories, but also these life stories have been collected in interviews that have been designed so as to encourage and elicit coherent and unified accounts. The search for and imposition of structure and unity in one's life story has been considered as part of a therapeutic process, and disjunctures, ruptures and lack of coherence have been seen as evidence of a life that has not been sufficiently assembled, reflected upon and rendered meaningful. Self and narrative have thus been typically brought together in ways that emphasize the ideas of autonomy, integration, consistency and coherence over those of fragmentation and relationality (cf. on this point, Roberts 2004). Fragmentation implies a view of the self as being discursively constructed as different things on different occasions that cannot be automatically reduced to a singular and coherent entity nor easily abstracted from local contexts. Relationality, on the other hand, includes the idea that the self derives its capacity for self-perception and self-definition through relations and interactional negotiations with others. Both these views have met with resistance within biographical narrative analysis where personal narrative seems to be presented as a model of how we should configure ourselves as selves striving for a purposeful and convincing whole (Parker 2003: 314). To many, this is a Western type of ideal encompassing neo-Cartesian individualist views of personhood and privileging unity and integration of a singular and "authentic" self through the piecing together of a well-structured and orderly life story (e.g. see De Peuter 1998: 32–4).

   The biographical view of narrative identity in the sense of the "storied self" has become a well-established and dominant paradigm across a wide array of disciplines. Overall, the paradigm has been slow to move away from representational accounts of the self (i.e. accounts of the type of person that a life story presents its teller to be) that treat stories as more or less authentic, transparent and unmediated records (see Atkinson and Delamont 2006) to interactional views of identity construction. As Shuman rightly points out, "the biggest challenge to the study of personal experience narrative continues to be to avoid the conflation of experience with the authentic and the real" (2005: 9).

   In contrast to this trend, as we will see in this chapter, interactional approaches to identities have become increasingly mainstream within sociolinguistics. Research on the communicative how of identities in talk has been flourishing, and recently there has been a proliferation of sociolinguistic studies of narrative and identities (e.g. De Fina 2003a; chapters in De Fina, Bamberg and Schiffrin 2006; Georgakopoulou 2007).[1] That said, biographical approaches to narrative have had a profound influence on linguistic analyses of narrative identities, particularly in the early stages of research. Such language-focused studies have drawn on the tradition of biographical research, for example, through the exploration of the discursive mechanisms by means of which tellers create coherent images of self over time and space. In this respect, as we will see in section 6.3.1 below, they have drawn on themes resonant within biographical studies of narrative identities.

6.2.1   Identities and positions

In line with what we suggested above, within biographical research of narrative and identities, there has been a long-standing tradition of investigating how socioculturally available – capital D – discourses (variously called "meta-narratives," "master-narratives," "scenarios," etc.) are drawn upon by tellers in order to make sense of themselves over time and of the defining events that happened to them (see, for example, Kerby 1991). A concept that has informed numerous studies of narrative and identity with this focus is that of *positioning*. Davies and Harré (1990: 48) introduced this concept in a seminal paper in which they defined it as "the discursive process whereby selves are located in conversations as observably and subjectively coherent participants in jointly produced story lines." This definition firmly locates the construction of selves and identities in interactional sites (*conversations*) and in this way subscribes to a discourse-based approach to identity. In fact, drawing attention to the dynamism of social interactions has been the starting point of this influential study. In this respect, positioning served as an alternative to purely cognitive and non-discursive concepts such as roles, norms and intentions. The idea was that such concepts could be made explicit and uncovered with a discursive methodology that allows analysts to look into how people realize them in their conversations. The notion of position thus has served as an umbrella concept that captures "clusters of rights and duties to perform certain actions" (Harré and Moghaddam 2003: 4) which are assigned, reassigned and dynamically negotiated in conversations. This stated interest in the interpersonal aspects of people's positioning of one another has nonetheless not been translated into a truly interactional approach. For one, Harré and his colleagues have routinely employed made-up examples of narratives rather than actual data, be they conversational or interview ones. Second, positions appear to have a cognitive status to the extent that there is an assumption that people mentally store sets of roles and rules, as a sort of non-discursive moral order, which can then be realized and traced (by the analysts) in discursive environments. This is a far cry from the vision of positions as discursively constructed and emergent, not as pre-existent entities, in interactional contexts that, as we will see below, has been adopted by recent interactional studies of positioning.

Although Harré's work is only one – albeit influential – of many strands of research on narrative identities and positioning, what brings most of these strands together is the tendency to postulate culturally available subject positions a priori of specific data and subsequently to look for how they impact on specific narratives. Within this tradition, the individual is seen as being assigned certain subject positions by pre-existing structures variously called "master narratives," "dominant discourses," "cultural texts" or, in Foucauldian terms, "culturally available subject positions" that are postulated a priori of specific interactions. The emphasis then is on "extracting" or "looking out for" how these positions are realized in particular instances of communication (see, for example, the discussion in Widdicombe 1998: 199ff.) in order to show their connection with wider cultural narratives. Participants in local storytelling events are seen as capable of engaging in various processes of negotiation: from drawing on and assigning positions to negotiating and resisting them. Thus, the fact that agency does come into play in the discursive "realization" of positions is not disputed by positioning analysts. However, the methodologically problematic assumption is that positions are independent, pre-discursive entities that exist out there ready to be taken off the shelf and to be reproduced and revealed in discursive action.

These assumptions have been heavily contested, among others, by discursive psychologists who, drawing on conversation-analytic premises, have called for attention to local contexts, that is, to how people locally accomplish identities through interactional and linguistic moves such as characterizations and person references (see the discussion in sections 6.3.3 and 6.3.4 below).

6.2.2   Interactional approaches to positioning

As suggested above, a great deal of positioning analysis has not been tuned into the emergence of positioning processes through details intrinsic to an interaction. It has also shied away from an exploration of the fleetingness and contingency of identity work in local storytelling contexts. Recently, however, there have been various moves to redefine positioning as an interactionally oriented mode of analysis. The assumption here is that, rather than being positioned in a deterministic way by out-there structures, speakers actively and agentively select, resist and revisit positions. These processes are more or less indirectly marked or cued in discourse by specific devices that can be subsequently used as an analytical platform for the exploration of speakers' identities (for examples, see Lucius-Hoene and Deppermannn 2000; Wortham 2000).

One of the most influential moves toward an interactional approach to positioning is traceable to Bamberg's (1997a) three analytically separable yet interrelated levels, which were postulated as heuristics for the ways in which tellers "do" self in narrative tellings. The first level explores positioning in the taleworld, i.e. it examines how the narrator as character is positioned vis-à-vis other characters in the world of the story. More specifically, this level involves the representation of characters (e.g. descriptions, evaluations) and event sequences and the ways in which these relate to social categories and their action potential. The second level looks at positioning as an interactional process and accomplishment, emerging from the ways in which the narrator as teller in the here-and-now positions himself vis-à-vis his interlocutors. What tellers do and which aspects or sense of self they present as relevant is co-drafted with their interlocutors in local contexts of storytelling. Finally, the third level seeks to provide an answer to the question of "who am I?" – attempting to define the teller's self as a more or less stable entity holding above and beyond the current storytelling situation. Here, the issue is to what extent the construction of a sense of self in the segment under analysis can be traced back to individual conversational moves and to what extent it depends on discourses that seemingly impose themselves onto participant structures and individual sense-making strategies.

With this model of positioning, Bamberg's aim has been to move to an analysis that grounds self and identity in the interactive engagement of storytelling. As he has repeatedly stressed, the basic point of departure in his model is the action orientation of the participants, not what is represented or reflected upon in the stories told. In this way, his focus is on how people use stories in their interactive engagements to convey a sense of who they are and not on how stories represent the world and identities.

Bamberg's model has been taken up in numerous studies of interview and conversational stories, as it affords an analytical apparatus for linking local telling choices to larger identities. However, exactly how the three levels relate to one another and particularly how the analyst arrives at the teller's sense of self as pertaining above and beyond the local telling context (level 3) remain open questions. More specifically, the analytical status of master discourses or story lines (level 3) is not entirely clear. How does level 3 differ from previous accounts of positioning that have been criticized as static and operating a priori of actual storytelling data? How can master discourses be locatable through fine-grained analysis of specific storytelling instances? These are questions with no fast and easy answers, but it is notable that interactional analyses of positioning, even if not converging with Bamberg's model, seem to draw upon its conceptualization, particularly the idea that positioning is connected with the double temporal logic or chronology of narrative: that of the *told* world (cf. level 1) and of the *telling world*, i.e. the here-and-now of storytelling (see section 1.1.1). Tellers position themselves in both these worlds, and as we will see below, they frequently draw strategically on the opportunities afforded by their coexistence for self-presentation. We can see positioning operating in both these worlds, for example in Lucius-Hoene and Deppermann's (2008) recent model. Like Bamberg, Lucius-Hoene and Deppermann explore the positioning of the told self as protagonist and of other actors as characters within the story and the positioning between the self as teller and the listener(s) in the here-and-now of the telling situation. Level 3 in Bamberg's model is absent here so there is no alternative proposal as to how one can get to the teller's more or less "constant" and "stable" self through identity analysis in storytelling instances.

Another proposal to use positioning as an analytical apparatus for an interactional account of autobiographical narrative has been developed by Wortham

(2000, 2001). In similar vein to Bamberg, Wortham offers his analysis as an example of how we can approach narrative not just as a vehicle of representation of denotational content but rather as a means for positioning narrator and audience interactionally (2000: 166). Wortham specifically identifies five types of positioning cues, that is, linguistic choices that narrators use to position themselves and others in storytelling events or, to put it in his terms, to present self and other as "socially relevant types" (p. 172). The first positioning device is the narrators' selection of words and expressions to denote their characters. Characterizations or categorizations are frequently studied as explicit ways of doing positioning (cf. Deppermann 2007). Wortham also claims that narrators in representing their characters when talking choose certain *metapragmatic verbs* (e.g. "negotiated," "was talked into," etc.) to describe the current event of speaking. Such verbs may be seen as a second positioning device. A third positioning cue is the attribution of *quoted speech* to characters. A fourth device involves *evaluative indexicals*, that is, implicit characterizations of situations or events that presuppose something about characters' social positions and position the narrator with respect to those. For instance, in the autobiographical narrative of a woman called Jane which Wortham analyses, the detail that at the academy she went to as a child "you were allowed to visit with your mother on Sundays only," acts as an evaluative indexical of the teachers' and administrators' ethos. In particular, the teachers are implicitly portrayed as "cruel and blinded by archaic notions of discipline" (p. 173). The fifth and final positioning cue involves *epistemic modalization*, that is, language choices which characterize the relative knowledge status of the teller vis-à-vis the characters. For example, the epistemic status of the narrator as teller in the here-and-now may well be presented as different to the epistemic status of the narrator as character in the told world. We can see how the distinction between the telling and the told world for positioning in narrative underlies Wortham's model too.

Broadly speaking, in the above studies, positioning has been employed as a meso-analytic concept, a means of establishing linkages between the tellings of stories – and specific interactional choices within them – on the one end, and larger processes beyond the here-and-now of interactions on the other end.[2] This is not an unprecedented analytical move. It is by now a truism that the business of establishing links between language choices and social processes, including identities, is no more straightforward than any connections between text and context can be. Similarly, such links are seen as complex, indirect and mediated. In the search for analytical tools for establishing those links, a number of related concepts have been invoked: e.g. *footing, frame, stance, evaluation* and *involvement*. When talking about stance as one concept "with unclear and overlapping reference," Coupland and Coupland make an argument that could be easily extended to all of them, namely that their value is to direct us to orders of discourse in the mid-range of social contextualization, somewhere between identities and the roles associated with the management of turns or particular communication genres.

In that respect, they can be seen as "a useful corrective to analytic approaches which assume that identities can be read off from the surface forms of talk" (Coupland and Coupland 2004: 29). Similarly to such concepts, positioning has exemplified the tension between micro- and macro-analytic projects by accounting for the details of interactions, without losing sight of extra-situational resources and processes (e.g. larger social roles and identities beyond the here-and-now). However, what exactly counts as a positioning cue is not uncontroversial (cf. Georgakopoulou 2000: 188). This is not helped by the broad remit of positioning as comprising all the "discursive practices which people use to present themselves and others as individuals or performers of roles, which claim and display certain roles, identity-properties, [and] group-membership" (Lucius-Hoene and Deppermann 2008: 2). This definition encompasses personal, social, role-related properties and, importantly, as we saw in Harré's model too, moral attributes. In other words, it somehow equates the scope of positioning with yet another elusive concept, that of identities, leaving considerable lack of clarity about the relationships between the two.

A related question is if there is anything specific or unique to positioning (cues) in narrative as opposed to other types of text/discourse. It is also the case that the analysts who have seen positioning as providing a bridge between local choices and larger identities tend to variously use it and call upon it as both a participants' and an analysts' resource (Georgakopoulou 2000: 189). The study of positioning seems to require that the analyst decide what counts as positioning and what type of dominant discourse is drawn upon or indexed in each case. As we will see below in more detail, this is a more generalized concern in interactional studies of narrative and identity. Finally, interactional studies of positioning are increasingly recognizing the need to analyze it in a range of stories other than the autobiographical narratives (see Bamberg and Georgakopoulou 2008) and with a focus on positioning not only self but also other (see Georgakopoulou 2005b).

6.3   Shift to narrative and identities-in-interaction

Interactional approaches to identities, also commonly characterized as approaches to identities-in-interaction, have become increasingly mainstream within sociolinguistics in general. What brings these approaches together is their dynamic conceptualization of social identities: Identities are viewed as locally occasioned, discursive projects that interrelate with language forms in indirect and mediated ways as opposed to one-to-one correspondences. Emphasis on the constitutive role of language in social identities, coupled with the recognition that identities can be multiple, fleeting and irreducibly contingent, has thus precipitated a shift of interest from category-bound research with a demographic basis, to practice-based research. This means that the focus is not on who people *are*, or who they are perceived to be a priori of language data analysis, but on what or who they *do being* in specific environments of language use for specific purposes. Instead of being seen as the speaker's properties, identities are taken to be articulated and constructed in talk where they can be negotiated, contested and redrafted (Androutsopoulos and Georgakopoulou 2003; Antaki and Widdicombe 1998). This shift represents a far cry from earlier views of identities as singular, static and given properties that at some point in one's life become finished projects.

As we will discuss below, a first step into an interactionally sensitive approach to narrative identity was taken by work on self-presentation which explored the use of a variety of semiotic resources for conveying a sense of self.

6.3.1   Identities as self-presentation

Narratives are often used by tellers to convey positive images of themselves or to counter negative perceptions that others may have about them. Within sociolinguistic studies of narrative, the exploration of self-presentation has been the first point of entry into how tellers do self. In the earlier, essentially post-Labovian, studies of self-presentation, the term *identity* was seldom used. Instead, the emphasis was on how storytellers create images of themselves and negotiate a certain kind of persona with interlocutors. Self-presentation is very much related to the teller's ability to "keep a narrative going" (Giddens 1991: 54), the assumption being that, by presenting themselves and others as characters in story worlds and by negotiating these self-images with interlocutors, tellers are able to portray themselves as people who think and act in specific ways without directly talking about who they are.

An example of how narratives may be used strategically to construct positive images of the self can be found in Charlotte Linde's (1993) study of life stories told by successful professionals in interviews about choice of profession. Linde singles out coherence as a central strategy in the construction of successful life stories. Coherence systems provided both a frame giving unity and continuity to professionals' life choices and a structure of values allowing them to cast their past actions against the background of widely shared beliefs and expectations about rights, obligations and roles of professionals in society. Amongst these complex coherence systems, which occupy "a position midway between common sense ... and expert systems" (p. 163), are cultural constructs such as astrology or Freudian psychology. Drawing on these frames to present their life choices, individuals are able to construct their current personas as the result of a series of connected developments.[3]

Another way of examining self-presentation in narrative has been proposed by Schiffrin in her analysis of stories told in sociolinguistic interviews by women talking about conflict in family matters (1996), Schiffrin showed that tellers construct and negotiate different aspects of their selves. Specifically, she drew on the distinction between epistemic and agentive selves originally proposed by Bruner (1990) to argue that tellers may present different facets of themselves depending on whether they report actions or feelings and beliefs. In her words: "We present ourselves epistemically when we state our beliefs, feelings and wants; agentive aspects of self are revealed when we report actions directed towards goals, including actions that have an effect on others" (p. 194).

Tellers usually display both aspects of the self in at times coherent and at times conflicting ways. For example, in one of the stories that Schiffrin analyzes, the teller, Zelda, recounts her difficulties, and eventual failure, in getting her daughter-in-law to address her using an acceptable address term such as "mom," or even to call her by her first name. Her epistemic position is that daughters-in-law should try to overcome any problems they may be having and accept to call their mothers-in-law "mom" as a way of breaking emotional barriers. However, her agentive self, as constructed through a consistent lack of confrontational actions in her story world, appears to be that of an accommodating person who tries to be understanding and to propose alternative solutions in order to maintain family harmony. Schiffrin shows in her analysis how epistemic selves are often (but not necessarily) constructed explicitly, i.e. through external evaluation and the open discussion of beliefs and opinions, while agentive selves are indexed through the actions of the teller as a character in the story world. She also argues that the concept of position captures the dialectic relation between epistemic and agentive selves on the one hand, and the self that emerges in interactional negotiations on the other. In her analysis, Schiffrin underscores the fact that self-presentation is conveyed through the form, the content and the performance of a narrative. At the level of linguistic forms, for example, narrators may use syntactic indicators (such as a contrast between direct and indirect reported speech) or contextualization cues (such as intonation contours) to convey a certain persona. At the level of content, they may manipulate the sequential order of actions in the story or the kinds of speech acts performed by characters. In terms of performance, they may alternate utterances from the story world and non-story world in order to create contrasts.

Research on self-presentation has in general showed how presenting an image of self in interaction relies on all these levels. People do not resort to a single strategy but use combinations of linguistic and paralinguistic structures to build their self-image in stories. Amongst these strategies, two have received special attention: the teller's alignment toward others and the negotiation of authorship and responsibility in order to assign and distribute blame and praise.

The analysis of both aspects owes a great deal to Goffman's work on footing and on participation frameworks (1981) that we discussed in Chapter 4. Goffman proposed that presenting oneself in interaction implies taking a certain footing or alignment toward other participants. In Schiffrin's example, one can argue that part of Zelda's self-presentation as tolerant and collaborative is related to her footing to the interviewer, to her effort to appear understanding and her appeal to commonly shared social norms. Let us go back to Goffman's deconstruction of the notion of speaker that we saw in Chapter 4. He distinguished between the following production roles: *author* (the person who created the utterance), *animator* (the person who physically produces an utterance), *figure* (somebody who belongs to the story world, a character) and *principal* (someone who is committed to what the utterance says).

This self-lamination has been central to the analysis of self-presentation, particularly in cases of reported speech. When speech is reported, the different interactive meaning-making contexts related to narrative are activated. Tellers are situated in a storytelling world in which they evoke a story world. However, they also animate the story world in which the interaction of the characters occurs. Tellers (and listeners) thus shift from one world to the other, creating multiple relations between themselves and the story world they are evoking. It is worth reminding ourselves at this point of the importance of reported speech as an evaluative device going back to Labov's model (1972). Post-Labovian studies further documented that, as an evaluative device, reported speech can contribute to the creation of a certain self-image for the teller. In particular, studies have related reported speech to two specific aspects of self-presentation: morality and agency.

In relation to this first point, Ochs and Capps have noted that: "tellers strive to represent themselves as decent, ethical persons who pursue the moral high road in contrast to certain other protagonists in their narratives" (2001: 284). A number of studies have shown how reported speech enables the tellers to present themselves as moral selves by allowing them to activate scenarios in which they can highlight their own ethical positions (Moita Lopes 2006; Relaño-Pastor and De Fina 2005; Vazquez 2007). It has been illustrated, for example, how tellers, instead of openly discussing their moral principles and beliefs, often voice them through dialogues in which they participate as story world characters. Such animations have the advantage of supporting their self-presentation as active and morally engaged, but also of highlighting the values they stand for. Reported speech has also been related to agency inasmuch as it has been shown that narrators may mobilize this strategy to emphasize or de-emphasize their own role, involvement and accountability in the reported situations, thus presenting themselves as agentive social actors. Indeed, often characters who speak are also characters who stand out and actively take particular roles in the story world. Hamilton (1998) described, for example, how patients' reports of speech acts initiated by them and by doctors and medical personnel in online narratives of conflict underscored their own role as active survivors. Conversely, reported speech may be used strategically so as to diffuse the teller's responsibility and accountability in the social field and to diminish their agency. By putting words into characters' mouths, the tellers can actually voice ("animate") their own opinions but without taking responsibility for them (Georgakopoulou 2005b).

Schiffrin's work is instructive here too. In comparing expressing opinions with telling stories (1990), she showed how narratives allow the tellers, particularly by means of reported speech, to assign certain aspects of themselves, including their views and beliefs, to characters and in that way to decrease their responsibility for them. In Goffman's terms, this means that tellers may keep the role of the animator for themselves but assign the roles of author, figure and principal to characters. This presents serious implications for how agency may be constructed. For example, De Fina (2003a) found that immigrants tended to downplay their agency in narratives about crossing the border to the United States by giving other characters greater speaking space and by attributing to them pro-active speech acts, such as suggestions and requests, while presenting themselves as silent. Such a strategy was one among others that tellers used to avoid presenting themselves as fully responsible for choosing to become undocumented immigrants.

It is not only when in the narrative and why tellers introduce reported speech that has attracted the attention of analysts in terms of self-presentation. It is also who is being quoted, how and how frequently that has been looked at as a marker of the teller's social identities. In Johnstone's corpus of middle-American stories (for details, see discussion in Chapter 4), the fact that women reported talk more frequently than men was linked to gendered differences in storytelling practices both at the level of action and at the level of reported interaction. Similarly, in Georgakopoulou's study (1997) of Greek stories, both male and female tellers were found to quote overwhelmingly men speaking. This was viewed as an index of socioculturally shaped notions of who counts as a source of evidence and/or as an expert. Put differently, the animation of male voices was a more powerful vehicle for constructing evidence for the teller's views.

Reported speech is a particularly well-studied strategy of self-presentation, but other discursive devices have also been examined as resources that the narrators deploy in order to convey certain images of who they are. In her study of male inmates talking about their own crimes, O'Connor (2000) talked about "authorial shaping" as the process through which tellers construct their narratives in ways that allow them to create a certain image of themselves. She argued that for prisoners it was important to show that they were changed persons and that they had in them the potential to become different people. Therefore, they often distanced themselves from the crimes that they had allegedly committed or tried to involve the addressee in their evoked story worlds as a way to create empathy. Among the strategies analyzed by O'Connor were irony, understatement and the construction of agentless crime stories as ways to deflect responsibility.[4] On the other hand, she pointed to switches between first and second person pronouns (*I* and *you*) as a prominent mechanism for involving the addressee into the story world, creating empathy and presenting a reflective self.

Although self-presentation is still a significant area of analysis, recent work has started to abandon the focus on the self and to favor analyses that take into account the interactional emergence of identity categories as a collaborative project between tellers and audiences. In much of this research, the concept of *indexicality* is a central one as it captures the process through which linguistic elements are connected to social meanings in ongoing processes of meaning creation. In the following sections we will explore these developments.

6.3.2   Identities as social categories

Although definitions and characterizations of identity vary widely, one main definitional criterion involves ascribing or claiming membership into groups. For example, according to a widely quoted definition by the social psychologist Tajfel, identity is "that part of an individual's self-concept which derives from his knowledge of his membership in a social group (or groups) together with the value and emotional significance attached to that membership" (1981: 255).

There would be much to say about identity being described as "self-concept," but the point we want to underscore here is that group membership is essential to a sense of identity. The delimitation of group boundaries is implicit in social identity categories such as those related to gender, age, occupation, etc., and it is for this reason that the study of categorization has recently come to occupy center stage in research about identities. Indeed, if identity has to do with belonging to social categories, the study of how they are used and negotiated in discourse becomes an important task for discourse analysts. Categorization is an extremely significant mechanism, not only in storytelling, but in discourse in general, as it lays bare the basic assumptions and stereotypical views that members of a group hold with respect to themselves and others. As Bucholtz and Hall (2005: 594) rightly observe:

The most obvious and direct way that identities can be constituted through talk is the overt introduction of referential identity categories into discourse. Indeed, a focus on social category labels has been a primary method that nonlinguistic researchers have used to approach the question of identity ... The circulation of such categories within ongoing discourse, their explicit or implicit juxtaposition with other categories, and the linguistic elaborations and qualifications they attract (predicates, modifiers, and so on) all provide important information about identity construction.

In the past, sociologists and anthropologists such as Durkheim (1954) and Lévi-Strauss (1963) highlighted the role of classification systems in cultural and social processes. They argued that such systems are the molds provided by culture within which individuals and groups construct oppositions and affiliations, similarities and differences. They are thus basic to the creation of social meanings in general and of identity in particular. The role of language in these processes of categorization is crucial in that it is through language that membership categories are constructed and negotiated. The analysis of how these processes are managed in discourse, i.e. of how categories for identification are produced and made relevant by participants in interaction, has become one of the main areas of interest within studies of identity and is central to the movement of Membership Categorization Analysis (hence MCA; see, for example, Antaki and Widdicombe 1998; Hester and Eglin 1997). The proponents of this approach have worked around ideas on categorization first developed by Sacks (1972b and [1966] 1992e) to explain the underlying assumptions according to which interactants create and use "membership categories," that is, employ a set of practices to refer to people and routinely link certain activities to them. Sacks, whose main interest is in how categories of membership figure in the common-sense worlds, describes the operation of generic reference categories in discourse. He says that categories such as "women," "blacks," "Jews" are used in a special way in that they are not seen just as designating individuals but as describing collections or sets of categories that go together (e.g. male/ female) and as generalized entities so that judgments and attributions made in relation to them cannot be falsified. He sees such collections of categories as grounded in relationships (e.g. mother/baby) but also in knowledge, in particular professional knowledge. He also sees such categories as intrinsically bound to social activities:

We have our category-bound activities, where, some activity occurring, we have a rule of relevance, which says "look first to see whether the person who did it is a member of the category to which the activity is bound." So that if somebody does being a fickle, or is observably being rich, you might then have a rule that permits you to select a preferred category to see who they are. And of course, using that procedure for finding the category, you may never come across occasions for seeing that it's "incorrect" in the sense that the first procedure I suggest would end up showing.

Now, one consequence of that procedure's use is, if it turns out that someone is a member of some category, then what you have is an explanation, X is fickle. Why? Use the relevance rule. It turns out that the one who did it is a woman, and women are fickle. One importance of these statements, then, is that they make some large class of activities immediately understandable, needing no further explanation. ([1966] 1992e: 337)

The MCA movement has strongly advocated a methodology of analysis of categorization processes in discourse centered on members' orientation to social identity categories and on local constructions of what belonging to those categories implies. In particular, Antaki and Widdicombe (1998) and Edwards (1997) have argued that analysts should not assume the relevance of political or social identity categories for a particular interaction unless such relevance is manifested by the participants themselves. Since Sacks' influential work, there has been an internal dialogue within conversation analysis about the validity and applicability of MCA, not helped by the fact that Sacks did not work with conversational data when he developed MCA. In reviewing the history of MCA in the field, Schegloff (2007: 464) states:

As the focus of CA work came increasingly to be on conversational materials, carefully transcribed, the work on categorization devices receded ... One key site for work on categorization has been story telling, and that may not be coincidental but worth pursuing. For example, a great deal of the subsequent work by others that draws on MCA is addressed to interview data, that is, data in which recounting is done, but which does not focus on the interview itself as a site of talk-in-interaction. Still, the relevance of membership categorization has seemed to many to extend past these boundaries to the very constitution and organization of perception, of understanding, of the character of stipulated reality, to the organization of experience. The question is whether it is possible to find a way to re-engage or adapt the early analytic work to the sort of data which the current state of the art requires – a constraint which Sacks himself insisted on. The answer to that question is by no means clear.

Recent studies of categorization in storytelling have pointed to the need to combine close attention to how identities are locally constructed with how larger constructs (e.g. ideologies) play within local interactional displays (see Bucholtz 1999a; De Fina 2000 and 2006; Flannery 2008; Kiesling 2006; Moita Lopes 2006). This work has shown how tellers give situated meanings to categories describing race, ethnicity and gender, how they align or distance themselves from groups that are "naturally" associated with them, how different categories are often interconnected in discourse, and how stories are used to back up and negotiate positions about the social characteristics of in-group and out-group members. They have also underscored the role of macro-social categories and processes such as practices of exclusion and discrimination for locally constructed identities. For example, in his analysis of narratives told by a Brazilian boy, Hans, during a fifth grade literacy event, Moita Lopes (2006) shows that race and gender categories are associated in his discourse and that those associations reflect mainstream discourses about sexuality. Hans tells, for instance, a brief story in which he depicts his father scolding his sister for being out in the street instead of staying home while at the same time instigating him going and finding a girlfriend. In the story, Hans uses his father's words to legitimize both his own masculinity and his vision of what it means to be a man in society by creating an opposition between men and women through a characterization of the former as hunters and the latter as prey. In addition, Hans indexes this vision about men and women by presenting his father as the most authoritative character in the narrative and as someone who dictates to members of the family what they should or should not do. These oppositions between "normal" and marked identities are built in the stories around stereotypical views of blacks as lazy, homosexuals as weird and pathetic, and women as sexual prey and are supported through the recounting of the actions that black, homosexual and feminine characters perform in the stories.

In other cases, commonly shared views about particular categories may become the object of critical scrutiny.

Conversation analysts have been particularly attuned to the study of categorization in institutional settings. For example, Stokoe (2006) and Stokoe and Edwards (2007) analyzed person formulations (cf. references) in neighbor dispute mediation (e.g. mediation sessions, telephone calls to mediation centers). They found that such person formulations did not occur as direct descriptions (e.g. "She is an X") but in reported speech, and ultimately in narrative accounts (e.g. "They called me an X"). These stories normally reported why the teller's previous attempts to solve problems with neighbors had failed and often served as scene-setting devices, which described a trouble-free, pre-dispute period of time. The important finding in Stokoe and Edwards' study is that identity-relevant categories such as person formulations were put to use methodically in specific interactional environments, presenting systematicity in their location and design as well as in the types of responses that follow them. For instance, a systematic practice for reporting racial insults involved pairing national or ethnic categories with another word (e.g. *Paki bastard*, *bitch Somali*) or editing the racial insults with generalizers and extenders (e.g. *black this*). In both cases though, the two-word formulation was maintained, either by indexing the swearword or by stating it next to the ethnic or racial category. Such person formulations received a continuum of response types from the mediation interviewers, from explicit assessments to minimal but aligned acknowledgments in mediation talk, to no affiliative response in police interviews. This work is a good example of how an identities-in-interaction approach can uncover systematicity in the use of categorizations in conversations by social actors. However, in this case as with other MCA analyses, little is said about how exactly telling a story is linked with the uses of categorizations and the types of responses they generate. This is despite the attested close association between person formulations and reported speech (which in itself is part of a story). As we have said previously (see Chapter 4), a certain lack of attention to stories in their own right characterizes most conversation analysis. As a result, here too there is much scope for exploring, from a conversation-analytic point of view, how identities as categorizations are worked up within the context of telling a story and how that differs from or compares with other discourse activities that take place in a conversation.

In an attempt to redress this balance, Georgakopoulou (2008) examined self- and other-categorizations, ascriptions and characterizations (cf. in her terms, identity claims) in stories as narrative-interactional resources. For the analysis, she postulated the distinction between *taleworld* and *telling* identity claims, recognizing that the immediate sequential context in a storytelling event in which claims occur is consequential for their interactional management. *Taleworld identity claims* pertain to characters (either third parties or the teller as a character) in the reported events and are embedded in the narrative (inter) action (e.g. they may occur in reported speech: as in *He was looking so sexy*). *Telling identity claims* on the other hand pertain to the interactional level of the here-and-now / you and I of the local storytelling situation and either suspend the narrative action (reminiscent of external evaluation; Labov 1972) or serve as a follow-up/coda to the reported action: e.g. *I'm too smart for sweet talk*.

The analysis showed that in the context of the classroom stories of 14-year-old female students in a London comprehensive school, such identity claims were predominantly about physical appearance and modes of conduct. They were also organized relationally, in contrastive pairs of positive and negative attributes (e.g. "pretty" – "ugly"). Finally, they were associated with likes and dislikes and with certain category-bound activities in plots and in that respect served as membership categorization devices. This system of organization comprised hierarchies of attributes and thus (re)constructed notions of normative value agreed upon in the local network: for example, what it is appropriate for a man or a woman to say, act like, where applicable wear, etc. in specific environments ranging from MSN (with web cam) to text-messaging and so on. The study also showed that taleworld identity claims supported the main teller's rights to tell the story's events and contributed to their tellability. Telling identity claims, on the other hand, were normally produced in relation to a story's evaluation and the overall assessment of the characters talked about. There, they set up spaces for co-construction between teller and interlocutors and a joint exploration of moral frames. Overall, identity claims were drawn upon as interactional resources, in order to justify, defend or challenge a point of view. In similar vein, the tellers did not always wholeheartedly subscribe to an identity claim made, but at times they playfully invoked it and distanced themselves from it.

Showing how identity claims in stories ultimately perform social actions and are sequentially managed stands in contrast to the tendency within biographical research on narratives to take identity claims at face value and in representational terms, when in actual conversations, identity claims are primarily interactional resources. In fact, as we will see in the following sections, looking at explicit identity ascriptions and categorizations is only one part of what the identities-in-interaction approach includes in its remit. There is also systematic attention to the ways in which semiotic resources and details in the conversational management more, or less, subtly index larger social roles.

6.3.3   Identities as semiotic resources: indexicality

We saw in the previous section that identities can be identified through social identity categories. Sometimes the criteria for membership into these categories or the social consequences of belonging to them are openly discussed and contested. However, a great deal of identity work is done much more indirectly, through the use of symbolic processes. Sounds, words, expressions of a language, styles are associated with qualities, ideas, social representations and entire ideological systems. These in turn are related to social groups and categories which are seen as sharing or representing them, in a process of meaning creation that rests upon accepted social meanings but at the same time constantly modifies them. This process of pairing of utterances with extra-linguistic categories has been called *indexicality* (Silverstein 1976) based on the idea that symbols (not only linguistic ones) "index," or point to something that is external to them. Phonological traits and styles of speaking may become symbolically associated with complex systems of meaning such as ideologies, social representations about group membership, social roles and attributes, presuppositions about all aspects of social reality, individual and collective stances, practices and organization structures. Thus, for example, dropping *-ing* endings may be associated with popular speech and may be used by a speaker as an index of authenticity. Or, speaking English with a French accent may be related with being sexy. Recent research on narrative (see, among others, Bucholtz 1999a; De Fina 2006; Georgakopoulou 2007; Kiesling 2006; Maryns and Blommaert 2001) has emphasized the importance of a close analysis of the ways in which these resources are deployed in narrative, arguing that such a detailed study of talk allows for a deeper understanding of the subtleties and complexities of identity work. Indexical processes are often revealing of the coexistence of conventional and creative ways in which people use social knowledge to construct themselves and others.

The analyses have shown that identities are projected through clusters of indexical resources that involve juxtapositions of narrated action, choice of words and syntax, metaphors and cues such as intonation, rhythm, code choice and switching, etc. Often these clusters amount to particular styles of telling that become associated with identities based on shared social knowledge. An example of the complexity of these mechanisms is provided by Mary Bucholtz (1999b) in her analysis of how masculine identities are managed and projected in a narrative told in a sociolinguistic interview. The story, told by a Californian male student, centers around a mugging perpetrated against him.

In the example, the narrator and protagonist is white while the story world opponent is African American, and race is signaled as an important construct by the teller himself. Bucholtz notes that in the first part of the narrative the teller reproduces stereotypical associations between language, race, gender and identity by presenting his African American opponent as violent and therefore reinforcing an ideological representation of black masculinity as characterized by physical brutality and aggressiveness. Bucholtz shows that at many points in the story, the white student uses African American Vernacular (henceforth AAVE) phonology, intonation and grammar in constructed dialogue to characterize his opponent. When his antagonist speaks, his use of AAVE together with word selection and intonation projects and indexes the identity of a physically and verbally abusive person. For example, after pushing the protagonist, the African American character is depicted as saying, "what you gonna do you little *punk* ass *whi:te bi:tch*" (1999b: 448). This utterance indexes the aggressiveness of the antagonist through the choice of words (the use of insults), syntax (AAVE copula deletion, i.e. the absence of the verb to be in "what you gonna do"), and the juxtaposition of the utterance with violent action (pushing). In the same scene, the narrator as character in the story world speaks in a colloquial variety of English and is depicted as non-confrontational through his actions. In other parts of the dialogue, the African American antagonist is characterized as using further typical AAVE features when his speech is reported. For example, he uses a monophthongal (ay) and glottalized word-final (d). These elements co-occur with a description of actions and utterances that index aggressiveness and violence. Thus, the stylization of the antagonist's AAVE speech in the story is central to his characterization as violent. Bucholtz notes that these associations between the use of AAVE and aggression are indexically produced via a widespread ideology of masculinity in which African American males are constructed as physically overbearing and violent. Allegiance to such ideology is presupposed by the teller. However, there are other points in the narrative in which the narrator himself crosses[5] into AAVE. These instances of language crossing co-occur with the description by the narrator of his encounter as a story world figure with two school friends who are African American and who save him from the grip of his antagonist. When reproducing his own words in the dialogue with these two friends, the narrator himself uses features of AAVE speech. In this case, then, the code shift indexes his identification and solidarity with African Americans, rather than his opposition to the group. As Bucholtz explains, identification with aspects of the African American culture is an aspect of the urban youth identity that many white boys embraced in the High school in which the research took place.

   The significance of this analysis lies in that it shows how tellers may use exactly the same linguistic resources to make completely different identity claims. In this case, switches into AAVE index in one case distancing and in another case alignment with members of the African American community. Another important point here is that identities can be complex and multilayered and can combine competing (dominant and non-dominant) ideologies (e.g. the view of black people as physically abusive and cool at the same time). Finally, the analysis also shows how the same narrator can switch between very different identity enactments in the same narrative.

Indexical cues can be very subtle. In their analysis of stories told by an asylum seeker in Belgium, Maryns and Blommaert (2001) discuss how speakers use patterns at different levels (linguistic, thematic, affective, epistemic, etc.) to organize the narration. They illustrate that stylistic shifts between distinct patterns are very subtle, both because the speaker uses a mixed language that incorporates elements of different varieties and because he plays with different voices that enact varied selves (the rebel, the victim, the black man in Europe, etc.). Thus, changes in identities and stances in this case get communicated through a clustering of indexical cues that belong to a variety of levels of structure. In the authors' words (p. 79):

the narration of experience is mediated through a number of micro-shifts and this at various levels: structure (intonation, grammar, etc.), mobilizing heavy stylistics, place-time articulations (narrative mode associated with place) and through identity work. Packages of performance can actually be identified as "voice" and identity building.

Work on indexicality has greatly contributed to our sense that the study of the enactment and production of identity within narrative cannot be reduced to the analysis of themes and explicit affiliations, but it still needs to delve into the immense richness of linguistic resources at all levels of expression.

6.3.4   Identities-in-interaction and telling roles

The current emphasis on the fluidity and emergence of identities in discourse, particularly in interactional sites, where they can present a multiplicity of meanings, brings together approaches to discourse as diverse as social constructionism and conversation analysis (Widdicombe 1998: 201). Nonetheless, there is far less convergence on how the discourse constructions of identities relate to factors that are external to a specific interactional situation (sic *exogenous*). Despite the focus on the communicative how of identities within identities-in-interaction, exactly how identities are located in interactions and how they can be linked with macro-social identities remain points of theoretical and methodological debate. The conversation-analytic view very much locates the macro in the micro and as such sees a person's identities as their display of, or ascription to, membership of some social category, with consequences for the interaction in which the display or ascription takes place. Which category or combination of categories, and which of the characteristics it affords are matters of changeable arrangements made locally. Membership of a category is ascribed (and rejected), avowed (and disavowed) and displayed (and ignored) in local places and at certain times, and it does these things as part of the interactional work that constitutes people's lives. In their introduction to the oft-quoted volume *Identities in talk*, Antaki and Widdicombe specify five principles which a conversation-analytic approach to identities endorses:

1. For a person to "have an identity" – whether he or she is the person speaking, being spoken to, or being spoken about – is to be cast into a category with *associated characteristics or features* (the sort of thing you'd expect from any member of that category; their actions, beliefs, feelings, obligations, etcetera).
2. Such casting is *indexical and occasioned*. That is, it only makes sense in its local setting.
3. The casting *makes relevant* the identity to the interactional business going on.
4. The force of "having an identity" is its *consequentiality* in the interaction – what it allows, prompts or discourages participants to do next.
5. All these things are visible in people's exploitation of the *structures of conversation*.

This nose-to-data approach and the single-minded focus on the specifics of a local interaction are not shared by all analysts. Drawing upon a wide range of social science and sociolinguistic approaches, Bucholtz and Hall (2005), for instance, propose a more synthetic, sociocultural linguistic, framework of identities analysis, which "focuses on both the details of language and the workings of culture and society" (p. 5). Their five principles are still premised on a view of identities "as intersubjectively rather than individually produced and interactionally emergent rather than assigned in a priori fashion" (p. 6). However, they also include local ethnographic categories and they aim at forging links between identities as discursively constructed in local contexts and larger, macro-social categorizations. The principles in question are as follows:

1. Emergence: Identities are viewed as emergent products, a fundamentally social and cultural phenomenon (p. 7).
2. Positionality: This principle stresses the fact that identities "encompass macrolevel demographic categories, local, ethnographically specific cultural positions and temporary and interactionally specific stances and participant roles" (p. 14).
3. Indexicality: By this principle, the links between language choices and social identities, instead of necessarily and automatically being direct, straightforward and explicit, are variously implicit, indirect and based on associations.

4. Relationality: In this case, identities are not seen "as autonomous or independent but always acquire social meaning in relation to other available identity positions and other social actors" (p. 26). Furthermore, identity relations include "sameness/difference, similarity/difference, genuineness/artifice, and authority/delegitimacy" (p. 26).
5. Partialness: This principle stresses the fact that any construction of identity is ever-shifting as the interaction unfolds, partly habitual, partly strategic and partly the outcome of interactional negotiation (p. 28). Taking this argument further, we can claim that no analytical account of identities construction can be complete and comprehensive.

This turn to identities-in-interaction within socially minded approaches to language has also been gaining currency within narrative analysis. As we have already suggested before (section 6.3.1), in this systematic turn to identities, one of the first domains to capture the analysts' attention was the ways in which tellers presented aspects of their self by making the most of the possibilities that the separation between the here-and-now of the narrative telling and the there-and-then taleworld (cf. told, narrated events) afforded them. More recently, however, there has been a shift toward exploring ways of connecting narrative tellings with larger social identities. This inquiry involves scrutinizing the narrative genres and their specific language and interactional choices for how they more, or less, subtly and indirectly point to (cf. index) aspects of the teller's identities, such as ethnicity, gender, age, etc. Context remains a key concept in this respect, and although there is an undeniably long-standing tradition of contextualized studies of narrative (e.g. ethnography of communication in studies such as Bauman 1986 and Hymes 1981, among others) there are distinct elements in this latest shift that, as we have argued elsewhere (De Fina and Georgakopoulou 2008a), qualify it as a "new" narrative turn:

1. An increasing acceptance of narrative as talk-in-social interaction informed by conversation analysis (e.g. Georgakopoulou 2007; chapters in Quasthoff and Becker 2005; Schegloff 1997).
2. An emphasis, derived from recent theories of context and genre (e.g. Bauman 2001), not just on the *contextualized* but also on the *contextualizing* aspects of narrative. In this sense, narrative is being studied both for the ways in which its tellings are shaped by larger sociocultural processes at work, including social identities, and for how it provides organization for the interactive occasions on which it occurs.
3. An increasing commitment to social theoretical concerns (mainly within the framework of cultural studies). This is particularly evident within studies that focus explicitly on narrative and identities (e.g. De Fina 2003a; De Fina, Bamberg, and Schiffrin 2006; Georgakopoulou 2002, 2007). One of the tasks here has been to problematize, de-essentialize or add nuance to

the widely held view that narrative is a privileged communication mode for making sense of the self.

This line of inquiry has already come a long way in forging links that are by no means presented as deterministic between narrative and identities through a focus on the action properties of language in narrative and away from the representational accounts of narrative studies in the social sciences.

This latest and more dynamic shift to narrative and identities-in-interaction has generated a renewed interest in co-construction. Within biographical research, it is fair to say that the researcher–researched co-construction has been widely acknowledged (e.g. Phoenix 2008; Squire 2008) as part of narrative interviews but mostly in general terms and not through painstaking, fine-grained analysis. On the other hand, a lot of the really groundbreaking work on teller–audience co-construction from an interactional point of view, which we discussed in Chapter 4, was carried out before the turn to identities-in-interaction and without a specific focus on identities. As a result, there is currently much scope for bringing the two together. Indeed, the premises of identities-in-interaction, as outlined above, necessitate a scrutiny of what kinds of local participation roles tellers assume in the course of a story's telling and in turn what roles they project for their audience. Zimmerman (1998) has developed the idea of identities as participation roles that can provide an empirical handle on social identities. He suggests the following three kinds of identity at play in any social encounter:

Discourse (or interactional) identities, such as "questioner," "answerer," "inviter," "invitee," etc., which may well shift in the course of an interaction. Discourse identities are tied to the sequentiality of a conversation (e.g. adjacency pairs). As they are formed in and by participants' actions, they constitute the type of activity underway and provide particular resources and constraints for the participants' display of values within it (pp. 90–1).

Situational identities, such as "teacher," "student," "doctor," "patient," which come into play in particular kinds of situation. These are brought about by local telling roles and are connected with the topic at hand and the activity underway. In turn, situational identities link the local with the distal context of social activity by proposing to the interlocutors how they should understand the relevance of an exchange (p. 89) and by invoking the participants' differential types and degrees of knowledge and skills regarding the activity underway.

Transportable identities (cf. exogenous, extra-situational) which are latent, travel with individuals across situations, and are potentially relevant at any time in a given interaction (e.g. "adolescent black girl," "middle-aged white woman," etc.).

Discourse identities have been shown to be one of the components of the conversational machinery that circumscribe and make salient the participants' larger social identities, constituted of such attributes as gender, age, professional status, etc. (Goodwin 1987). As such, they provide a point of entry into the exploration of the connection between the micro- and the macro-level of any interaction, in other words, of how details intrinsic or endogenous to the specific situation of the interaction make available or visible extra-situational resources. Put differently, these are assumed to furnish for the participants "a continuously evolving framework within which their actions … assume a particular meaning, import, and interactional consequentiality" (Zimmerman 1998: 88). In this way, they provide not just the relevant proximal turn-by-turn context but also the distal context for social activities, that is, the oriented-to extra-situational agendas and concerns accomplished through such endogenously developing sequences of interaction. In general terms, according to Zimmerman, identities-in-interaction can either be "oriented to," actively influencing the way that people try to shape both their own actions and the subsequent actions of others, or merely "apprehended" – tacitly noticed but not treated as immediately relevant to the interaction on hand. In turn, the interactional and institutional identities that a person projects at any moment may be ratified, reformulated or resisted in the immediately following actions of their interlocutors.

This intimate link between discourse and social identities has formed an object of inquiry mainly in talk in institutional contexts (see, for example, papers in Drew and Heritage 1992), where it has been shown how institutionally prescribed and pre-allocated roles, at best, shape and, at worst, constrain the participants' organization of talk (i.e. turn-taking, turn design, sequence organization). As we have argued elsewhere (Georgakopoulou 2006), however, discourse identities (in the sense of local participation roles) have remained largely unexplored in the case of stories.

In a study of the pairing of storytelling participation roles (*sic* discourse identities) with social identities, Georgakopoulou showed how at the local level, different participants contributed in varying degrees to different story components, particularly plot line and evaluation. Furthermore, the participants were differentiated in the degree in which their contributions were ratified and taken on board by others or, equally, challenged and delegitimated. More specifically, the qualitative analysis of the data suggested that there were three types of telling roles that were important as platforms for the participants' larger social roles and identities:

a. The roles that participants assumed vis-à-vis a story's emerging structure
b. The action performed with each of the contributions vis-à-vis prior story talk
c. The shape of a participant's story turn, that is, the local linguistic choices and devices in operation.

A quantitative analysis of the above-mentioned aspects in a corpus of selected stories showed that there were systematic and significant differences in the ways in which each of the four participants (female adolescent friends) tended to contribute to different parts of the story. Another difference involved who ratified or challenged others' contributions more, and by the same token whose contributions were accepted or challenged more. What was perhaps more important was how these distinct telling roles for each participant brought into focus certain situational identities, again systematically assumed by each of them. These identities had to do with role-relevant and topic-relevant knowledge, that is, advice-seeking and -giving on one hand and expertise (in this case, in the topic of male/female relationships) on the other hand. These arrangements were visible in the participants' turn design and choice as well as in their storytelling contributions. For instance, Fotini, a participant who regularly assumed the identity of an advice-seeker and a novice tended to elicit stories from the other – more expert – participants and to pose clarification questions about the plot in the course of a story's telling. In turn, Vivi, who assumed the role of an advice-giver, provided by way of emplotment, solutions and suggestions to such questions.

But the co-articulation of telling with situational identities made also visible certain wider social identities: in the case of this study, gender identities, and the participants' relational identities as close friends. Overall then, the study showed the usefulness of extending Zimmerman's approach to identities-in-interaction to the analysis of stories. It also showed that a close link can be found between identity construction in narrative and a story's (emerging) structure. Looking into this relationship further would build on the interactional line of inquiry to narrative structure, as we discussed it in Chapter 4, which sees structure as raising alternative tasks and types of action for different participants (see Goodwin 1984: 245). Further studies in this direction could shed more light on how the relation between locally enacted participation roles and story parts bears on the tellers' identity construction.

The above suggests that there is still much scope for attempting to tie identities to particular kinds of story sequence and furthermore to examine the kinds of social action that they locally perform.

6.4   Sample analysis

Below, we will illustrate some of the discursive mechanisms for presenting self and others that we discussed above in an excerpt taken from a sociolinguistic interview with a Mexican undocumented worker, Antonio, 36 years old, which focused on his experience with migration. The interview was part of a corpus collected for a study on identity construction through narrative discourse among Mexican immigrants to the United States that we have quoted at different points in this book (De Fina 2003a; see section 3.6). The interviews were centered on questions about the life trajectory of interviewees: why they had migrated, what kind of jobs they had in Mexico, how they had arrived into the USA, found work, etc. and about their perceptions about life in the USA: what they liked or didn't like, whether they had adapted and/or changed as the result of this experience. The interviews were semi-structured: They loosely followed a set of questions but were rather open-ended since the interviewer tended to follow up on answers given by interviewees. The recordings took place at the interviewees' homes and were mostly done in the presence of an assistant researcher who was also a member of the community.

Antonio, the interviewee here, had been coming to the USA on a temporary basis and then going back to Mexico for around ten years. Before the point where the transcript starts, the researcher had asked Antonio about his work experience in Mexico, and about how he had found jobs in the USA. When the excerpt begins, the interviewer is asking him about his impressions of the country when he first arrived.

(6.1)
Participants: (A)ntonio, R(esearcher), I (Assistant researcher)

1	R:	Y qué impresión le hizo el país cuando llegó?
2	A:	(.)
3	R:	Qué pensó cuando llegó aquí, qué era muy distinto qué no era muy distinto?
4	A:	No, en todo es muy distinto,
5		en todo.
6		porque por ejemplo en el pueblo de uno puede andar uno a las dos
7		tres de la mañana en la calle y nunca le falta nada,
8		y aquí no puede usted andar a las tres de la mañana, dos de la mañana,
9		solo,
10		sOlo, verdad?
11		porque pasan muchas cosas y allá en el pueblo de uno, no!
12		allá puede uno andar a la hora que quiera.
13	R:	A usted le ha pasado algo aquí?
14	A:	Nada más una vez (.)
15		nos asaltaron trabajando en un apartamento,
16	R:	Uhu.
17	A:	remodelando un apartamento, entraron y nos asaltaron ahí mismo,
18		a mí y a un patrón,
19		uh?
20		y con pistola y se imagina qué hacíamos,
21		a mí me quitaron veinte dólares que traía nada más,
22		a mi patrón su reloj y su dinero,
23		y toda la herramienta se la llevaron,

24		y y fueron morenos verdad? morenos,
25		y todavía cuando fuimos a poner la demanda,
26		nos dice el policía, 'Y cuántos hispanos eran?'
27	I:	@[@
28	R:	[@@@
29	A:	A ver.
30	R:	Directamente.
31	A:	Uhu.
32		y, y, y se enojó porque, el policía era moreno,
33		le digo "No, eran puros morenos, puros negros,"
34		verdad? (.)
35		ahora por ejemplo aquí ya no se puede salir ya ni en paz-,
36		ya no se vive en paz aquí,
37		por tanta droga que hay, tanta, tanta drogadicción, tanta cosa.
38	R:	Entonces, esa fue una diferencia.
39		y qué otras cosas notó que le parecen diferentes en su país?

Translation

1	R:	And what impression of the country did you have when you came?
2	A.:	(.)
3	R:	What did you think when you came, that it was very different, it wasn't different?
4	A:	No, everything it is very different,
5		everything.
6		because for example in one's village one can go around at two three
7		in the morning, in the street and never miss anything,
8		and here no you cannot go around at three in the morning, two in the morning.
9		alone,
10		alOne, right?
11		because many things happen and there in one's village, they don't!
12		there you can go around at the time you want.
13	R:	Has something happened to you here?
14	A:	Just once (.)
15		they robbed us while working in an apartment,
16	R:	Uhu.
17	A:	remodeling an apartment, they came in and robbed us right there,
18		me and an employer,
19		uh?
20		and with a pistol and can you imagine what could we do,
21		they took from me just the twenty dollars that I carried,

22		from my employer his watch and his money,

22   from my employer his watch and his money,
23   and all the tools they took them,
24   and it was dark-skinned people, right? dark-skinned people,
25   and on top of it when we went to notify the police,
26   the policeman says to us, "How many Hispanics were they?"
27 I: @[@
28 R: [@@@
29 A: Let's see.
30 R: Directly.
31 A: Uhu.
32   and, and, and the policeman got mad because he was dark skinned,
33   I tell him, "No they were all dark skinned, all blacks,"
34   right? (.)
35   now for example here one cannot go out in peace any more-
36   one does no longer live in peace here,
37   because of so much drug that there is, so much so much drug addiction,
        so much stuff happening.
38 R: Then, this was one difference.
39   and what other things did you notice that look different from your
        country to you?

As we can see from the transcript, Antonio does not answer the interviewer's
question about his impressions of the country right away (line 2). However,
in line 4 he starts arguing that everything is different in the USA with respect
to Mexico. We see that he proposes a first opposition between his village and
"here." In his village people can go around freely at any time in the night, while
in the USA many things happen (lines 6–12). At this point, the researcher asks
Antonio a narrative-eliciting question, i.e. if something specific has happened
to him. In response, Antonio produces a typical story-opening device ("just
once," line 14) followed by a Labovian abstract in which he gives the gist
of the narrative: "they robbed us while working in an apartment" (line 15).
As we can see, Antonio does not describe the assailants in the beginning of
the narrative. He simply refers to them as "they" (lines 15 and 17). In line
20, Antonio provides further details on his assailants: he describes them as
being armed with pistols and comments, "Can you imagine what could we
do." In Labovian terms, this utterance functions as external evaluation in that
the narrator stops the action of the story to insert details and comments on the
characters and their actions that convey his point of view on what was happening. In this case, he conveys his and his employer's sense of impotence in
dealing with people who were armed. He then goes on to describe the things
that were taken from him ("twenty dollars") and his employer (his "watch and
some money plus all the tools," lines 21–23). Until line 23, there is not much

evaluation of the events and the robbers have not been identified. However, in line 24, almost as if adding a detail, Antonio identifies the robbers as "morenos" ('dark skinned'). Such a term was used by the Mexicans interviewed in the study as a more "politically correct" label for *negro* ('black'). It is interesting to note that this description has, again, an evaluative function signaled by the repetition of the qualifier at the end of the line. Antonio starts building on the relevance of this description of his assailants in racial terms for the development of the story world action when he recounts that the police that they notified of the assault asked "how many Hispanics" there were (lines 25–26). Notice the function of the expression "on top of it" in the same line to signal Antonio's evaluation of the police intervention as something that "topped" the negativity of the experience. Although nothing explicit is said here about relations between ethnic/racial groups, Antonio is implicitly conveying the idea that the policeman was prejudiced against Hispanics. Such an implicit meaning is partly being conveyed through the use of the expression "on top of it," which, as we saw, implies that the police increased the problematic nature of the situation. It is also communicated through a selective use of reported speech. Indeed the policeman is presented as having uttered exclusively the question about the perpetrators of the robbery. The selection of this particular line of reported speech can be seen as creating an image of the policeman as prejudiced on the basis that it violates a generally shared expectation about police behavior in these circumstances, i.e. that policemen would try to seek information on the identity of the robbers instead of presupposing it. That this implication is understood is clear from the reactions of the audience. Both the researcher and the research assistant laugh here (lines 27–28), and then the researcher comments, "Directly" (line 30), thus indexing that she has understood what Antonio is trying to say. The preceding laughter coupled with this comment shows both an awareness of his interpretation of the behavior of the police as prejudiced and an alignment of the audience with Antonio's implicit rejection of it. At this point Antonio has signaled, and his interlocutors have accepted, the relevance of the identification of the assailants as black for the unfolding of the action in the narrative and its evaluation. He has already indexed the relevance of the opposition black/Hispanic through both external evaluation (his identification of his assailants as "morenos" in line 24) and reaffirms it through use of constructed dialogue. In fact, the characters themselves voice their own understanding of how being black or Hispanic affects the interpretation of events. In particular, as we have seen, the policeman is presented as presupposing that if there is a robbery it must have been carried out by Hispanics (line 26), while Antonio is presented as emphatically contesting that interpretation. The emphasis is achieved through repetition of the robber's race ("puros morenos, puros negros" [all dark skinned, all black], line 33). The relationship between being black or Hispanic and the action in the story world is also emphasized in the external evaluation in line 32 since Antonio explains the policeman's anger with the fact that he was black (notice the use of the connective *because* in "the policeman got mad because he was dark skinned"). The use of these storytelling strategies allows Antonio to convey his stance toward the particular events and characters, but also toward interracial relationships more in general.

Antonio's use of identity descriptors based on race ("morenos," "negros") in this narrative is a good illustration of the way narrators use membership category devices to convey stances and attitudes about identities. In this case, the category "black" is related to the activity of "robbing" and members of the category are also attributed the characteristics of "being prejudiced" (at least against Hispanics) through a variety of devices. In this way, membership categorization devices are used to construct categories that are related to actions and properties in systematic ways and are therefore important in the construction of "us" versus "them" categories. In this case, the "them," i.e. black people, are constructed as criminals and as prejudiced. As we have seen, the narrator stresses the racial origin of the assailants through repetition at different points (lines 24, 32), thus emphasizing the opposition between the facts and the interpretation of the policeman. However, the repetition also has the effect of underscoring the importance of race and ethnicity to understand some further implications of the narrative. In fact, after the end of the story (lines 35–37), Antonio speaks of the difficulty of living in peace in his neighborhood. These lines seem to provide a further evaluation of the story as an example of the kinds of things that happen in the neighborhood based on the experience of the narrator as a victim of robbery. Since, in this case, the narrator underlines the race of the robbers, the meaning of the narrated events changes: it is not just a robbery, but a robbery carried out by blacks. This information creates a relevance space not only with respect to the action in the story world, but also with respect to the more general evaluation of the story: since the narrative has at its center black people acting in a criminal way, all the other criminal activities going on in the neighborhood, such as drug consumption and violence, can also be more easily attributed to them.

In the light of the above, we can say that Antonio is discursively constructing identities indexically, rather than directly or explicitly. A typical mechanism of identity construction in discourse is opposition and Antonio builds an opposition between blacks and Hispanics which is centered on the description of blacks as criminals (the robbers) or in any case dishonest (the policeman) and of Hispanics as victims. These meanings are conveyed indirectly. Nothing is said openly about ethnicity or race relations, but Antonio's stance is indexed, as we have seen, through evaluation, constructed dialogue, repetition, emphasis, and temporal ordering of actions and reactions. Together these linguistic strategies help convey his point on the story and his vision of how having a certain identity implies acting in a certain way toward other individuals categorized as members of specific social groups. However, Antonio is also relying on the mobilization of indexical associations between identities and social characteristics that are part of circulating discourses and representations. For example, the idea that black people are prone to criminal activity is widely circulated in US public discourses.[6] Also the idea that black people do not like Hispanic people is both shared among members of this group and part of circulating stereotypes about minority relations. Thus, although our analysis started from local identity negotiations, it has led us to the consideration of the role of stereotypes that are brought to bear in the interaction. Given the audience responses during the storytelling, the presuppositions sustaining these stereotypes appear to be shared among the three participants. That said, it is also important to note that the researcher was not familiar with prevailing views about race relations in this particular community at the beginning of her research. She reached a certain understanding of how people felt about other ethnic or racial groups through the process of interviewing different members of the community, discussing her observations with them and with the research assistant who also was a member of the community, and gathering other kinds of data and information on Mexican immigrants in the area. In brief, the analyst's interpretation of identity construction in discourse depended on a close analysis of interaction data, but it also went beyond them to the wider context of social relationships, ideologies and stances that may be shared by members of a particular community (for details, see De Fina 2003a, chapters 5 and 6). Making these connections necessitates some form of ethnographic work.

How different would the above analysis be if it had been done from a conversation-analytic perspective? CA analysts would devote attention to the identities constructed within the interactional occasion, pointing, for example, to the situational orientation of the participants as interviewer/interviewee and as teller/audience as elicited by the interview format. The analysis of the use of MCA would have probably pointed to the type of implicit meanings that we have signaled in the construction of black people as a category defined by certain kinds of actions, but there would have been no attempt to relate those meanings to Antonio's macro-identity as a member of a community of Mexican undocumented workers and to circulating discourses in this and the larger community. Indeed, these kinds of generalizations would be seen as illustrations of the analyst imposing her own categories on the data.

In this respect, the two approaches would produce quite different readings of the same data and different answers to the question of how far one can go with an interactional analysis without needing to invoke the concept of identities. However, there are advantages in trying to find a middle ground and in attempting to reduce the distance between more macro- and more micro-oriented approaches. While the consideration of what Coupland and Coupland have called middle-range contextualization (see above pp. 165–6) may allow discourse analysts to understand how local identity construction depends a great deal on processes that lie outside it, greater attention to the local level can prevent them from reaching unwarranted conclusions. In this case, for example, a fine-grained analysis of the discourse management and construction of local roles by participants allows for a more nuanced understanding of categorization processes as it sheds light on the fact that portable identities, such as racial or ethnic ones, are often invoked as part of strategic negotiations with the interlocutor, rather than as categories with absolute and fixed meanings. The balance between an orientation to the local and an understanding of how it relates to the global remains a focal concern in any interaction-focused study of narrative. Answers to this question are bound to shape the direction and synergies of narrative analysis as well as its place in the social sciences.

Notes

1   Narrative definitions, issues and approaches

1 We distinguish here between "classical" narratologists, that is, the founders of the narratological approach to literary texts such as Bal, Genette and Prince, and "post-classical narratologists" who, according to Prince (2008: 115), share the same commitment to formalism as their predecessors but are more interested in studying narrative as "contextually situated practice."
2 However, this assumption is not shared by transmedial narratologists who are interested in the study of narratives in different media. See Herman (2010: 196) who argues that "Unlike classical, structuralist narratology, transmedial narratology disputes the notion that the fabula or story level of a narrative (= what is told) remains wholly invariant across shifts of medium (= an aspect of how that 'what' is presented)."
3 We refer to these authors as structuralists in that they followed some basic principles first laid out by Ferdinand de Saussure. Amongst those, the most important was that languages are systems of elements which can be described based on their combinations and oppositions independently of their concrete use and realization.
4 Prince ([1987: 65] 2003) defines it as "The set of properties characterizing NARRATIVE and distinguishing it from non-narrative: the formal and contextual features making a (narrative) text more or less narrative, as it were."
5 Hortatory discourse in Longacre's terms is any discourse that attempts to persuade the addressee to fulfill commands, and typical examples of it include sermons, political speeches and warnings to children.
6 The definition of genre is yet another complicated and controversial issue. We will, however, discuss the view of narrative as genre within sociolinguistic perspectives in section 3.0.

2   Narrative as text and structure

1 See Mishler (1995) for a discussion of this point.
2 We reproduce the coding proposed by Labov and Waletzky. Note that the authors divide the narrative into lines corresponding to independent clauses, or independent clauses + their dependent clauses, whenever those exist.
3 On this point see Edwards (1997: 141–2).
4 Bauman (1986) showed that dog hunters expect their interlocutors to make up stories. The ability to recount tall tales is regarded as an art among them.

5 Keller-Cohen and Dyer (1997) go as far as arguing that Labov and Waletzky in fact took active steps to constrain the intertextuality of the stories in their data by controlling, for example, the context of the story occurrence (i.e. by means of elicitation) and the type of story (they chose personal stories). In their view, Labov and Waletkzy saw intertextuality as "a resource to manage in such a way as to not infringe into a kind of analysis aimed at drawing generalizations across narrative structures and abstracting a stable structure across contexts" (p. 150).

6 *The Journal of Narrative and Life History*, vol. VII (1997), a retrospective of Labov and Waletzky 1967, makes reference to several of those. Polanyi (1989) is a notable case inasmuch as it was one of the earlier studies to bring into sharp focus the context-specificity of the model, evaluation in particular.

7 The obvious parallels between the notion of involvement (Tannen 1989) and evaluation are a case in point (see Chapter 3 for a discussion). Attempts to formalize "positioning strategies" (see discussion in Chapter 6) have also had to use Labov and the notion of evaluation as a point of departure (e.g. Bamberg 1997a; Wortham 2000). It is notable too that multilevel analyses that introduce narrative dimensions such as teller-tale-telling or narrated vs. narrative event (see Bamberg 1997; Blum-Kulka 1997) that were neglected in Labov's model still more or less explicitly appeal to a notion of narrative structure.

8 The idea that storytelling, even in its everyday forms, has a poetic quality and aesthetic functions has been fruitfully developed by narrative analysts. Polanyi (1982), for example, talked of "literary complexity" as a characteristic of everyday stories, showing that narrators use devices such as indeterminacy, polyphony or indirect free style that are typical of literary forms of language. Tannen (1989) also argued that literary narrative is a refinement of everyday storytelling, that the devices used by everyday narrators to manipulate different voices within a story are close to the ones employed in novels and short stories, and that storytelling, because of its aesthetic qualities, creates involvement in audiences. Building on the tradition of uncovering (instead of erasing) the verbal artistry involved in everyday talk, Georgakopoulou (1997) analyzed performance devices in conversational storytelling, grouping them into theatrical and poetic devices. We will come back to this point in Chapter 3.

9 For example, Poveda (2002) proposes an ethnopoetic reading of a narrative told by a Gipsy child during sharing time (*la ronda*) in a Spanish kindergarten classroom. In similar vein as Gee, Poveda uses ethnopoetics to demonstrate both the high communicative skills possessed by a child belonging to a group that is normally classified as less proficient than other groups in the educational setting, and the existence of storytelling traditions and practices that are profoundly different from the ones known and taught in the Western world.

10 The terms *emic* and *etic*, first introduced by the linguist Kenneth Pike (1967), refer to interpretations produced from the point of view of a member of a specific culture (emic) as opposed to those produced by external observers (etic).

11 See Hutchby and Wooffitt (1998) for an accessible introduction to the conversation analysis.

12 Emergence is discussed in Hanks (1996), and it originates in linguistic research by, among others, Hopper (1987).

3   Narrative and sociocultural variability

1 For a comparison between the two scholars, see Dundes (1997).

2 Hufford (1995: 528) describes contextualist theories of language and culture as emerging from a "pandisciplinary shift from an explanatory quest for universal principles to an interpretive exploration of situated communication."

3 The term *formalist* here is used to refer to views of language in which the focus of attention is on the form, seen as an autonomous level that can be studied in its own merit. Formalism was typical of linguistic models that dominated in the 1960s and 1970s. For example, in his grammar model (1965), Chomsky posited a rigid division between levels of linguistic description: syntax was independent from semantics (the level of meaning) and phonetics (the level of sound). The effect of formalism was seen in the emphasis on the creation of descriptive systems that addressed each individual linguistic level.

4 For a discussion of context in different discourse approaches, see Schiffrin 1994: 365–78.

5 See section 2.2.1, for an explanation of the distinction between *emic* and *etic*.

6 See Darnell (1974: 315) on this point. The author argues that traditional performers change and adapt their performances to different audiences (including researchers) and social occasions.

7 Bauman also aims at an extension and a deepened understanding of the concept of performance relating it not to an idea of "folklore," but to concepts such as verbal art and oral literature. The concept ties verbal art with ways of speaking. In his words: "Verbal art may comprehend both myth narration and the speech expected of certain members of society whenever they open their mouths, and it is performance that brings them together in culture-specific and variable ways, ways that are to be discovered ethnographically within each culture and community" (1969: 5).

8 Similarly, Katherine Young distinguished between different narrative frames that are embedded in what she calls *the realm of conversation*: *the story realm* (i.e. the world of the telling) and *the taleworld* (or the world of the story) (1987: 28).

9 A discussion of the role of detail (particularly orientation detail) in building up audience participation can also be found in Lavandera (1981). The author argued that orientations, besides providing temporal, spatial and personal coordinates for the story, also reflect social expectations about what is relevant to a particular group of speakers. By calculating such expectations, the speaker can create specific pragmatic effects such as audience involvement.

10 A case in point is Georgakopoulou's study (1997) of performance devices in Greek conversational stories. The analysis showed that the sustained use of narrative present and constructed dialogue (two of the main involvement strategies in Tannen's study of Greek storytelling, 1989) was far from a clear-cut culturally shaped performance choice. As it happened, the use of the devices also fulfilled organizational purposes: it demarcated different narrative parts. It was thus difficult to suggest that the devices in question acted as solely or primarily performance or involvement mechanisms.

11 In the original project, narratives were transcribed based on a division in clauses. We reproduced the coding used in the study.

12 The notion of a socio-centric conception of the self, proposed by Hill in connection with pronominal choice, has also been used by social psychologists who have

looked at the degree of social orientation in the discourse of different social groups such as ethnic communities or children (see Dreyer, Dreyer and Davis 1987; and Veroff, Chadiha, Leber and Sutherland 1993).

4   Narrative as interaction

1 Following a sequential approach such as that proposed by Jefferson (1978), Kjaerbeck and Asmuss (2005), observe that story closings often follow a three-step sequence that starts with the punch line, that is the climax of the story. First, the punch line is produced, then the recipient acknowledges the modality of the story, i.e. the kind of story the teller is producing (whether it is a funny, sad, ridiculous story, etc.) and finally the teller acknowledges the recipient's comprehension. The function of this sequence is to negotiate the frame of understanding of the story. Then a post-punch line sequence starts. In this second sequence storyteller and participants negotiate understanding, i.e. they jointly produce Labov's story evaluation (see section 2.1).
2 As we discussed in section 3.4, Blum-Kulka distinguished between three different socioculturally shaped modes of performance based on audience participation and distribution of rights, namely the monologic, the dialogic and the polyphonic mode.
3 Another angle on retellings has been recently proposed by Bamberg (2008) who locates their importance in their ability to put together a sense of self and rework it on different occasions, and therefore regards them as an ideal basis for a developmental look into the formation of self and identity.
4 Norrick (2000) has used the term *diffuse* for those half-tales.
5 The data come from an ERC Identities and Social Action Project entitled 'Urban Classroom Culture and Interaction' (2005–8). The project team comprised Ben Rampton (Director), Roxy Harris, Alexandra Georgakopoulou, Constant Leung, Caroline Dover and Lauren Small.

5   Narrative power, authority and ownership

1 In Bourdieu's terms: "In a determinate social formation, the stabler the objective structures and the more fully they reproduce themselves in the agents' dispositions, the greater the field of doxa, of that which is taken for granted. When, owing to the quasi-perfect fit between the objective structures and the *internalized* structures which results from the logic of simple reproduction, the established political and cosmological order is perceived not as arbitrary, i.e. as one possible order among others, but as a self-evident and natural order which goes without saying and therefore goes unquestioned, the agents' aspirations have the same limits as the objective conditions of which they are the product" (1977: 176).
2 Critical Discourse Analysis, or CDA, whose prominent proponents are van Dijk, (1984, 1993), Fairclough (1989) and Wodak (1999), focuses on the study of language as a form of social practice and has amongst its objectives the use of linguistic analysis to fight social injustice and power abuse. "CDA sees itself as politically involved research with an emancipatory requirement: it seeks to have an effect on social practice and social relationships, for example in teacher development, in the elaboration of guidelines for non sexist language use or in proposals to increase the intelligibility of news and legal texts" (Tischer, Meyer, Wodak and Vetter 2000: 147).

Critical discourse analysts are particularly interested in public discourse such as political discourse, the language of the press and of the mass media.

3 See, for example, Goodwin (1990) and Shuman (1986) on the use of stories to create alignments among groups of adolescents.

4 We use the term *index* to refer to a process through which sounds, words, expressions of a language, and styles are associated with qualities, social roles, ideas, social representations and entire ideological systems. We will discuss indexicality in depth in section 6.3.3.

5 Studies of the inclusion of voices in stories, particularly in instances of reported speech, routinely draw on Bakhtin's (1981) concepts of *heteroglossia* and *polyphony* to describe the stratification of a variety of different and at times conflicting (as in the case of heteroglossia) voices within utterances, and even within the same word (see, for example, Hill 1995).

6 For a review of work connecting the use of reported speech to authority building see Briggs (1996a: 27).

7 Bash, D. McCain tells his story to voters. CNNpolitics.com, March 31, 2008 www.cnn.com/2008/POLITICS/03/31/mccain.tour/index.html. Site accessed 4/5/08.

8 Both these authors talk about the persistence of the political motif of the regular guy, the anti-intellectual and anti-snob in Republican political campaigns. They also argue that both Ronald Reagan and George Bush have been presented this way by their party and gained popularity because of their association with average people. For a press story applying the idea of the regular guy to one of the 2008 Republican presidential candidates (Fred Thompson), see Rodrick (2007).

9 Blommaert's (2005) summary of definitions of ideology is comprehensive and clear. He discusses certain fundamental antinomies, such as those between ideologies as cognitive systems versus ideologies as practices, or between ideologies as monolithic wholes versus ideologies as diffused elements of common sense and proposes some alternatives.

10 See, for example, the following text from the Introduction to a special issue of *Narrative Inquiry* on power and narrative: "The development of each of these three conceptual frameworks [Postmodern, postcolonial and feminist theories], albeit variously expressed, has been founded to a significant degree upon the recognition of the myriad narratives that make up any reality, and all three are thus intricately intertwined. While perhaps not the first, postmodern theorists have been the most influential in articulating and focusing attention on the question of meta-narratives" (Daya and Lau: 2007: 6).

11 See, for example, Fowler (1991) and Hodge and Kress (1993).

12 Taking the case of an indigenous woman unjustly accused of infanticide, Briggs (2007) details, for example, the extremely homogeneous (and, in his view ideologically biased) depiction of infanticide in news stories in the Venezuelan press. According to him, the press criminalized all episodes of infanticide by: placing news stories that focused on this topic in the crime section of the paper and framing them in the lead as stories of crime, embedding them in textual fields that indexically linked them to violent crimes, setting up contrasts between dehumanized parents and romanticized children, selectively quoting witnesses, judges and legal professionals, not giving voice to the accused. Briggs concludes that, "ideological constructions of communication enable powerful actors to determine what will count as silences, lies, and surpluses, just as they create silences of their own – these

cartographies of communication write issues of critical poverty, domestic violence and sexual abuse, and the violence of the state out of infanticide narratives" (2007: 328).

13 Baynham and De Fina defend this political stance in the introduction to their edited volume on displacement in narratives: "In an era in which public discourses, particularly in the media, increasingly present displacements through the lenses of nationalist and racist rhetoric (Wodak and Riesegl 1999), creating atmospheres of social panic in which migrants and refugees are seen as threatening the stable borders of national identities, there is an urgent need for accounts of such processes 'from the inside,' emphasizing through micro discourse analysis the subjective construction of these movements of human beings, rather than the objectivist 'othering' of these in nationalist or racist mainstream discourses, and offering an 'emic' perspective (Harris 1999) on them" (2005: 2).

6   Narrative and identities

1 This turn to identities has been slow, as shown by the fact that the focal concerns of the area looked very different in 1996 when Schiffrin made a plea for sociolinguistic studies of narrative and identities (in her terms, narratives act as "self-portraits").

2 Micro-meso-macro should be understood here as a metaphor, a heuristic for analysis. Not only is the distinction a continuum rather than a trichotomy; there are also multiple levels involved on each end.

3 For a more recent study on self-presentation amongst successful professional women, see Wagner and Wodak (2006).

4 See Anderson (2008) for an analysis of similar strategies in narratives of violence.

5 The term *crossing* is used here to designate the use by a speaker of the language variety of a group that the teller is not demonstrably a member of (Rampton 1995).

6 In his book *A Country of strangers: Blacks and whites in America*, David Shipler writes, for example, "The image of black violence spins through daily life like a dust devil across a plain. It filters so thoroughly into the American consciousness that non blacks actually argue among themselves about whether or not they are justified in discriminating against all black males as a shortcut to security. A *Washington Post* columnist, Richard Cohen, wrote sympathetically of jewelers who refuse to buzz blacks through the locked glass doors of their downtown stores. A public radio host in Washington allowed, without comment or objection, the assertion by Dynesh D'Souza, a right-wing writer originally from India, that taxi drivers should be legally permitted to refuse black men as passengers; this, he claimed, was 'rational discrimination'" (1997: 358–9).

References

Abbott, A. 1988. Transcending general linear reality. *Sociological Theory* **6**: 169–86.

Abell, J., E. Stokoe and M. Billig 2000. Narrative and the discursive (re)construction of events. In M. Andrews (ed.) *Lines of narrative: Psychosocial perspectives*. London: Routledge, pp. 180–92.

Adams, J. K. 1996. *Narrative explanation*. Frankfurt: Peter Lang.

Anderson, K. 2008. Constructing young masculinity: a case study of heroic discourse on violence. *Discourse & Society* **19**(2): 139–61.

Andrews, M. 2002. Introduction: counter-narratives and the power to oppose. *Narrative Inquiry* **12**: 1–6.

  2008. Never the last word: revisiting data. In M. Andrews, C. Squire and M. Tamboukou (eds.) *Doing narrative research*. Thousand Oaks/London: SAGE Publications, pp. 86–101.

Andrews, M., C. Squire and M. Tamboukou (eds.) 2008. *Doing narrative research*. London: Sage

Androutsopoulos, J. and A. Georgakopoulou (eds.) 2003. *Discourse constructions of youth identities*. Amsterdam/Philadelphia: John Benjamins.

Antaki, C. 1994. *Explaining and arguing: The social organization of accounts*. Thousand Oaks/London: SAGE Publications.

Antaki, C. and S. Widdicombe (eds.) 1998a. *Identities in talk*. Thousand Oaks/London: SAGE Publications.

  1998b. Introduction. In C. Antaki and S. Widdicombe (eds.) *Identities in talk*. Thousand Oaks/London: SAGE Publications, pp. 1–14.

Appadurai, A. 2004. The capacity to aspire: culture and the terms of recognition. In V. Rao and M. Walton (eds.) *Culture and public action*. Stanford University Press, pp. 59–84.

Aristotle 1927. *Poetics. Longinus: on the sublime. Demetrius: on style*. S. Halliwell (ed.) Cambridge, MA: Harvard University Press.

  1970. *Poetics*. G. E. Else (ed. and trans.) Ann Arbor: University of Michigan Press.

Arnett, J. 2004. *Emerging adulthood: The winding road from the late teens through the twenties*. Oxford/New York: Oxford University Press.

Aronsson, K. and A. Cederborg 1994. Co-narration and voice in family therapy: voicing, devoicing and orchestration. *Text* **14**(3): 345–70.

Atkinson, P. and S. Delamont 2006. Rescuing narrative from qualitative research. *Narrative Inquiry* **16**: 173–81.

Atkinson, R. 1995. *The gift of stories: Practical and spiritual applications of autobiography, life stories, and personal mythmaking*. Westport, CT: Bergin & Garvey.

197

Baker, C. D. and G. Johnson 2000. Stories of courtship and marriage: orientations in openings. *Narrative Inquiry* **10**(2): 377–401.

Bakhtin, M. 1981. *The dialogic imagination: Four essays*. Austin: University of Texas Press.

1986. *Speech genres and other late essays*. C. Emerson and M. Holquist (eds.), V. W. McGee (trans.) Austin: University of Texas Press.

Bal, M. 1985. *Narratology: Introduction to the theory of narrative*. University of Toronto Press.

Bamberg, M. 1997a. Positioning between structure and performance. *Journal of Narrative and Life History* **7**(1–4): 335–42.

(ed.) 1997b. *Narrative development: Six approaches*. Mahwah, N.J.: Lawrence Erlbaum.

2004. Talk, small stories, and adolescent identities. *Human Development* **47**: 331–53.

2006a. Stories: big or small? Why do we care? *Narrative Inquiry* **16**: 147–55.

2006b. Biographic-narrative research, quo vadis? A critical review of "big stories" from the perspective of "small stories." In K. Miles, C. Horrocks, N. Kelly, B. Roberts and D. Robinson (eds.) *Narrative, memory and knowledge: Representations, aesthetics and contexts*. University of Huddersfield Press, pp. 1–16.

2008. Twice-told tales: small story analysis and the process of identity formation. In T. Sugiman, K. J. Gergen, W. Wagner and Y. Yamada (eds.) *Meaning in action*. New York: Springer, pp. 183–204.

Bamberg, M. and A. Georgakopoulou 2008. Small stories as a new perspective in narrative and identity analysis. *Text & Talk* **28**: 377–96.

Barthes, R. 1977. Introduction to the structural analysis of narrative. In *Image, Music, Text*. S. Heath (trans.) New York: Hill and Wang, pp. 79–124.

Bascom, W. 1965. The forms of folklore: prose narratives. *Journal of American Folklore* **78**: 3–20.

Bash, D. 2008. McCain tells his story to voters. CNN politics.com, March 31, 2008. www.cnn.com/2008/POLITICS/03/31/mccain.tour/index.html. Accessed April 5, 2008.

Bauman, R. 1969. *Verbal art as performance*. Rowley, MA: Newbury House.

1986. *Story, performance and event*. Cambridge University Press.

2001. The ethnography of genre in a Mexican market: form, function, variation. In P. Eckert and J. Rickford (eds.) *Style and sociolinguistic variation*. Cambridge University Press, pp. 55–77.

2004. *A world of others' words: Cross-cultural perspectives on intertextuality*. Oxford: Blackwell.

Bauman, R. and C. Briggs 1990. Poetics and performances as critical perspectives on language and social life. *Annual Review of Anthropology* **19**: 59–88.

Bauman, Z. 2005. *Work, consumerism, and the new poor*. London: Open University Press.

Baynham, M. 2003. Narrative in space and time: beyond "backdrop" accounts of narrative orientation. *Narrative Inquiry* **13**(2): 347–66.

2005. Network and agency in the migration stories of Moroccan women. In M. Baynham and A. De Fina (eds.) *Dislocations/relocations: Narratives of displacement*. Manchester: St. Jerome Publishing, pp. 15–35.

Baynham, M. and A. De Fina (eds.) 2005. *Dislocations/relocations: Narratives of displacement*. Manchester: St. Jerome Publishing.

Bell, A. 1991. *The language of news media*. Oxford: Blackwell.

1998. The discourse structure of news stories. In A. Bell and P. Garrett (eds.) *Approaches to media discourse*. Oxford: Blackwell, pp. 64–104.

Bell, S. 1999. Narratives and lives: women's health politics and the diagnosis of cancer for DES daughters. *Narrative Inquiry* **9**(2): 1–43.

2006. Becoming a mother after DES: intensive mothering in spite of it all. In A. De Fina, D. Schiffrin and M. Bamberg (eds.) *Discourse and identity*. Cambridge: Cambridge University Press, pp. 233–52.

Ben-Amos, D. 1993. Context in context. *Western Folklore* **52**: 209–26.

Benjamin, W. 1968. The storyteller: reflections on the works of Nikolai Leskov. In H. Arendt (ed.) *Illuminations: Essays and reflections*. London: Jonathan Cape, pp. 83–109.

Benveniste, E. [1966] 1971. L'appareil formel de l'énonciation. In E. Benveniste (ed.) *Problèmes de linguistique générale*. Paris: Gallimard, pp. 79–90.

Benwell, B. and E. Stokoe 2006. *Discourse and identity*. Edinburgh University Press.

Beran, E. and Z. Unoka 2005. Construction of self-narrative in a therapeutic setting: an analysis of the mutual determination of narrative perspective taken by patient and therapist. In U. M. Quasthoff and T. Becker (eds.) *Narrative interaction*. Amsterdam/Philadelphia: John Benjamins, pp. 223–42.

Bercelli, F., F. Rossano, and M. Viaro 2008. Different place, different action: clients' personal narratives in psychotherapy. *Narrative analysis in the shift from text to practices*. A. De Fina and A. Georgakapoulou (eds.). Special issue *Text and Talk* **28**(3): 283–305.

Berger, A. 1996. *Narratives in popular culture, media and everyday life*. Thousand Oaks/London: SAGE Publications.

Berger, P. L. and T. Luckmann 1966. *The social construction of reality: A treatise in the sociology of knowledge*. Garden City, NY: Doubleday.

Berman, R. A. and D. Slobin 1994. *Relating events in narrative: A crosslinguistic developmental study*. Hillsdale, NJ: Lawrence Erlbaum.

Blommaert, J. 2001. Reflections on ethnography. Online: www.ling-ethnog.org.uk/ Leicester. Retrieved June 6, 2008.

2005. *Discourse: A critical introduction*. Cambridge University Press.

Blum-Kulka, S. 1993. "You gotta know how to tell a story": telling, tales, and tellers in American and Israeli narrative events at dinner. *Language in Society* **22**: 361–402.

1997. *Dinner talk: Cultural patterns of sociability and socialization in family discourse*. Mahwah, NJ: Lawrence Erlbaum.

Blum-Kulka, S. and C. Snow (eds.) 2002. *Talking to adults*. Hillsdale, NJ: Lawrence Erlbaum.

Blumer, H. 1969. *Symbolic interactionism: Perspective and method*. London: Prentice Hall.

Boas, F. 1927. *Primitive art*. Oslo: Instituttet for Sammenlignende Kulturforksning, H. Ashehoug and Co.

Bourdieu, P. 1977. *Outline of a theory of practice*. Cambridge University Press.

Bourguignon, E. 1979. *Psychological anthropology*. New York: Holt, Rinehart & Winston.

Branner, R. 2005. Humorous disaster and success stories among female adolescents in Germany. In U. M. Quasthoff and T. Becker (eds.) *Narrative interaction*. Amsterdam/Philadelphia: John Benjamins, pp. 113–48.

Bremond, C. 1973. *Logique du récit*. Paris: Seuil.

Brewer, W. F. and E. H. Lichtenstein 1981. Event schemas, story schemas, and story grammars. In J. Long and A. Baddeley (eds.) *Attention and performance* IX. Hillsdale, NJ: Lawrence Erlbaum, pp. 363–79.

Briggs, C. (ed.) 1996a. *Disorderly discourse: Narrative, conflict and inequality.* Oxford University Press.

1996b. Introduction. In C. Briggs (ed.) *Disorderly discourse: Narrative, conflict and inequality.* Oxford University Press, pp. 3–40.

1997. Sequentiality and temporalization in the narrative construction of a South American cholera epidemic. *Oral versions of personal experience: Three decades of narrative analysis.* M. Bamberg (ed.). Special issue of *Journal of Narrative and Life History* **7**(1–4): 177–84.

2007. Mediating infanticide: theorizing relations between narrative and violence. *Cultural Anthropology* **22**(3): 315–56.

Bright, W. 1982. Poetic structure in oral narrative. In D. Tannen (ed.) *Spoken and written language: Exploring orality and literacy.* Norwood, NJ: Ablex, pp. 171–91.

Brockmeier, J. and D. Carbaugh 2001. Introduction. In J. Brockmeier and D. Carbaugh (eds.) *Narrative and identity: Studies in autobiography, self and culture.* Amsterdam/Philadelphia: John Benjamins, pp. 1–22.

Bruner, J. 1986. Two modes of thought. In *Actual minds possible worlds.* Cambridge, MA: Harvard University Press, pp. 11–43.

1990. *Acts of meaning.* Cambridge MA: Harvard University Press.

1991. The narrative construction of reality. *Critical Inquiry* **18**: 1–21.

1994. Life as narrative. *Social Research* **71**(3): 691–710.

1996. *The culture of education.* Cambridge MA: Harvard University Press.

1997. Labov and Waletzky thirty years on. *Journal of Narrative and Life History* **7**(1–4): 61–8.

2001. Self-making and world-making. In J. Brockmeier and D. Carbaugh (eds.) *Narrative and identity: Studies in autobiography, self and culture.* Amsterdam/Philadelphia: John Benjamins, pp. 25–37.

2010. Narrative, culture and mind. In D. Schiffrin, A. De Fina and A. Nylund (eds.) *Telling stories: Language, interaction and social life.* Washington DC: Georgetown University Press, pp. 45–50.

Bucholtz, M. 1999a, "Why be normal?": Language and identity practices in a group of nerd girls, *Language in Society* **28**: 203–23.

1999b. You Da man: narrating the racial other in the production of white masculinity. *Journal of Sociolinguistics* **3**(4): 461–79.

Bucholtz, M. and K. Hall 2005. Identity and interaction: a sociocultural linguistic approach. *Discourse Studies* **7**(4–5): 585–614.

Bucholtz, M., A. Liang, and L. Sutton (eds.) 1999. *Reinventing identities.* Oxford University Press.

Burke, K. [1950] 1969. *A rhetoric of motives.* Berkeley: University of California Press.

Burr, V. 2002. *The person in social psychology.* Hove, East Sussex: Psychology Press.

Butler, J. 1990. *Gender trouble: Feminism and the subversion of identity.* New York: Routledge.

Capps, L. and E. Ochs 1995. Out of place: narrative insights into agoraphobia. *Discourse Processes* **19**: 407–39.

Carr, D. 1991.*Time, narrative and history*. Bloomington: Indiana University Press.

Carranza, I. 1996. Argumentation and ideological outlook in storytelling. Unpublished Ph.D. thesis, Georgetown University.

1998. Low narrativity narratives and argumentation. *Narrative Inquiry* **8**(2): 287–317.

1999. Winning the battle in private discourse: rhetorical–logical operations in story-telling. *Discourse and Society* **10**(4): 509–41.

2010. Truth and authorship in textual trajectories. In D. Schiffrin, A. De Fina and A. Nylund (eds.) *Telling stories: Language, narrative and social life*. Washington, DC: Georgetown Roundtable in Language and Linguistics, Georgetown University Press, pp.173–80.

Cattell, R. B. 1966. *The scientific analysis of personality*. Chicago: Aldine.

Cavallaro Johnson, G. 2006. The discursive construction of teacher identities in research interviews. In A. De Fina, D. Schiffrin and M. Bamberg (eds.) *Discourse and identity*. Cambridge University Press, pp. 213–32.

2008. Making visible an ideological dilemma in an interview narrative about social trauma. *Narrative Inquiry* **18**(2): 187–205.

Cazden, C. 1988. *Classroom discourse: The language of teaching and learning*. Portsmouth: Heinemann.

Cederborg, A. C. and K. Aronsson 1994. Co-narration and voice in family therapy: voicing, devoicing and orchestration. *Text* **14**: 345–70.

Chafe, W. (ed.) 1980. *Pear stories: Cognitive, cultural, and linguistic aspects of narrative production*. Norwood, NJ: Ablex.

1990. Some things that narratives tell us about the mind. In B. Britton and A. Pellegrini (eds.) *Narrative thought and narrative language*. Hillsdale NJ: Lawrence Erlbaum, pp. 79–98.

Chatman, S. 1990. *Coming to terms: The rhetoric of narrative in fiction and film*. Ithaca: Cornell University Press.

Chomsky, N. 1965. *Aspects of the theory of syntax*. Cambridge, MA: MIT Press.

Clegg, S. R. 1993. Narrative, power and social theory. In D. Mumby (ed.) *Narrative and social control*. Thousand Oaks/London: SAGE Publications, pp.15–45.

Coates, J. 2001. My mind is with you: story sequences in the talk of male friends. *Narrative Inquiry* **11**: 1–21.

2002. *Men talk: Stories in the making of masculinity*. Oxford: Blackwell.

2005. Masculinity, collaborative narration and the heterosexual couple. In J. Thornborrow and J. Coates (eds.) *The sociolinguistics of narrative*. Amsterdam/Philadelphia: John Benjamins, pp. 89–106.

Coles, R. 1989. *The call of stories: Teaching and the moral imagination*. Boston: Houghton Mifflin.

Conley, J. M. and W. O'Barr. 1990. *Rules versus relationships: The ethnography of legal discourse*. University of Chicago Press.

Connelly, F. M. and D. J. Clandinin 1990. Stories of experience and narrative inquiry. *Educational Researcher* **19**: 2–14.

Cortazzi, M. 1993. *Narrative analysis*. London: Falmer Press.

Coupland, J. and N. Coupland 2004. A place for stance? Stance, role, frame and identity in geriatric medicine. Paper presented to the Sociolinguistics Symposium 15, Newcastle upon Tyne, 1–4 April 2004.

Coupland, N., P. Garrett and A. Williams 2005. Narrative performance, cultural demands and evaluation. In J. Thornborrow and J. Coates (eds.) *The sociolinguistics of narrative*. Amsterdam/Philadelphia: John Benjamins, pp. 67–88.

Dahlgreen, P. 1992. Introduction. In P. Dahlgreen and C. Spark (eds.) *Journalism and popular culture*. Thousand Oaks/London: SAGE Publications, pp. 1–23.

Daiute, C. and C. Lightfoot (eds.) 2004. *Narrative analysis: Studying the development of individuals in society*. Thousand Oaks: SAGE Publications.

Darnell, R. 1974. Correlates of Cree narrative performance. In R. Bauman and J. Sherzer (eds.) *Explorations in the ethnography of speaking*. Cambridge University Press, pp. 315–36.

Davies, C. and R. Harré. 1990. Positioning: the discursive construction of selves. *Journal for the Theory of Social Behaviour* **20**: 43–63.

Daya, S. and L. Lau. 2007. Introduction. *Power and narrative*. Special issue of *Narrative Inquiry* **17**(1): 1–11.

De Beaugrande, R. 1982. The story of grammars and the grammar of stories. *Journal of Pragmatics* **6**: 383–422.

De Beaugrande, R. and B. Colby. 1979. Narrative models of action and interaction. *Cognitive Science* **3**(1): 43–66.

De Fina, A. 2000. Orientation in immigrant narratives: the role of ethnicity in the identification of characters. *Discourse Studies* **2**(2): 131–57.

   2003a. *Identity in narrative: A study of immigrant discourse*. Amsterdam/Philadelphia: John Benjamins.

   2003b. Crossing borders: time, space and disorientation in narrative. *Narrative Inquiry* **13**(2): 1–25.

   2006. Group identity, narrative and self representations. In A. De Fina, D. Schiffrin and M. Bamberg (eds.) *Discourse and identity*. Cambridge University Press, pp. 351–75.

   2008. Who tells the story and why? Micro and macro contexts in narrative. *Narrative analysis in the shift from text to practices*. A. De Fina and A. Georgakopoulou (eds.). Special issue of *Text and Talk* **28**(3): 421–42.

   2009a. From space to spatialization in narrative studies. In J. Collins, M. Baynham and S. Slembrouck (eds.) *Globalization and language in contact scale, migration, and communicative practices*. Harrisburg, PA: Continuum, pp. 109–29.

   2009b. Narratives in interview – the case of accounts: for an interactional approach to narrative genres. *Narrative Inquiry* **19**(2): 233–58.

   2011. Researcher and informant roles in narrative interactions: constructions of belonging and foreign-ness. *Narratives in interviews, interviews in narrative studies*. A de Fina and S. Perrino (eds.). Special issue of *Language in Society* **40**: 1–12.

De Fina, A. and A. Georgakopoulou 2008a. Analysing narratives as practices. *Qualitative Research* **8**(3): 379–87.

   (eds.) 2008b. Narrative analysis in the shift from text to practices. Special issue of *Text and Talk* **28**(3).

De Fina, A., D. Schiffrin and M. Bamberg (eds.) 2006. *Discourse and identity*. Cambridge University Press, pp. 1–23.

Deppermann, A. 2007. Using the other for oneself: conversational practices of representing out-group members among adolescents. In M. Bamberg, A. De Fina and D. Schiffrin (eds.) *Selves and identities in narratives and discourse*. Amsterdam/Philadelphia: John Benjamins, pp. 273–302.

De Peuter, J. 1998. The dialogics of narrative identity. In M. M. Bell and M. Gardiner (eds.) *Bakhtin and the human sciences: No last words*. Thousand Oaks/London: SAGE Publications, pp. 30–48.

Dolezel, L. 1998. *Heterocosmica: Fiction and possible worlds*. Baltimore: Johns Hopkins University Press.

Drew, P. and J. Heritage (eds.) 1992. *Talk at work: Interaction in institutional settings*. Cambridge University Press.

Dreyer, A., C. Dreyer and J. Davis. 1987. Individuality and mutuality in the language of families of field-dependent and field-independent children. *Journal of Genetic Psychology* **148**: 105–17.

Dundes, A. 1964. *The morphology of North American Indian folktales. FF Communications 195*. Helsinki: Suomalainen Tiedeakatemia.

Dundes, A. 1997. Binary opposition in myth: the Propp/Lévi-Strauss debate in retrospect. *Western Folklore* **56**(1): 39–50.

Duranti, A. 1986. The audience as co-author. *Text* **6**: 239–48.

1993. Intentions, self, responsibility: an essay in Samohan ethnopragmatics. In J. Hill and J. Irvine (eds.) *Responsibility and evidence in oral discourse*. Cambridge University Press, pp. 24–47.

1997. *Linguistic Anthropology*. Cambridge University Press.

Durkheim, E. 1954. *The elementary forms of the religious life*. London: Allen & Unwin.

Dyer, J. and D. Keller-Cohen 2000. The discursive construction of professional self through narratives of personal experience. *Discourse studies* **2**(3): 283–304.

Eckert, P. and S. McConnell-Ginet. 1999. New generalizations and explanations in language and gender research. *Language in Society* **28**(2): 185–202.

Eco, U. 1979. *The role of the reader*. Bloomington: Indiana University Press.

1994. *Six walks in the fictional woods*. Cambridge, MA: Harvard University Press.

Edwards, D. 1997. Structure and function in the analysis of everyday narratives. *Oral versions of personal experience: Three decades of narrative analysis*. M. Bamberg (ed.). Special issue of the *Journal of Narrative and Life History* **7**: 139–46.

Edwards, D. and J. Potter 1992. *Discursive psychology*. Thousand Oaks/London: SAGE Publications.

Eelen, G. 1999. Politeness and ideology: a critical review. *Pragmatics* **9**: 163–73.

Ehrenhaus, P. 1993. Cultural narratives and the therapeutic motif: the political containment of Vietnam veterans. In D. Mumby (ed.) *Narrative and social control*. Thousand Oaks/London: SAGE Publications, pp. 77–96.

Ehrlich, S. 2001. *Representing rape: Language and sexual consent*. London: Routledge.

2007. Legal discourse and the cultural intelligibility of gendered meanings. *Journal of Sociolinguistics* **11**: 452–77.

Ekström, M. 2000. Information, storytelling and attractions: TV journalism in three modes of communication. *Media, culture and society* **22**: 465–92.

Elliott, J. 2005. *Using narrative in social research: Qualitative and quantitative approaches*. London: SAGE Publications.

Fairclough, N. 1989. *Language and power*. London: Longman.

1995. *Media discourse*. London: Edward Arnold.

Fasulo, A. 1999. Life narratives and the construction of normality. In W. Maiers, B. Bayer, B. Duarte Esgalhado, R. Jorna and E. Schraube (eds.) *Challenges to theoretical psychology*. Concord, Ontario: Captus Press, pp. 235–44.

Fasulo, A. and C. Zucchermaglio. 2008. Narratives in the workplace: facts, fictions and canonicity. *Narrative analysis in the shift from text to practices*. A. De Fina and A. Georgakopoulou (eds.). Special issue of *Text and Talk* **28**(3): 421–42.

Ferrara, K. 1988. Variation in narration: retellings in therapeutic discourse. In K. Ferrara, B. Brown, K. Walters and J. Baugh (eds.) *Linguistic change and contact: Proceedings of the sixteenth annual conference on new ways of analyzing variation*. Austin: University of Texas, Department of Linguistics, pp. 100–112.

Finnegan, R. [1966] 1981. *Limba stories and storytelling*. Oxford: Clarendon Press. Reprinted by Westport, CT: Greenwood Press.

Fisher, A. 1988. *The logic of real arguments*. Cambridge University Press.

Fisher, W. R. 1987. *Human communication as narration: Toward a philosophy of reason, value, and action*. Columbia: University of South Carolina University Press.

Fivush, R. 1998. The stories we tell: how language shapes autobiography. *Applied Cognitive Psychology* **12**: 483–7.

Flannery, M. 2008. "She discriminated against her own race": voicing and identity in a story of discrimination. *Narrative Inquiry* **18** (1): 111–30.

Fludernik, M. 1996. *Towards a 'natural' narratology*. London: Routledge.

  2009. *An introduction to narratology*. London: Routledge.

Foucault, M. 1972. *The archeology of knowledge*. New York: Harper and Row.

  1978. *The history of sexuality*. Robert Hurley (trans.) New York: Pantheon Books.

  1979. *Discipline and punish*. New York: Vintage.

Fowler, R. 1991. *Language in the news: discourse and ideology in the press*. London: Routledge.

Frank, T. 2004. *What's the matter with Kansas? How conservatism won the heart of America*. New York: Henry Holt and Company.

Freeman, M. 2006. Life "on holiday"? In defense of big stories. *Narrative Inquiry* **16**: 131–8.

  2010. *Hindsight: The promise and peril of looking backward*. Oxford University Press.

Freeman, M. and J. Brockmeier 2001. Narrative integrity: autobiographical identity and the meaning of the "good life." In J. Brockmeier and D. Carbaugh (eds.) *Narrative and identity: Studies in autobiography, self and culture*. Amsterdam/Philadelphia: John Benjamins, pp. 75–99.

Gabriel, Y. 2000. *Storytelling in organizations: Facts, fictions, and fantasies*. Oxford University Press.

Garfinkel, H. 1967. *Studies in ethnomethodology*. Englewood Cliffs, NJ: Prentice Hall.

Gee, J. P. 1986. Units in the production of narrative discourse. *Discourse Processes* **9**: 391–422.

  1989. Two styles of narrative construction and their linguistic and educational implications. *Discourse Processes* **12**: 287–307.

  1991. A linguistic approach to narrative. *Journal of Narrative and Life History* **1**: 15–40.

Geertz, C. 1983. *Local knowledge: Further essays in interpretive anthropology*. New York: Basic Books.

Genette, G. 1980. *Narrative discourse*. J. E. Lewin (trans.) Ithaca: Cornell University Press.

Georgakopoulou, A. 1997. *Narrative performances: A study of modern Greek storytelling*. Amsterdam/Philadelphia: John Benjamins.

1998. Conversational stories as performances: the case of Greek. *Narrative Inquiry* **8**(2): 319–50.

2000. Analytical positioning vis-à-vis narrative positioning. Commentary of Wortham, S. "Interactional positioning and narrative self-construction" (pp. 157–84). *Narrative Inquiry* **10**: 185–90.

2001. Arguing about the future: on indirect disagreements in conversations. *Journal of Pragmatics* **33**: 1881–900.

2002. Greek children and familiar narratives in family contexts: *en route* to cultural performances. In S. Blum-Kulka and C. E. Snow (eds.) *Talking to adults*. Mahwah, NJ: Lawrence Erlbaum, pp. 33–54.

2004a. Reflections on language-centered perspectives on modern Greek society and culture. *Kampos: Cambridge Papers in Modern Greek* **12**: 45–68.

2004b. To tell or not to tell? Email stories between on- and off-line interactions. Language @ Internet 1. Available online: www.languageatinternet.com.

2005a "Same old story?" On the interactional dynamics of shared narratives. In U. M. Quasthoff and T. Becker (eds.) *Narrative interaction*. Amsterdam/Philadelphia: John Benjamins, pp. 223–41.

2005b. Styling men and masculinities: interactional and identity aspects at work. *Language in Society* **34**: 163–84.

2006. Small and large identities in narrative (inter)action. In A. De Fina, D. Schiffrin and M. Bamberg (eds.) *Discourse and identity*. Cambridge University Press, pp. 83–102.

2007. *Small stories, interaction and identities*. Amsterdam/Philadelphia: John Benjamins.

2008. "On MSN with buff boys": self- and other- identity claims in the context of small stories. *Journal of Sociolinguistics* **15**: 597–626.

Georgakopoulou, A. and D. Goutsos 2000. Revisiting discourse boundaries: the narrative and non-narrative modes. *Text* **20**: 63–82.

2004. *Discourse analysis* (2nd edn.). Edinburgh University Press.

Gergen, M. 1994. The social construction of personal histories: gendered lives in popular autobiographies. In R. T. Sarbin and I. J. Kitsuse (eds.) *Constructing the social*. Thousand Oaks/London: SAGE Publications, pp. 19–44.

Giddens, A. 1991. *Modernity and self-identity: Self and society in the late modern age*. Stanford University Press.

Giles, H., and N. Coupland 1991. *Language: Contexts and consequences*. Pacific Grove, CA: Brooks/Cole.

Gledhill, C. 1993. Women reading men. In P. Kirkhamp and J. Thumim (eds.) *Me Jane: Masculinities, movies and women*. London: Lawrence and Whishart, pp. 73–93.

Goffman, E. 1967. *Interaction ritual: Essays on face to face behavior*. New York: Pantheon.

1981. Footing. In *Forms of talk*. Philadelphia: University of Pennsylvania Press, pp. 124–59.

Goodwin, C. 1979. The interactional construction of a sentence in natural conversation. In G. Psanthas (ed.) *Everyday language: Studies in ethnomethodology*. New York: Irvington Press, pp. 97–121.

1984. Notes on story structure and the organization of participation. In M. Atkinson and J. Heritage (eds.) *Structures of social action*. Cambridge University Press, pp. 225–46.

1986. Audience diversity, participation and interpretation. *Text* **6**(3): 283–316.

1987. Forgetfulness as an interactive resource. *Social Psychology Quarterly* **50**: 115–30.

Goodwin, C. and A. Duranti 1992. Rethinking context: an introduction. In A. Duranti and C. Goodwin (eds.) *Rethinking context.* Cambridge University Press, pp. 1–42.

1990. Tactical uses of stories: participation frameworks within girls' and boys' disputes. *Discourse processes* **13**: 33–72.

1997a. Toward families of stories in context. *Oral versions of personal experience: Three decades of narrative analysis.* M. Bamberg (ed.). Special issue of *Journal of Narrative and Life History* **7**: 139–46.

1997b. By-play: negotiating evaluation in story-telling. In G. R. Guy, C. Feagin, D. Schiffrin and J. Baugh (eds.) *Towards a social science of language: Papers in honor of William Labov,* vol. II: *Social interaction and discourse structures.* Amsterdam/Philadelphia: John Benjamins, pp. 77–102.

Grabe, W. and R. B. Kaplan 1996. *Theory and practice of writing: An applied linguistics perspective.* London: Longman.

Gramsci, A. 1971. *Selections from the prison notebooks of Antonio Gramsci.* Q. Hoare and G. N. Smith (eds.) London: Lawrence & Wishart.

Greenhalgh, T. and B. Hurwitz (eds.) 1998. *Narrative-based medicine: Dialogue and discourse in clinical practice.* London: BMJ Books.

Greenwald, G. 2008. *Toppling the big myths of Republican politics.* New York: Crown Publishing Group.

Greimas, A. J. [1966] 1983. *Structural semantics: An attempt at a method.* Daniele McDowell, Ronald Schleifer and Alan Velie (trans.) Lincoln: University of Nebraska Press.

Gubrium, J. F. and J. A. Holstein 2009. *Analyzing narrative reality.* Thousand Oaks/London: SAGE Publications.

Gumperz, J. 1982. *Discourse strategies.* Cambridge University Press.

Günthner, S. 1995. Exemplary stories: the cooperative construction of indignation. *Versus* **70/71**: 147–75.

Hall, S., C. Critcher, T. Jefferson, J. Clarke and B. Roberts 1978. *Policing the crisis: Mugging, the state, and law and order.* London: Macmillan.

Hamilton, H. 1998. Reported speech and survivor identity in on-line bone marrow transplantation narratives. *Journal of Sociolinguistics* **2**(1): 53–67.

Hanks, W. 1990. *Referential practice: Language and lived space among the Maya.* University of Chicago Press.

1996. *Language and communicative practices.* Oxford: Westview Press.

Harré, R. and F. M. Moghaddam 2003. Introduction: the self and others in traditional psychology and in positioning theory. In R. Harré and F. M. Moghaddam (eds.) *The self and others: Positioning individuals and groups in personal, political, and cultural contexts.* Westport, CT: Praeger Publishers, pp. 1–12.

Harris, M. 1999. *Theories of culture in postmodern times.* Walnut Creek: Altamira Press.

Harris, R. and B. Rampton 2003. *The language, ethnicity and race reader.* London: Routledge.

Harris, S. 2001. Fragmented narratives and multiple tellers: witness and defendant accounts in trials. *Discourse Studies* **3**(1): 53–74.

Haviland, J. 1996. "We want to borrow your mouth." Tzotzil marital squabbles. In C. Briggs (ed.) *Disorderly discourse: Narrative, conflict and inequality.* New York/ Oxford: Oxford University Press, pp. 158–203.

Heath, S. B. 1983. *Ways with words.* Cambridge University Press.

Herman, D. 2001. Spatial reference in narrative domains. *Text* **21**: 515–41.

    2002. *Story logic: Problems and possibilities of narratives.* Lincoln/London: University of Nebraska Press.

    2010. Multimodal storytelling and identity construction in graphic narratives. In D. Schiffrin, A. De Fina and A. Nylund (eds.) *Telling stories: Building bridges among language, narrative, identity, interaction, society and culture.* Washington, DC: Georgetown University Press, pp. 195–208.

Herman, L. and B. Vervaeck 2005. *Handbook of narrative analysis.* D. Herman (trans.) Lincoln/London: University of Nebraska Press.

Hester, S. and P. Eglin (eds.) 1997. *Culture in action: Studies in membership categorization analysis.* London/Lanham, MD: International Institute for Ethnomethodology and University Press of America.

Heyd, T. 2009. *Email hoaxes. Form, function, genre relations.* Amsterdam/Philadelphia: John Benjamins.

Hicks, D. 1990. Narrative skills and literacy learning. *Penn Working Papers in Educational Linguistics* **6**(1). Available online: www.wpel.net/v6/v6n1Hicks1. pdf. Retrieved September 5, 2009.

Hill, J. 1989. The cultural (?) context of narrative involvement. In R. Graczyk and C. Wiltshire (eds.) *Papers from the twenty-fifth annual regional meeting of the Chicago Linguistic Society.* Chicago Linguistics Society, pp. 138–56.

    1995. The voices of Don Gabriel. In Bruce Mannheim and Dennis Tedlock (eds.) *The dialogic emergence of culture.* Urbana: University of Illinois Press, pp. 97–147.

Hodge, R. and G. Kress 1993. *Language as ideology.* London: Routledge.

Hoffmann, C. 2008 "Once upon a blog": paradigms of narrative interaction. Paper presented to the Stylistic Workshop – The State of the Art, ISLE 2008, October 8–11, 2008, Freiburg.

Hoffmann, C. and V. Eisenlauer 2010. "Once upon a blog": collaborative narration in weblogs. In C. Hoffman (ed.) *Narrative revisited: Telling a story in the age of new media.* Amsterdam/Philadelphia: John Benjamins, pp. 1–18.

Hogg, M. A. and D. Abrams 1988. *Social identifications: A social psychology of intergroup relations and group processes.* London: Routledge.

Holland, D., W. Lachicotte, D. Skinner and C. Cain 1998. *Identity and agency in cultural worlds.* Cambridge, MA: Harvard University Press.

Hollway, W. 1984. Gender difference and the production of subjectivity. In J. Henriques, W. Hollway, C. Urwin, C. Venn and V. Walkerdine (eds.) *Changing the subject: Psychology, social regulation, and subjectivity.* London: Methuen. pp. 227–63.

Holmes, J. 1997. Struggling beyond Labov and Waletzky. In M. Bamberg (ed.) *Oral versions of personal experience: Three decades of narrative analysis.* M. Bamberg (ed.). Special issue of *Journal of Narrative and Life History* **7**: 139–46.

    2006. Workplace narratives, professional identity and relational practice. In A. De Fina, D. Schiffrin and M. Bamberg (eds.) *Discourse and identity.* Cambridge University Press, pp. 166–87.

Holstein, J. A. and J. F. Gubrium 2000. *The self we live by: Narrative identity in a post-modern world*. Oxford University Press.

Hopper, P. 1987. Emergent grammar. *Berkeley Linguistics Conference* **13**: 139–57.

Hufford, M. 1995. Context. *Journal of American Folklore* **108** (430): 528–49.

Hutchby, I. and R. Wooffitt 1998. *Conversation analysis*. Cambridge: Polity Press.

Hymes, D. 1974. *Foundations of sociolinguistics: An ethnographic approach*. Philadelphia: University of Pennsylvania Press.

1981. *"In vain I tried to tell you": essays in Native American ethnopoetics*. Philadelphia: University of Pennsylvania Press.

1996. *Ethnography, linguistics, narrative inequality: Toward an understanding of voice*. London: Taylor and Francis.

1998. When is oral narrative poetry? Generative form and its pragmatic conditions. *Pragmatics* **8**(4): 475–500.

2004. *Now I know so far: Essays in ethnopoetics*. Lincoln/London: University of Nebraska Press.

Hymes, D. and V. Hymes 2002. Enlisting patterns, enlisting members. In D. C. S. Li (ed.) *Discourses in search of members: In honor of Ron Scollon*. Lanham/New York: University Press of America, pp. 541–58.

Jacobs, R. 2000. Narrative, civil society and public culture. In M. Andrews (ed.) *Lines of narrative: Psychosocial perspectives*. London: Routledge, pp. 18–35.

Jacquemet, M. 2005. The registration interview: restricting refugees' narrative performances. In M. Baynham and A. De Fina (eds.) *Dislocations/relocations: Narratives of displacement*. Manchester: St. Jerome Publishing, pp. 194–216.

Jakobson, R. 1968. Poetry of grammar and grammar of poetry. *Lingua* **21**: 597–609.

Jefferson, G. 1978. Sequential aspects of storytelling in conversation. In J. Schenkein (ed.) *Studies in the organization of conversation*. New York: Academic Press, pp. 79–112.

1979. A technique for inviting laughter and its subsequent acceptance/declination. In G. Psathas (ed.) *Everyday language: Studies in ethnomethodology*. New York: Irvington Press, pp. 79–96.

Johnson, A. 2008. "From where we're sat …": negotiating narrative transformation through interaction in police interviews with suspects. *Narrative analysis in the shift from text to practices*. A. De Fina and A. Georgakopoulou (eds.). Special issue of *Text and Talk* **28**(3): 327–50.

Johnson, N. S. and J. M. Mandler 1980. A tale of two structures: underlying and surface forms in stories. *Poetics* **9**: 51–86.

Johnson-Laird, P. N. 1983. *Mental models: Towards a cognitive science of language, inference and consciousness*. Cambridge University Press.

Johnstone, B. 1990. *Stories, community and place: Narratives from middle America*. Bloomington: Indiana University Press.

1996. *The linguistic individual: Self-expression in language and linguistics*. Cambridge University Press.

Josselson, R. 2004. The hermeneutics of faith and the hermeneutics of suspicion. *Narrative Inquiry* **14**: 1–29.

Juzwik, M. 2004. What rhetoric can contribute to an ethnopoetics of narrative performance in teaching: the significance of parallelism in one teacher's narrative. *Linguistics and Education* **15**(4): 359–86.

Keller-Cohen, D. and J. Dyer 1997. Intertextuality and the narrative of personal experience. *Oral versions of personal experience: Three decades of narrative analysis.* M. Bamberg (ed.). Special issue of *Journal of Narrative and Life History* **7**(1–4): 147–54.

Kerby, A. 1991. *Narrative and the self.* Bloomington/Indianapolis: Indiana University Press.

Kiesling, S. 2006. Hegemonic identity-making in narrative. In A. De Fina, D. Schiffrin and M. Bamberg (eds.) *Discourse and identity.* Cambridge University Press, pp. 261–87.

Kirshenblatt-Gimblett, B. 1974. The concept and varieties of narrative performance. In R. Bauman and J. Sherzer (eds.) *Explorations in the ethnography of speaking.* Cambridge University Press, pp. 283–310.

Kjaerbeck, S. and B. Asmuss 2005. Negotiating meaning in narratives: an investigation of the interactional construction of the punchline and the post punchline sequences. *Narrative Inquiry* **15**(1): 1–24.

Kölbl, C. 2002. Blame it on psychology!? *Narrative Inquiry* **12**: 29–35.

Kotthoff, H. 2000. Gender and joking: on the complexities of women's image politics in humorous narratives. *Journal of Pragmatics* **32**: 55–80.

Kroskrity, P. 2000. Identity. *Journal of Linguistic Anthropology* **9**(1–2):111–14.

Kyratzis, A. 2000. Tactical uses of narratives in nursery school same-sex groups. *Discourse Processes* **29**: 269–99.

Labov, W. 1997. Some further steps in narrative analysis. *Oral versions of personal experience: Three decades of narrative analysis.* M. Bamberg (ed.). Special issue of *Journal of Narrative and Life History* **7**(1–4): 395–415.

1972. The transformation of experience in narrative syntax. In W. Labov (ed.) *Language in the inner city: Studies in the Black English Vernacular.* Philadelphia: University of Pennsylvania Press, pp. 354–96.

1981. Speech actions and reactions in personal narrative. In D. Tannen (ed.) *Analyzing discourse: Text and talk.* Washington, DC: Georgetown University Press, pp. 217–47.

2003. Uncovering the event structure of narrative. In D. Tannen and J. Alatis (eds.) *Georgetown University round table on languages and linguistics 2001.* Washington, DC: Georgetown University Press, pp. 63–83.

Labov, W. and J. Waletzky 1967. Narrative analysis: oral versions of personal experience. In J. Helm (ed.) *Essays on the verbal and visual arts.* Seattle/London: University of Washington Press, pp 12–44.

Langellier, K. M. 2001. "You're marked": breast cancer, tattoo, and the narrative performance of identity. In J. Brockmeier and D. Carbaugh (eds.) *Narrative and identity: Studies in autobiography, self and culture.* Amsterdam/Philadelphia: John Benjamins, pp. 145–84.

Langellier, K. M. and E. Peterson 2004. *Storytelling in daily life: Performing narratives.* Philadelphia: Temple University Press.

Lavandera, B. 1981. Lo quebramos, but only in performance. In P. R. Duran (ed.) *Latino language and communicative behavior.* Norwood, NJ: Ablex, pp. 49–68.

Lerner, G. 1992. Assisted storytelling: deploying shared knowledge as a practical matter. *Qualitative Sociology* **15**(3): 247–71.

Lévi-Strauss, C. 1963. The structural study of myth. In *Structural anthropology.* New York: Basic Publishers, pp. 206–31.

1969. *The raw and the cooked.* J. Weightman and D. Weightman (trans.) New York: Harper and Row.

Linde, C. 1993. *Life stories: The creation of coherence.* Oxford University Press.

Longacre, R. E. 1976. *An anatomy of speech notions.* Lisse: Peter de Ridder.

1989. Two hypotheses regarding text generation and analysis. *Discourse Processes* **12**: 413–60.

Lucius-Hoene, G. and A. Deppermann 2000. Narrative identity empiricized: a dialogical and positioning approach to autobiographical research interviews. *Narrative Inquiry* **10**(1): 199–222.

2008. Levels of positioning in narrative interaction. Paper presented at Georgetown Roundtable of Language and Linguistics on Telling Stories: Building bridges among Language, Narrative, Identity, Society, Interaction and culture. Washington, DC, March 14–16, 2008.

Lyotard, J. F. 1984. *The postmodern condition: A report on knowledge.* Minneapolis: University of Minnesota Press.

McAdams, D. P. 1988. *Power, intimacy and the life story: Personological inquiries into identity.* New York: The Guilford Press.

1993. *The stories we live by: Personal myths and the making of the self.* New York: William C. Morrow and Co.

1996. Personality, modernity, and the storied self: a contemporary framework for studying persons. *Psychological Inquiry* **7** (4): 295–321.

McCabe, A. 1996. *Chameleon readers: Teaching children to appreciate all kinds of good stories.* New York: McGraw-Hill.

McCabe, A. and C. Bliss 2003. *Patterns of narrative discourse: A multicultural life span approach.* Boston/New York: Pearson Education.

Machin, D. and T. Van Leeuwen 2004. Global media: generic homogeneity and discursive diversity. *Continuum* **18**(1): 99–120.

MacIntyre, A. 1981. *After virtue: A study in moral theory.* Notre Dame, IN: University of Notre Dame Press.

Mandelbaum, J. 1987. Couples sharing stories. *Communication Quarterly* **35**(4): 144–70.

Mandler, J. M. 1982. Another story of grammars: comments on Beaugrande's "The story of grammars and the grammar of stories." *Journal of Pragmatics* **6**(5–6): 433–40.

1984. *Stories, scripts, and scenes: Aspects of schema theory.* Hillsdale, NJ: Lawrence Erlbaum.

Mandler, J. M. and M. Goodman 1980. On the psychological validity of story structure. La Jolla: University of California technical report. Presented at the Psychonomic Society Meeting, St. Louis.

Mandler, J. M. and N. Johnson 1977. Remembrance of things parsed: story structure and recall. *Cognitive Psychology* **9**: 111–51.

1980. On throwing out the baby with the bathwater: a reply to Black and Wilensky's evaluation of story grammars. *Cognitive Science* **4**: 305–12.

Manzoni, C. 2005. The use of interjections in Italian conversation. In U. M. Quasthoff and T. Becker (eds.) *Narrative interaction.* Amsterdam/Philadelphia: John Benjamins, pp. 197–220.

Maryns, K. 2005. Displacement and aylum seekers narratives. In M. Baynham and A. De Fina (eds.) *Dislocations/relocations: Narratives of displacement.* Manchester: St. Jerome Publishing, pp. 174–93.

Maryns, K. and J. Blommaert 2001. Stylistic and thematic shifting as a narrative resource. *Multilingual* **20**(1): 61–84.

Matheson, D. M. 2005. *Media discourses.* Berkshire: McGraw-Hill Education.

Matsumoto, D. 1994. Culture and emotion. In L. Loeb Adler and U. Gielden (eds.) *Cross-cultural topics in psychology.* Westport, CT: Praeger Publishers, pp. 115–24.

Mattingly, C. 1998. *Healing dramas and clinical plots: The narrative structure of experience.* Cambridge University Press.

Mayers, M. 1949. *Frog, where are you?* New York: Dial Books.

Mead, G. 1956. Self and other. In A. Strauss (ed.) *The social psychology of George Herbert Mead.* Chicago University Press, pp. 212–60.

Meyers, D. T. 1997. Introduction. In D. T. Meyers (ed.) *Feminists rethink the self.* Boulder, CO: Westview Press, pp. 1–11.

Michaels, S. 1981. "Sharing time": children's narrative styles and differential access to literacy. *Language in Society* **10**(4): 423–42.

Michaels, S. and J. Collins 1984. Oral discourse style: classroom interaction and the acquisition of literacy. In D.Tannen (ed.) *Coherence in spoken and written discourse.* Norwood, NJ: Ablex, pp. 219–44.

Miller, G. 1997. Building bridges: the possibility of analytic dialogue between ethnography, conversation analysis and Foucault. In D. Silverman (ed.) *Qualitative research: Theory, method and practice.* Thousand Oaks/London: SAGE Publications, pp. 24–44.

Miller, J. H. 1990. Narrative. In F. Lenticchia and T. M. McLaughlin (eds.) *Critical terms for literary studies.* University of Chicago Press, pp. 66–79.

Miller, P. and L. L. Sperry 1988. Early talk about the past: the origins of conversational stories of personal experience. *Journal of Child Language* **15**: 293–316.

Mills, S. and C. A. White 1997. Discursive categories and desire: feminists negotiating relationships. In K. Harvey and C. Shalom (eds.) *Language and desire: Encoding sex, romance and intimacy.* London: Routledge, pp. 222–44.

Minami, M. 2002. *Culture-specific language styles: The development of oral narrative and literacy.* Clevedon: Multilingual Matters.

Minami, M. and A. McCabe 1991. Haiku as a discourse regulation device: a stanza analysis of Japanese children's personal narratives. *Language in Society* **20**(4): 577–99.

Mishler, E. G. 1986. *Research interviewing: Context and narrative.* Boston: Harvard University Press.

1995. Models of narrative analysis: a typology. *Journal of Narrative and Life History* **5**(2): 87–123.

1999. *Storylines: craftartists' narratives of identity.* Cambridge, MA: Harvard University Press.

Mitchell, W. J. T. 1980. On narrative. *Critical Inquiry* **6**(4): 1–4.

Mitra, A. 1999. Characteristics of the WWW text: tracing discursive strategies. *Journal of Computer-Mediated Communication* **5**. Available online: www.ascusc.org/jcmc/vol5/issue1/mitra.html. Retrieved July 15, 2008.

Moita Lopes, L. 2006. On being white, heterosexual and male in a Brazilian school: multiple positionings in oral narrative. In A. De Fina, M. Bamberg and D. Schiffrin (eds.) *Discourse and identity.* Cambridge University Press, pp. 288–313.

Mühlhausler, P. and R. Harré 1990. *Pronouns and people: The linguistic construction of social and personal identity.* Oxford: Blackwell.

Mulholland, J. 1996. A series of story turns: intertextuality and collegiality. *Text* **16**(4): 535–55.

Müller, F. and A. Di Luzio 1995. Stories as examples in everyday argument. *Versus* **70/71**: 115–45.

Mumby, D. 1993a. Introduction. In D. Mumby (ed.) *Narrative and social control*. Thousand Oaks/London: SAGE Publications, pp. 1–14.

    (ed.) 1993b. *Narrative and social control*. Thousand Oaks/London: SAGE Publications.

Murray, C. 1994. The stolen woman: oral narrative, postmodernism and the feminist turn in anthropology. *Canadian Review of Comparative Literature* **21**(3): 295–309.

Murray, M. 1997. A narrative approach to health psychology. *Journal of Health Psychology* **2**(1): 9–20.

Narajan, K. and K. George 2001. Personal and folk narratives as cultural representations. In J. F. Gubrium and J. A. Holstein (eds.) *Handbook of interview research*. Thousand Oaks/London: SAGE Publications, pp. 815–32.

Nash, C. (ed.) 1990. *Narrative in culture: The uses of storytelling in the sciences, philosophy, and literature*. London/New York: Routledge.

Nealon, J. 2008. *Foucault beyond Foucault*. Stanford University Press.

Norrick, N. 1993. *Conversational joking: Humor in everyday talk*. Bloomington: Indiana University Press.

    1997. Collaborative narration of familiar stories. *Language in Society* **26**: 199–220.

    2000. *Conversational narrative: Storytelling in everyday talk*. Amsterdam/Philadelphia: John Benjamins.

Oatley, K. 1999. Why fiction may be twice as true as fact: fiction as cognitive and emotional simulation. *Review of General Psychology* **3**: 101–17.

Ochs, E. and L. Capps 1996. Narrating the self. *Annual Review of Anthropology* **25**(1): 25–44.

    2001. *Living narrative*. Cambridge MA: Harvard University Press.

Ochs, E. and C. Taylor 1995. The "father knows best" dynamic in dinnertime narrative. In K. Hall and M. Bucholtz (eds.) *Gender articulated: Language and the socially constructed self*. New York/London: Routledge, pp. 97–120.

O'Connor, P. 1994. You could feel it through the skin: agency and positioning in prisoners' stabbing stories. *Text* **14**(1): 45–75.

    2000. *Speaking of crime: Narratives of prisoners*. Lincoln: University of Nebraska Press.

Oppenheim, D. R. N. Emde and F. S. Wamboldt 1996. Associations between 3-year-olds' narrative co-constructions with mothers and fathers and their story completions about affective themes. *Early Development and Parenting* **5**: 149–60.

Page, R. 2009. Trivia and tellability: storytelling in status updates. Paper presented to the Centre for Language, Discourse & Communication Research Seminars, October, 14, 2009, King's College London.

Pander Maat, H. 2008. Editing and genre conflict: how newspaper journalists clarify and neutralize press release copy. *Pragmatics* **18**(1): 97–114.

Parker, I. 2003. Psychoanalytic narratives: writing the self into contemporary cultural phenomena. *Narrative Inquiry* **13**(2): 301–15.

Perelman, C. and L. Olbrechts-Tyteca 1979. *The new rhetoric: A treatise on argumentation*. London: University of Notre Dame Press.

Perrino, S. 2005. Participant transposition in Senegalese oral narrative. *Narrative Inquiry* **15**(2): 345–75.

Peterson, C. and A. McCabe 1983. *Developmental psycholinguistics: Three ways of looking at a child's narrative.* New York: Plenum.

Phoenix, A. 2008. Analysing narrative contexts. In M. Andrews, C. Squire and M. Tamboukou (eds.) *Doing narrative research.* London: SAGE Publications, pp. 64–77.

Pike, K. L. 1967. *Language in relation to a unified theory of structure of human behavior* (2nd edn.). The Hague: Mouton.

Polanyi, L. 1981. What stories can tell us about their tellers' world. *Poetics Today* **2**: 97–112.

1982. Literary complexity in everyday storytelling. In D. Tannen (ed.) *Spoken and written language: Exploring orality and literacy.* Norwood, NJ: Ablex, pp. 155–70.

1985. Conversational storytelling. In T. van Dijk (ed.) *Handbook of discourse analysis.* London: Academic Press, pp. 183–201.

1989. *Telling the American story: A structural and cultural analysis of conversational storytelling.* Norwood, NJ: Ablex.

Polkinghorne, D. E. 1988. *Narrative knowing and the human sciences.* Albany: State University of New York Press.

1991. Narrative and self-concept. *Journal of Narrative and Life History* **1**(2–3): 135–53.

Potter, J. and Wetherell, M. 1997. *Discourse and social psychology.* Thousand Oaks/London: SAGE Publications.

Poveda, D. 2002. Quico's story: an ethnopoetic analysis of a Gypsy boy's narratives at school. *Text* **22**(2): 269–300.

Prince, G. 1973. *A grammar of stories.* The Hague: Mouton.

1982. *Narratology: the form and functioning of narrative.* The Hague: Mouton.

[1987] 2003. *A dictionary of narratology.* Lincoln: University of Nebraska Press.

2008. Classical and/or postclassical narratology. *L'Esprit Créateur* **48**(2): 115–23.

Propp, V. 1968. *Morphology of the folktale* (2nd edn.). Ed. Louis A. Wagner. Trans. Laurence Scott. Austin: University of Texas Press.

Quasthoff, U. 1980. *Erzählen in Gesprächen.* Tübingen: Narr.

Quasthoff, U. M. and T. Becker (eds.) (2005). *Narrative interaction.* Amsterdam: John Benjamins.

Rampton, B. 1995. *Crossing: Language and ethnicity among adolescents.* London: Longman.

(ed.) 1999. *Styling the other.* Special issue of *Journal of Sociolinguistics* **3/4**.

2000. Speech community. In J. Verschueren, J.-O. Östman, J. Blommaert and C. Bulcaen (eds.) *Handbook of pragmatics.* Amsterdam/Philadelphia: John Benjamins, pp.1–34.

Rampton, B., K. Tusting, J. Maybin, R. Barwell, A. Creese and V. Lytra 2005. UK linguistic ethnography. A discussion paper. Available online: www.ling-ethnog.org. uk. Retrieved July 8, 2009.

Reddy, M. 1979. The conduit metaphor: a case of frame conflict in our language about language. In A. Ortony (ed.) *Metaphor and thought.* Cambridge University Press, pp. 284–324.

Relaño-Pastor, M. and A. De Fina 2005. Contesting social place: narratives of language conflict. In M. Baynham and A. De Fina (eds.) *Dislocations/relocations: Narratives of displacement.* Manchester: St. Jerome Publishing, pp. 36–60.

Richardson, J. E. 2004. *(Mis)Representing Islam: The racism and rhetoric of British broadsheet newspapers*. Philadelphia: John Benjamins.

Richardson, L. 1992. Resisting resistance narratives: a representation for communication. *Studies in Symbolic Interaction* **13**: 77–83.

Ricoeur, P. 1984. *Narrative and time*. University of Chicago Press.

[1983–5] 1990. *Time and narrative*. University of Chicago Press. Translation of *Temps et récit*, vols. 1–3. Paris: Seuil.

Riessman, C. K. 1990. *Divorce talk: Women and men make sense of personal relationships*. New Brunswick, NJ: Rutgers University Press.

1991. Beyond reductionism: narrative genres in divorce accounts. *Journal of Narrative and Life History* **1**: 41–68.

1993. *Narrative analysis*. Thousand Oaks/London: SAGE Publications.

1997. A short story about long stories. *Oral versions of personal experience: three decades of narrative analysis*. M. Bamberg (ed.). Special issue of *Journal of Narrative and Life History* **7**(1–4): 155–8.

2002. Doing justice: positioning the interpreter in narrative work. In W. Patterson (ed.) *Strategic narrative*. Lanham, MD/Boulder, CO: Lexington Books, pp. 193–214.

2004. A thrice-told tale: new readings of an old story. In B. Hurwitz, T. Greenhalgh and V. Skultans (eds.) *Narrative research in health and illness*. Oxford: Blackwell, pp. 309–24.

2008. *Narrative methods in the social sciences*. Thousand Oaks/London: SAGE Publications.

Roberts, B. 2004. Poetics and the composition of life. *Narrative Inquiry* **14**: 261–73.

Rodrick, S. 2007. Fred Thompson bills himself as a true southern conservative and a plain-ol'-folks regular guy. But is he just playing a part? *New York Magazine*, July 23, 2007. Available online: http://nymag.com/news/features/34992/ Retrieved May 18, 2008.

Rogers, Carl 1959. A theory of therapy, personality and interpersonal relationships as developed in the client-centered framework. In S. Koch (ed.) *Psychology: A study of a science,* vol. III: *Formulations of the person and the social context*. New York: McGraw Hill, pp. 184–256.

Rosaldo, R. 1986. Hongot hunting as story and experience. In V. W. Turner and E. M. Bruner (eds.) *The anthropology of experience*. Urbana/Chicago: University of Illinois Press, pp. 97–138.

1993. *Meaning and truth: The remaking of social analysis*. Boston: Beacon Press.

Rosch, E. and C. B. Mervis 1975. Family resemblances: studies in the internal structure of categories. *Cognitive Psychology* **7**: 573–605.

Rosenwald, G. and R. Ochberg 1992. *Storied lives*. New Haven: Yale University Press.

Rothemberg, J. 1985. *Technicians of the sacred*. Berkeley: University of California Press.

Ruesch, J. and G. Bateson 1968. *Communication: The social matrix of psychiatry*. New York: Norton.

Rumelhart, D. 1975. Notes on a schema for stories. In D. Bobrow and A. Collins (eds.) *Representation and understanding*. New York: Academic Press, pp. 211–36.

1977. Understanding and summarizing brief stories. In D. LaBerge and J. Samuels (eds.) *Basic processes in reading: Perception and comprehension*. Hillsdale, NJ: Lawrence Erlbaum, pp. 265–303.

1980. On evaluating story grammars. *Cognitive Science* **4**: 313–16.

Ryan, M. L. 1991. *Possible worlds, artificial intelligence and narrative theory.* Bloomington: Indiana University Press.

2004a. Introduction. In M. L. Ryan (ed.) *Narrative across media: The languages of storytelling.* Lincoln/London: University of Nebraska Press, pp. 1–46.

2004b. Will new media produce new narratives? In M. L. Ryan (ed.) *Narrative across media: The languages of storytelling.* Lincoln/London: University of Nebraska Press, pp. 329–37.

Ryave, A. L. 1978. On the achievement of a series of stories. In J. Schenkein (ed.) *Studies in the organization of conversational interaction.* New York: Academic Press, pp. 113–32.

Sacks, H. 1972a. An initial investigation of the usability of conversational data for doing sociology. In D. Sudnow (ed.) *Studies in social interaction.* New York: Free Press, pp. 31–74.

1972b. On the analyzability of stories by children. In J. Gumperz and D. Hymes (eds.) *Directions in sociolinguistics.* New York: Holt, Rinehart & Winston, pp. 325–45.

1974 An analysis of the course of a joke's telling in conversation. In R. Bauman and J. F. Sherzer (eds.) *Explorations in the ethnography of speaking.* Cambridge University Press, pp. 337–53.

1992a. *Harold Sacks: Lectures on conversation.* G. Jefferson (ed.) Oxford: Blackwell.

[1970] 1992b. Second stories; "Mm hm"; story prefaces; "local news"; tellability. In G. Jefferson (ed.) *Harold Sacks: Lectures on conversation*, vol. I. Oxford: Blackwell, pp. 3–16.

[1970] 1992c. Stories take more than one utterance: story prefaces. In G. Jefferson (ed.) *Harold Sacks: Lectures on conversation*, vol. II. Oxford: Blackwell, pp. 222–38.

[1970] 1992d. Storyteller as 'witness': entitlement to experience. In G. Jefferson (ed.) *Harold Sacks: Lectures on conversation*, vol. I. Oxford: Blackwell, pp. 242–6.

[1966] 1992e. "We"; category-bound activities. In G. Jefferson (ed.) *Harold Sacks: Lectures on conversation*, vol. I: Oxford: Blackwell, pp. 333–40.

Sacks, H., E. Schegloff and G. Jefferson 1974. A simplest systematics for the organization of turn-taking in conversation. *Language* **50**(4): 696–735.

Santa Ana, O. 1999. Like an animal I was treated: anti-immigrant metaphor in U.S. public discourse. *Discourse and Society* **10**(2): 192–224.

Sarbin, T. R. (ed.) (1986). *Narrative psychology: The storied nature of human conduct.* New York: Praeger Publishers.

Savage, M. and R. Burrows 2007. The coming crisis of empirical sociology. *Sociology* **41**(6): 885–99.

Sawin, P. 1999. Gender, context, and the narrative construction of identity: rethinking models of women's narratives. In M. Bucholtz, A. C. Liang and L. A. Sutton (eds.) *Reinventing identities: The gendered self in discourse.* New York: Oxford University Press, pp. 241–58.

Schank, R. 1990. *Tell me a story: A new look at real and artificial memory.* New York: Scribner.

Schank, R. and R. P. Abelson 1977. *Scripts, plans, goals, and understanding: An inquiry into human knowledge structures.* Hillsdale, NJ: Lawrence Erlbaum.

Schegloff, E. A. 1968. Sequencing in conversational openings. *American Anthropologist* **70**(6): 1075–95.

1979. Identification and recognition in telephone conversation openings. In G. Psathas (ed.) *Everyday language: Studies in ethnomethodology*. New York: Irvington Publishers, pp. 23–78.

1997. "Narrative analysis" thirty years later. *Oral versions of personal experience: Three decades of narrative analysis*. M. Bamberg (ed.). Special issue of *Journal of Narrative and Life History* **7**: 97–106.

2007. A tutorial on membership categorization. *Journal of Pragmatics* **39**: 462–82.

Schiffrin, D. 1981. Tense variation in narrative. *Language* **57**(1): 45–62.

1984. How a story says what it means and does. *Text:* **4**(4): 313–46.

1985. Everyday argument: the organization of diversity in talk. In T. A. van Dijk (ed.) *Handbook of discourse analysis*. London: Academic Press, pp. 35–45.

1988. Sociolinguistic approaches to discourse: topic and reference in narrative. In K. Fererra, B. Brown, K. Walters and J. Baugh (eds.) *Linguistic change and contact*. Austin: University of Texas Press, pp. 1–28.

1990. The management of a cooperative self during argument: the role of opinions and stories. In A. D. Grimshaw (ed.) *Conflict talk*. Cambridge University Press, pp. 241–59.

1994. *Approaches to discourse*. Oxford: Blackwell.

1996. Narrative as self portrait: sociolinguistic constructions of identity. *Language in society* **25**: 167–203.

2000. Mother/daughter discourse in a Holocaust oral history: "Because then you admit that you're guilty." *Narrative Inquiry* 10(1): 1–44.

2006. *In other words: Variation in reference and narrative*. Cambridge University Press.

Schutz, A. 1967. *The phenomenology of the social world*. Evanston, IL: Northwestern University Press.

Schwandt, T. A. 1997. *Qualitative inquiry: A dictionary of terms*. Thousand Oaks/London: SAGE Publications.

Scollon, R. and S. Scollon 1981. *Narrative, literacy, and face in interethnic communication*. Norwood, NJ: Ablex.

Scott, M. and S. Lyman 1986. Accounts. *American Sociological Review* **33**(1): 46–62.

Sheldon, A. 1996. You can be the baby brother, but you aren't born yet: preschool girls' negotiations for power and access in pretend play. *Research on Language & Social Interaction* **29**: 57–80.

Sherzer, J. 1983. *Kuna ways of speaking: An ethnographic perspective*. Cambridge, MA: MIT Press.

Shipler, D. K. 1997. *A country of strangers: Blacks and whites in America*. New York: Alfred A Knopf.

Shklovsky, V. [1965] 1917. Art as technique. In L. T. Lemon and M. Reis (eds.) *Russian formalist criticism*. Lincoln: University of Nebraska Press.

Shuman, A. 1986. *Storytelling rights: The uses of oral and written texts by urban adolescents*. Cambridge University Press.

1993. "Get outa my face": entitlement and authoritative discourse. In J. Hill and J. Irvine (eds.) *Responsibility and evidence in oral discourse*. Cambridge University Press, pp. 135–60.

2005. *Other people's stories*. Urbana/Chicago: University of Illinois Press.

Sidnell, J. 2003. Constructing and managing male exclusivity in talk-in-interaction. In
  J. Holmes and M. Meyerhoff (eds.) *Handbook of Language and Gender*. Oxford:
  Blackwell, pp. 327–52.
Silverstein, M. 1976. Shifters, linguistic categories, and cultural description. In
  K. Basso and H. A. Selby (eds.) *Meaning in anthropology*. Albuquerque: University
  of New Mexico, pp. 11–55.
Skinner, B. 1953. *Science and human behavior*. New York: McMillan.
Slembrouck, S. 2003. What the map cuts up, the story cuts across. *Narrative Inquiry*
  13(2): 459–67.
Somers, M. and G. Gibson 1994. Reclaiming the epistemological "other": narrative and
  the social construction of identity. In C. Calhoun (ed.) *Social theory and the polit-
  ics of identity*. Oxford: Blackwell, pp. 37–99.
Squire, C. 2008. Experience-centred and culturally-oriented approaches to narrative.
  In M. Andrews, C. Squire and M. Tamboukou (eds.) *Doing narrative research*.
  London: SAGE Publications, pp. 41–63.
Stein, N. 1982. The definition of a story. *Journal of Pragmatics* **6**: 487–507.
Stein, N. and M. Policastro 1984. The concept of a story: a comparison between
  children's and teachers' viewpoints. In H. Mandl, N. Stein and T. Trabasso (eds.)
  Learning and comprehending text. Hillsdale, NJ: Lawrence Erlbaum, pp. 113–55.
Stokoe, E. 2006. Public intimacy in neighbour relationships and complaints. *Sociological
  Research Online* **11**(3). September 30, 2006. Available online: www.socresonline.
  org.uk/11/3/stokoe.html. Retrieved April 30, 2008.
Stokoe, E. and D. Edwards 2007. 'Black this, black that': racial insults and reported
  speech in neighbour complaints and police interrogations. *Discourse and Society*
  18(3): 337–72.
Strawson, G. 2004. Against narrativity. *Ratio* **17**: 428–52.
Strömquist, S. and Verhoven, L. (eds.) 2004. *Relating events in narrative*, vol. II:
  Typological and contextual perspectives. Mahwah, NJ: Lawrence Erlbaum.
Svennevig, J. 1999. *Getting acquainted in conversation: A study of initial interactions*.
  Amsterdam/Philadelphia: John Benjamins.
Swales, J. 1990. *Genre analysis*. Cambridge University Press.
Tajfel, H. 1981. *Human groups and social categories: Studies in social psychology*.
  Cambridge University Press.
Tannen, D. 1979. What's in a frame? Surface evidence for underlying expectations. In
  R. O. Feedle (ed.) *New directions in discourse processing*. Norwood, NJ: Ablex,
  pp. 137–81.
  1980. A comparative analysis of oral narrative strategies. In W. Chafe (ed.) *Pear stories: Cognitive, cultural and linguistic aspects of narrative production*. Norwood, NJ:
  Ablex, pp. 51–87.
  1983. "I take out the rock – dok!": how Greek women tell about being molested (and
  create involvement). *Anthropological Linguistics* **25**: 359–74.
  1984. *Conversational style: Analyzing talk among friends*. Norwood, NJ: Ablex.
  1986. Introducing constructed dialogue in Greek and American conversational and
  literary narrative. In F. Coulmas (ed.) *Direct and reported speech*. Berlin: Mouton,
  pp. 311–32.
  1989. *Talking voices: Repetition, dialogue, and imagery in conversational discourse*.
  Cambridge University Press.

Tannen, D. and C. Kakava 1992. Power and solidarity in modern Greek conversation: disagreeing to agree. *Journal of Modern Greek Studies* **10**: 11–34.

Taylor, C. 1989. *Sources of the self: The making of modern identity*. Cambridge, MA: Harvard University Press.

Tedlock, D. 1972. *Finding the center: Narrative poetry of the Zuni Indians*. New York: Dial Books.

1983. *The spoken word and the work of interpretation*. Philadelphia: University of Pennsylvania Press.

Thompson, S. 1961. *The types of the folktale*. FFC 184. Helsinki: Suomalainen Tiedeakatemia.

Thornborrow, J. 2007. Narrative, opinion and situated argument in talk show discourse. *Journal of Pragmatics* **39**: 1436–53.

Thorndyke, P. W. 1977. Cognitive structures in comprehension and memory of narrative discourse. *Cognitive Psychology* **9**: 77–110.

Tischer, S., M. Meyer, R. Wodak and E. Vetter (2000) *Methods of text and discourse analysis*. London: Sage.

Todorov, T. 1969. *Grammaire du Décameron*. The Hague: Mouton.

Toolan, M. 2001. *Narrative: A critical linguistic introduction* (2nd edn.). London: Routledge.

Toulmin, S., R. Rieke and A. Janik 1979. *An introduction to reasoning*. New York: Macmillan.

Trabasso, T. and P. W. van den Broek 1985. Causal thinking and the representation of narrative events. *Journal of Memory and Language* **24**: 612–30.

Trabasso, T., P. W. van den Broek and S. Suh 1989. Logical necessity and transitivity of causal relations in the representation of stories. *Discourse Processes* **12**: 1–25.

Triandis, H. C. (ed.) 1972. *The analysis of subjective culture: comparative studies in behavioral science*. New York/ London: Wiley.

Trinch, S. and S. Berk-Seligson 2002. Narrating in protective order interviews: a source of interactional trouble. *Language in Society* **31**: 383–418.

Ungerer, F. 2000. News stories and news events: a changing relationship. In F. Ungerer (ed.) *English media texts, past and present: Language and textual structure*. Amsterdam/Philadelphia: John Benjamins, pp. 177–95.

Van Dijk, T. A. 1984. *Prejudice in discourse*. Amsterdam: John Benjamins.

1991. *Racism and the press*. London: Routledge.

1993. Stories and racism. In D. Mumby (ed.) *Narrative and social control: Critical perspectives*. Thousand Oaks/London: SAGE Publications, pp. 121–42.

1998. *News as discourse*. Hillsdale, NJ: Lawrence Erlbaum.

Van Dijk, T. A. and W. Kintsch 1983. *Strategies in discourse comprehension*. New York: Academic.

Van Hout, T. and G. Jacobs 2008. News production theory and practice: fieldwork notes on power, interaction and agency. *Pragmatics* **18**(1): 59–86.

Vazquez, C. 2007. Moral stance in the workplace narratives of novices. *Discourse Studies* **9**: 653–75.

Veroff, J., L. Chadiha, D. Leber and L. Sutherland 1993. Affect and interactions in newlyweds' narratives: black and white couples compared. *Journal of Narrative and Life History* **3**(4): 361–90.

Virtanen, T. 1992. Issues of text-typology: narrative – a "basic" type of text? *Text* **12**: 293–310.

Voloshinov, V. N. 1973. *Marxism and the philosophy of language*. L. Matejka and R. Titunik (trans.) New York/London: Seminar Press.

Wagner, I. and R. Wodak 2006. Performing success: identifying strategies for self-presentation in women's biographical narratives. *Discourse and Society* **17**(3): 385–411.

Walker, J. 2004 Distributed narrative: telling stories across networks. Paper presented to AoIR 5.0, September 2004. Available online: http://huminf.uib.no/~jill/talks/DistributedNarr.html.

Werlich, E. 1976. *A text grammar of English*. Heidelberg: Quelle and Meyer.

Werth, P. 1999. *Text worlds: Representing conceptual space in discourse*. Michael Short (ed.) London: Longman.

Wetherell, M. 1998. Positioning and interpretative repertoires: conversation analysis and post-structuralism in dialogue. *Discourse and Society* **9**: 387–412.

White, H. 1978. *Tropics of discourse: Essays in cultural criticism*. Baltimore: Johns Hopkins University Press.

    1987. *The content of the form: Narrative, discourse and historical representation*. Baltimore/London: Johns Hopkins University Press.

Widdicombe, S. 1998. Identity as an analyst's and participant's resource. In C. Antaki and S. Widdicombe (eds.) *Identities in talk*. Thousand Oaks/London: SAGE Publications.

Witten, M. 1993. Narratives and obedience at the workplace. In D. Mumby (ed.) *Narrative and social control*. Thousand Oaks/London: SAGE Publications, pp. 97–118.

Wodak, R. 1999. Critical discourse analysis at the end of the 20th century. *Research on Language and Social Interaction* 32(1–2): 185–93.

Wodak, R. and M. Reisigl 1999. *Discourse and discrimination: The rhetoric of racism and antisemitism*. London: Routledge.

Wolfson, N. 1978. A feature of performed narrative: the conversational historical present. *Language in Society* **7**: 215–37.

Woodbury, A. 1985. The functions of rhetorical structure: a study of Central Alaskan Yupic Eskimo discourse. *Language in Society* **14**(2): 153–90.

Woolard, K. A. 1998. Introduction: language ideology as a field of enquiry. In B. Schieffelin, K. Woolard and P. Kroskrity (eds.) *Language ideologies: Practice and theory*. Oxford University Press, pp. 3–47.

Wortham, S. 2000. Interactional positioning and narrative self-construction. *Narrative Inquiry* **10**(1): 157–84.

    2001. *Narratives in action*. New York: Teachers College Press.

Young, K. G. 1987. *Taleworlds and storyrealms*. Dordrecht: Martinus Nijhoff Publishers.

Zimmerman, D. 1998. Identity, context and interaction. In C. Antaki and S. Widdicombe (eds.) *Identities in talk*. Thousand Oaks/London: SAGE Publications, pp. 87–106.

Zimmerman, D. and D. L. Weider 1970. Ethnomethodology and the problem of order: comment on Denzin. In J. D. Douglas (ed.) *Understanding everyday life: Toward the reconstruction of sociological knowledge*. Chicago: Aldine, pp. 285–98.

Zwaan, R. A. and G. A. Radvansky. 1998. Situation models in language comprehension and memory. *Psychological Bulletin* **123**: 162–85.

Index

For EU product safety concerns, contact us at Calle de José Abascal, 56–1°, 28003 Madrid, Spain or eugpsr@cambridge.org.

www.ingramcontent.com/pod-product-compliance
Ingram Content Group UK Ltd.
Pitfield, Milton Keynes, MK11 3LW, UK
UKHW020329140625
459647UK00018B/2078